Independence

Independence

A Guide to Historic Philadelphia

George W. Boudreau

WESTHOLME

Yardley

Title page: *A View of Several Public Buildings in Philadelphia* (detail). This view of Independence Hall and the buildings flanking it, attributed to artist Charles Willson Peale and engraved by James Trenchard, dates to early 1790. Philadelphia was enjoying postwar prosperity following the American Revolution, allowing for new buildings (including the County Court House, later known as Congress Hall). By the end of that year, these buildings would host the members of the first federal government when the city became the United States capital for the following decade.

Page ix: "Costume des Quakers, Bibliotheque de Philadelphia," an early nine-teenth-century engraving shows members of the Society of Friends in their distinctive clothing, viewed from the lawn of Independence Hall with Library Hall in the background.

Copyright ©2012 George W. Boudreau
Map by Tracy Dungan ©2012 Westholme Publishing

Westholme Publishing, LLC
904 Edgewood Road
Yardley, Pennsylvania 19067

ISBN: 978-1-59416-143-8

Printed in the United States of America.

Book Club Edition

For David and Becky Waas,
Mentors and friends,
and for my parents,
Everette and Beverly Boudreau,
for a lifetime of love and support.

Contents

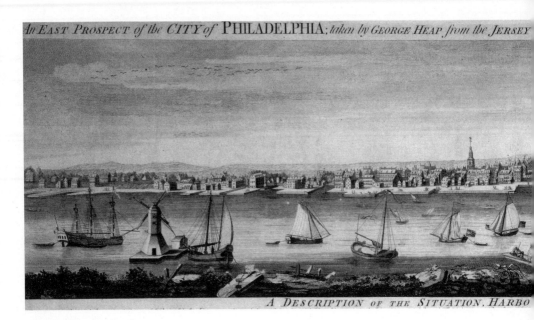

An EAST PROSPECT of the CITY of PHILADELPHIA; taken by GEORGE HEAP from the JERSEY

A DESCRIPTION OF THE SITUATION, HARBO

"An east prospect of the city of Philadelphia; taken by George Heap from the Jersey shore, under the direction of Nicholas Scull surveyor general of the Province of Pennsylvania." Surveyor General Nicholas Scull captured the rise and prosperity of Philadelphia in 1754, when he sketched the city from the New Jersey side of the Delaware River. The numerous ships' masts in the river, and the public buildings' steeples (some of which were not complete by the time this engraving by George Heap was published in London) all reveal that the city had become the largest and most diverse in British North America.

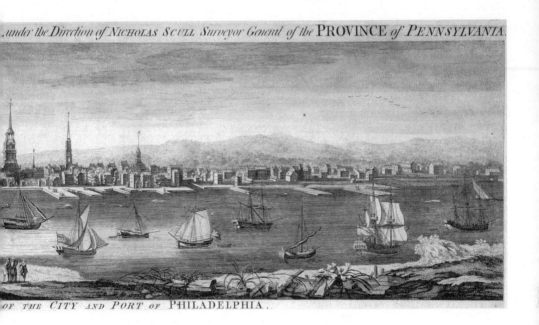

Introduction:
Philadelphia, City of Independence

"The City of Philadelphia is perhaps one of the wonders of the World, if you consider its Size, the Number of Inhabitants, the regularity of its Streets, their great breadth and length, they cutting one another all at Right Angles, their Spacious publick and private buildings, Quays and Docks, the Magnificence and diversity of places of Worship," Lord Adam Gordon wrote, after visiting the city in 1765. He went on to praise "the plenty of provisions brought to Market, and the Industry of all its Inhabitants, one will not hesitate to Call it the first town in America, but one that bids fair to rival any in Europe."

This English lord's account was far from unique. The eighteenth century was an age that prized published accounts of foreign places, written guides that told the reader what he or she might see there, even if the sights and sounds described were only to be encountered on paper, from hundreds or thousands of miles away. In this era, travelers wrote of Philadelphia's size and sophistication, its design and architecture, and the cultural advantages that lined its streets. But beyond these factors, visitors noted Philadelphia's people. From its founding, Philadelphia differed from most English and colonial towns because of the diversity that greeted a person as he or she walked the neatly arranged streets of Philadelphia's grid-plan cityscape. Dr. Alexander Hamilton, a Scots-born physician living in Annapolis, Maryland (and no relation to George Washington's secretary of the treasury), visited in 1744, and was struck by the city's pluralism: "I dined at a tavern with a very mixed company of different nations and religions. There were Scots, English, Dutch, Germans, and Irish; there were Roman Catholics, Church [of England] men, Presbyterians, Quakers, Newlightmen, Methodists, Seventh day men, Moravians, Anabaptists, and one Jew." As the doctor learned that day, the diverse people of the town could provide what one historian described as a "cacophony of voices."

This book is organized by key sites, yet the lives of these people and their role in securing the country's independence form its narrative. While historians have long understood the diversity of the residents of eighteenth-century Philadelphia, that message has only recently begun to be part of the story told to the millions

The ACCIDENT in LOMBARD-STREET PHILAD: 1787

Charles Willson Peale, early Philadelphia's most prominent artist, captured a street scene outside his home at Fourth and Lombard streets in 1787. Peale's "Accident in Lombard Street" shows a girl in a moment of crisis, when she dropped the pie she was carrying home from the bakery. Peale's inscription reads: "The pye from Bake-house she had brought/But let it fall for want of thought/ And laughing [chimney] sweeps collect around/The Pye that's scatter'd on the ground"

of visitors to the city's historic district. Officials estimate that more than five million people a year visit the area surrounding Independence Hall, but many of them still hear only about the founding fathers who gathered in that building in 1776 and 1787.

The story of the men who wrote the Declaration of Independence and the Constitution is fascinating, and vital to the heritage of Americans and people around the world. But to tell their story as if they existed in a vacuum is a disservice to them as well as to the men and women who interacted with them every day during those pivotal moments. This book seeks to recover more voices from the city where America was born.

President-elect Abraham Lincoln at Independence Hall on February 22, 1861, where he was presented with an American flag showing a star for the new state of Kansas. This is one of only a handful of photographs of Lincoln taken during his journey by rail from Springfield, Illinois, to his inauguration in Washington, D.C. All are from his stop in Philadelphia.

This book is also a story about spaces: the area laid out by William Penn and his surveyor in 1682 that would become the heart of Philadelphia, where the Continental Congress created the United States in 1776. These blocks now constitute Independence National Historical Park and the historic areas immediately adjacent to it. Philadelphia has more surviving early American buildings than any other city in the nation, and each of these spaces is the result of historic preservation and interpretation. Sadly, many buildings were lost in the century following the nation's founding. William Penn's house, Benjamin Franklin's houses and shops, the house where Thomas Jefferson wrote the Declaration of Independence, the early courthouse and market sheds, and hundreds of others made way for progress as the city grew and developed.

Indeed, Independence Hall—or the old State House, as it was actually known— might easily have joined the list, had Americans not begun to attach sentiment to it in the 1820s, the country's fiftieth birthday and the decade that saw the last of the Declaration's signers die. The Marquis de Lafayette's visit to "the hall of independence" in 1824 gave a new name and new meaning to the old office building. In the decades that followed, local citizens and national officials slowly realized the area's importance to history. Early preservationists later commissioned noted architect John Haviland to re-panel the room. Haviland created a look that was considered beautiful and majestic by nineteenth-century standards, but had nothing to do with the tastes of the Quaker-dominated colonial Assembly. Likewise, when the city decided to build a new tower on the hall, to replace the one that had rotted in the late eighteenth century, they commissioned William Strickland to create a new spire, but one that was quite different from the original. Strickland took his inspiration from earlier artworks, but added clock faces, decorative elements, and size. Once the last of Philadelphia's city offices moved to the newly built City Hall in 1900, preservation groups moved in to turn Independence Hall into a national shrine.

Ideas like social and cultural history were still years away in the mid-nineteenth century, and while the government buildings were preserved and "restored," private spaces associated with the founding era were still being lost. It was not until the 1930s that Philadelphians began to make a concerted effort to preserve houses as a central part of America's story. In 1931, Frances

I am filled with deep emotion at finding myself standing in this place, where were collected the wisdom, the patriotism, the devotion to principle, from which sprang the institutions under which we live. . . . I have never had a feeling politically that did not spring from the sentiments embodied in the Declaration of Independence.

—President-elect Abraham Lincoln February 22, 1861

The Powel House was threatened with demolition when it was purchased by the newly founded Philadelphia Society for the Preservation of Landmarks in 1931. The picture at top shows the house's east side with the dependency wing to the left. The first floor front parlor is below; the original mantle for the fireplace had been removed by this time.

Anne Wister founded the Philadelphia Society for the Preservation of Landmarks, saving the Powel House. Not far from the Powel House, but distant on the social scale, was Dorothy Ottey, a working-class woman who led her neighbors in a campaign starting in 1934 to preserve their street, Elfreth's Alley.

Increased patriotism at the start of World War II led to the creation of the Independence Hall Association in 1942, and on June 28, 1948, President Harry S Truman signed Public Law

795, creating Independence National Historical Park. In the decades since, historians, curators, architects, archaeologists, archivists, and literary scholars have sifted the evidence of the past, uncovering the stories of the people who lived and worked in these spaces when the United States was founded.

We are all visitors to the past, stepping into moments that are unfamiliar, among people who are strangers. This book seeks to serve as a guide to the place and time that was early Philadelphia, from the first European settlements through the years when the city played host to America's "great experiment" in federal government. Men and women of a variety of backgrounds provide us with snapshots of these years, leaving diaries, letters, published accounts, and government documents. The narrative that follows would not have been possible without the records they left behind. Together, they allow us to step into Philadelphia's familiar grid-patterned streets, and get to know the men and women who helped create a city and a nation.

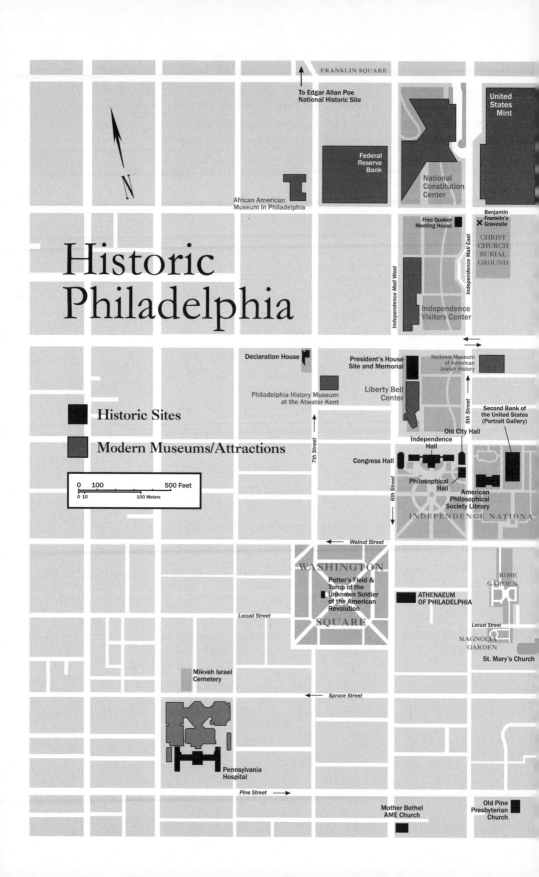

Historic
Philadelphia

FRANKLIN SQUARE

To Edgar Allan Poe
National Historic Site

Federal
Reserve
Bank

African American
Museum in Philadelphia

National
Constitution
Center

United
States
Mint

Free Quaker
Meeting House

Benjamin
Franklin's
✕ Gravesite

CHRIST
CHURCH
BURIAL
GROUND

Independence
Visitors Center

Declaration House

President's House
Site and Memorial

National Museum
of American
Jewish History

Philadelphia History Museum
at the Atwater Kent

Liberty Bell
Center

Second Bank of
the United States
(Portrait Gallery)

■ **Historic Sites**

■ **Modern Museums/Attractions**

Old City Hall

Independence
Hall

Congress Hall

Philosophical
Hall

American
Philosophical
Society Library

INDEPENDENCE NATIONAL

7th Street

6th Street

5th Street

0   100   500 Feet
0 10   100 Meters

Walnut Street

WASHINGTON

Potter's Field &
Tomb of the
■ Unknown Soldier
of the American
Revolution

ATHENAEUM
OF PHILADELPHIA

ROSE
GARDEN

Locust Street

SQUARE

Locust Street

MAGNOLIA
GARDEN

St. Mary's Church

Mikveh Israel
Cemetery

Spruce Street

Pennsylvania
Hospital

Pine Street →

Mother Bethel
AME Church

Old Pine
Presbyterian
Church

N

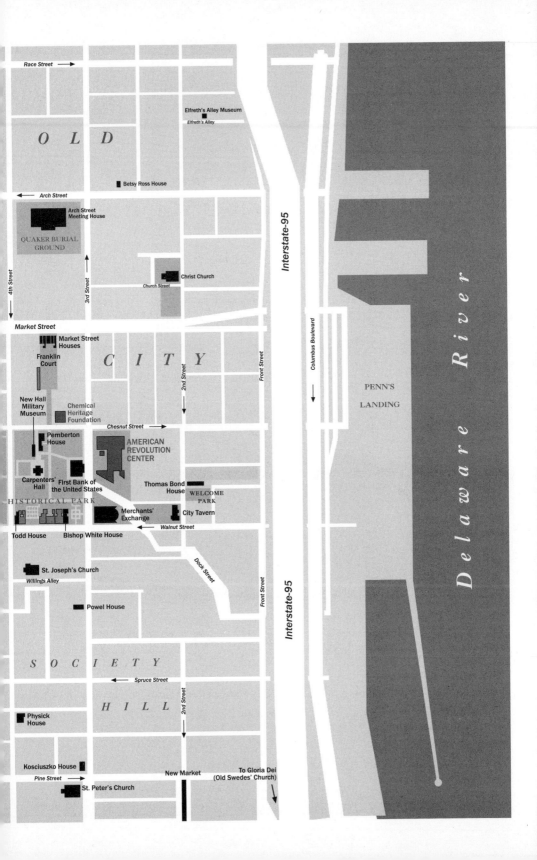

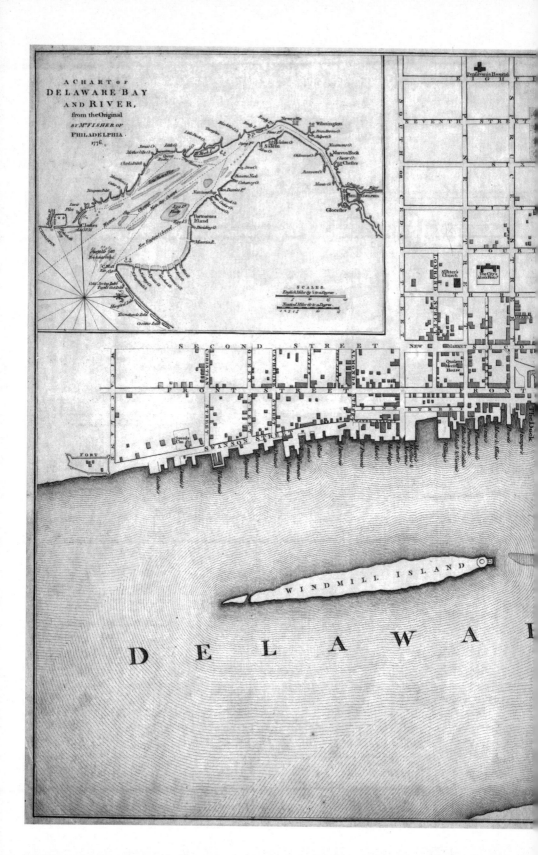

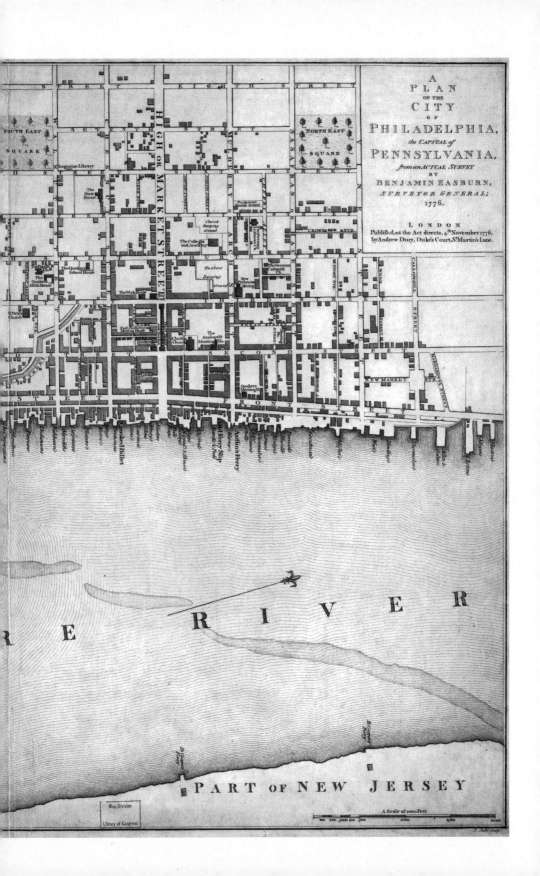

William Penn's statue in Welcome Park sits at the center of Thomas Holmes's 1684 map of Philadelphia (*see page 7*), on the site where City Hall stands at Broad and Market streets today. To the left, a model of Penn's Slate Roof House residence sits on the map's Second Street, between Chestnut and Walnut.

Welcome Park
and
William Penn

F ROM ITS FIRST DAYS as an English colony,
Pennsylvania and its capital, Philadelphia, had
a unique history. The king of England granted the
province, one of the largest land grants made to an
individual in history, as a proprietorship to an elite
Englishman who had converted to one of the
country's most radical religious sects. It was a religious group that defied England's standard beliefs
about social hierarchy, gender roles, and the nature
of warfare and fighting in the modern world, as
well as how humans should know and interpret
God. That proprietor, William Penn, founded a
colony so that his fellow members of the Society of
Friends, or Quakers, would find a safe space in the
New World; the results of his "Holy Experiment"
would influence Pennsylvania, Philadelphia, and
the world for centuries to come.

William Penn might glory in having brought down upon earth the so much boasted golden age, which in all probability never existed but in Pennsylvania.

—Voltaire, *Letters on the English*, 1734

Today Welcome Park, named for the *Welcome*, the ship that brought Penn to his colony for the first time in 1682, sits on the site of the Slate Roof House, Penn's final residence in Philadelphia. The layout of the park copies the city plan Penn and his surveyor created: slabs of white marble represent Philadelphia's wide streets. City blocks are shown as pieces of gray granite. Trees symbolize Penn's four city commons, and a copy of Alexander Milne Calder's famous statue of "Billy Penn" stands on center square, marking the spot on the map where the original statue stands atop City Hall. The park itself is clearly visible on the map, with a small model of the Slate Roof House at Second Street between Walnut and Chestnut. The map commemorates Penn's city. His life is retold on the panels that surround the park on two sides. While the house was destroyed in 1867, this site remembers Penn's legacy for the people of Pennsylvania and the United States.

Pennsylvania's founder was a complex character, a product of a political, cultural, and economic world vastly different from today's. Penn lived in one of the most tumultuous eras in English history, and that era profoundly shaped both his life and his colony. He was born in London on October 14, 1644. By that time, the English capital was already witnessing the turmoil as Parliament argued with King Charles I over issues of taxation and religion. The king—whom many Parliamentary Protestants thought was too pro-Catholic—demanded taxation for military support, and conflict broke out. When William Penn was four years old, the Puritan leaders of Parliament tried, convicted, and beheaded the king. For the next decade, England was ruled by Parliament and the Lord Protector, Oliver Cromwell.

During that period, William Penn's father rose to prominence and wealth as a naval officer, gaining military and governmental prestige in 1655 by capturing the sugar islands of Jamaica from the Spanish. He was a canny politician, supporting first Cromwell and then shifting his allegiance to the monarchy when King Charles II ascended the throne in 1660. He even loaned money to the new king. Eventually, the monarch rewarded him with both military and social titles, becoming Admiral Sir William Penn.

The same year England restored the monarchy, the younger William Penn entered Oxford, to prepare for a place among England's gentry. But his life was about to take a profoundly different path. The era of the English Civil War witnessed the creation of several religious sects that questioned the teachings of the state-supported Church of England. Early in his college studies he began experimenting with some of these religions. In 1662, young Penn was expelled for dissenting against the church. His father sent him on a tour of the European continent, hoping that it would end his religious dissent. On his return, Penn studied law at Lincoln's Inn in London. In 1666, he went to Ireland and took charge of some family estates.

The next year, exposure to one of England's most radical religious groups would change Penn's life. In an era of religious conflict, the Society of Friends, also known as the Quakers, stood out. Quakers believed in the innate quality of all people, in an inward light that revealed divinity to each person, and in the duty of Friends to challenge authority as one way to achieve salvation. They questioned the teachings of the Church of England on social class, gender, wealth, and military conflict. English authorities persecuted this

William Penn, like many early members of the Society of Friends, or Quakers, believed that sitting for portraits was a vanity. Only two life images of Penn are known to exist: a youthful painting showing him in the military tradition of his father, and this one, by Francis Place, a crayon-and-chalk sketch done when Penn was middle-aged.

Friends, or "Quakers," were one of seventeenth-century England's most controversial religious sects, hated by other groups for their beliefs that an inward light led them to an understanding of God, and because they allowed women, the poor, and others to preach. This English cartoon from the period shows the level of anti-Quaker hatred: a Quaker female preaches while Satan whispers in her ear.

dissenting sect, and English critics called Friends "Quakers," ridiculing their enthusiasm during religious meetings.

Penn became an active Quaker and wrote and preached Quakerism's message. For those acts, he was imprisoned in the Tower of London. There, he began writing his famous work, *No Cross, No Crown,* where he condemned luxury, frivolity, violent entertainments like bear baiting and cock fighting, and economic oppression.

When Admiral Penn died in 1670, King Charles faced an embarrassing situation. William

William Penn's Charter of Privileges, which he signed under pressure from the colonists prior to his return to England in 1701, gave widespread rights to the people of Pennsylvania, including freedom of religion and annual elections for the assembly. It served as the colony's constitution until 1776.

Penn was now wealthy, and the crown owed the Penn family a considerable amount of money. This member of the "better sort" was also a member of a radical religious group. New wealth and position did not change Penn's behavior, and he was imprisoned again in 1671 for preaching Quaker ideals.

In 1681, the king got rid of both the embarrassment that Quakers caused him and his debt to the Penn family when he granted a piece of land in North America almost as large as England to William Penn. Pennsylvania—which King Charles named in honor of his friend the admiral—would be a proprietary colony, an almost feudal state where Penn would be both the largest landowner and the governor answerable only to the crown.

Quakerism would profoundly shape Pennsylvania's development. Quakers opposed war and killing in an era of intense international warfare; they refused to follow English society's rules of manners and deference; and their perceptions of class, gender, and race flew in the face of all that seemed to identify the individual and the group in

I doe Call the City to be layed out by the Name of Philadelphia, and soe I will have it Called.

—William Penn
October 28, 1681

Let every House be placed, if the Person pleases in the middle of its platt as to the breadth way of it, that so there may be ground on each side, for Gardens or Orchards or fields, that it may be a greene country towne, which will never be burnt, and allways be wholesome.

—William Penn,
September 30, 1681

that era. Penn intended to be guided by these principles as he laid the foundations for his new city.

Penn hoped that his "holy experiment" would meet the needs and desires of his fellow Quakers from the British Isles. Quakers had been persecuted for religious and financial causes in the old world, and his guarantee that anyone could purchase property in his new colony and its capital was thus quite attractive. Friends also emphasized the family, already calling for a loving sense of domesticity that was very different than any other religion's beliefs in the seventeenth century.

William Penn carefully planned out many aspects of his new colony and its capital, named for the biblical "city of brotherly love," even before he left England aboard the *Welcome* on August 30, 1682. In September 1681 he had instructed the three Quakers who served as his first commissioners "That having taken what Care you can for the Peoples good . . . let the Rivers and Creeks be sounded . . . to Settle a great Towne, and be sure to make your choice in the most Navigable, high, dry, and healthy. That is where most Ships may best ride, of deepest draught of Water, if possible to Load, or unload at the Bank, or Keyside, without boating and Litering of it. It would do well if the River Comeing into the Creek be navigable, at least for Boats up into the Country, and that the Scituation be high, at least dry and sound, and not swampy." The land they chose, on a peninsula of land between the Delaware and Schuylkill rivers, already had a few Swedish farmers settled on it when the English began to lay out their town.

The *Welcome* landed at New Castle in the "three lower counties"—as Delaware, a part of Penn's colony, was then called—on October 28, 1682. In the weeks that followed, Penn visited Chester, Pennsylvania, where the first colonial

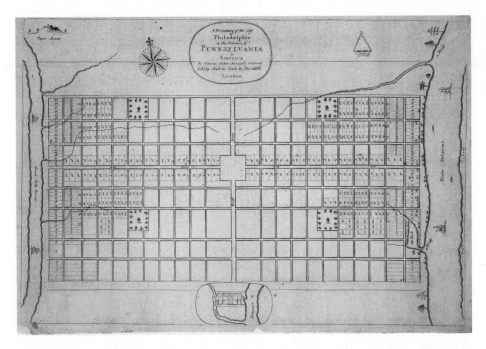

Assembly convened in December. In the months that followed, twenty-three additional ships brought colonists to the Quaker colony on the Delaware River. In January 1683, members of the Society of Friends began to hold their weekly "First Day" (Sunday) services in Philadelphia, and the County Court began to sit.

William Penn was a man of many contrasts, and one of the most striking of these is the fact that he was a religious mystic who was also comfortable in the physical world and enthusiastic about the emerging field of science. An elected member of the Royal Society of London—the group of English gentlemen who sought a deeper understanding of the natural world—Penn used new developments in science and urban planning in creating Philadelphia. He had lived through the Great Fire of London in September 1666, a blaze that destroyed the homes of 70,000 Londoners, eighty-seven churches, and St. Paul's Cathedral.

Thomas Holme, William Penn's surveyor general, drew this map of Philadelphia that was subsequently published in London and reproduced in several other languages, showing potential settlers and investors the colonial capital's grid plan of large lots and wide streets, with five squares or "commons" and two rivers that were navigable to sailing ships.

He believed that in a "greene country towne" houses should be far enough apart that fire could not jump from one neighbor to another.

Immediately upon arriving in the new colony, Thomas Holme, Penn's surveyor general, set about turning 2,000 acres of forest and meadow into an orderly colonial capital. Holme staked out a grid consisting of High (now Market), Mulberry (Arch), Walnut, and Chestnut streets, designated where Broad Street would lie, and began laying out the east-west streets, which had to contend with Dock Creek's interruption of the street plan in the south and that of another creek in the northern part of the city.

As Philadelphia grew over the next century, the grid plan was one of the most commented-upon aspects of the city. Thomas Jefferson, himself an amateur architect, saw classical influence in Holme's work and compared it to major cities: "They are none of them comparable to the old, revived in Philadelphia, and exemplified." Others guessed that Holme was inspired by other grid-patterned towns, or that Holme (a former military man who had converted to Quakerism) laid out the city based on a well-ordered camp. For whatever reason Holme chose, it is certain that the plan lasted. While Penn's visions of a bucolic city were quickly abandoned by the settlers in his colony, Holme's plan for Philadelphia survives almost intact.

Penn's creation of Pennsylvania reflected both Quakerism and his personal experiences. The colony would be diverse, because Penn believed in religious toleration but also because he needed a large number of settlers to purchase land and pay taxes. English, Irish, and Welsh settlers would arrive from the British Isles; Pennsylvania would also welcome Dutch colonists, and large numbers

---

The country was then called Pennsylvania from William Penn, who there founded Philadelphia, now the most flourishing city in that country. The first step he took was to enter into an alliance with his American neighbours, and this is the only treaty between those people and the Christians that was not ratified by an oath, and was never infringed. The new sovereign was at the same time the legislator of Pennsylvania, and enacted very wise and prudent laws, none of which have ever been changed since his time. The first is, to injure no person upon a religious account, and to consider as brethren all those who believe in one God.

—Voltaire, *Letters on the English* (1734)

of Germans began to arrive in 1683. Swedes and Finns who were already on site as part of the New Sweden colony would stay, too. Indeed, the French *philosophe* Voltaire, who learned of the colony while he was exiled in London in 1707, praised Pennsylvania and its founder for the colony's religious liberty and just dealings with Native Americans.

The king of the Contry where I live, hath given me a great Province; but I desire to enjoy it with your Love and Consent, that we may always live together as Neighbors and friends.
—William Penn to the Lenni Lenape, 1681

Quaker pacifism was one of the most significant aspects of Philadelphia's early history. Pennsylvania's leaders built no wall around the city in an era when other colonies experienced bloody warfare. Just before Penn founded Pennsylvania, King Philip's War of 1675–1676 had devastated the New England colonies, while conflict with Native Americans had been a leading cause of Bacon's Rebellion in Virginia in 1676. Hundreds of white settlers had been killed or wounded, as many Indians had been hurt or displaced, towns along the frontier destroyed, captives taken, economies damaged. This violence did not happen in Pennsylvania. For half a century, while Friends maintained their control over the Pennsylvania Assembly, peace continued on the frontier. Philadelphia prospered greatly as a result. The city's hinterlands developed into rich farmlands settled by people of diverse religious convictions from throughout Europe. The city, with its large port on the Delaware River, became a major trading center. Many Quakers became leaders of the transatlantic trading community as they exported grains, furs, and lumber from Pennsylvania to ports around the world.

Penn's American Indian policies would set his colony apart from other English settlements in America. Pennsylvania's first English colonists encountered the Lenni Lenape ("true people," in their Unami or Munsee language), an Algonquian people who lived in the area between modern-day Trenton, New Jersey, and Wilmington, Delaware. In this matrilineal culture, people's economic lives were based on the growing of the "three sisters" (corn, beans, and squash). The Lenape were used to European colonists long before Penn's experiment began. Early Virginia settlers had named both the native people and the river the "Delaware," in honor of Governor De La Warr of Jamestown. But William Penn was the only European colonizer who paid Native Americans for the land he acquired, maintaining a colonial policy based on negotiation rather than force. Penn's Indian policy worked so well that, despite the rapid growth of white settlements, Native Americans also moved to the areas as refugees from other parts of Anglo-America.

But Penn's toleration also brought trouble. By 1720, the population of Pennsylvania was 31,000 people, many of whom were German and Scots-Irish settlers who did not share Quaker pacifist views and were land hungry. This led to beginnings of white-Indian conflict in the eighteenth century.

William Penn planned a political system where he, and eventually his heirs, would act as governor, with a Provincial Council and an elected bicameral legislature, made up of the lower Assembly and the upper house, to propose and pass laws. That plan lasted only a year, and under pressure Penn created a new constitution in 1683 that expanded the power of the Assembly beyond just approving legislation written by the upper house. When Penn returned to the colony from England in 1699, colonial leaders again demanded a revised form of government, and he created the Charter of

☞ Architecture: The Slate Roof House

As William Penn prepared to return to England in August 1684, he enthused about the structures being constructed in his new colony's capital. They were "large, well-built, with good Cellars, three stories, and some with balconies." Penn may have let enthusiasm cloud his observations. After all, he was both a proud town father who was viewing his newborn village, as well as a businessman who wanted to see his investment thrive.

Few buildings from Penn's era survive in Philadelphia. The eighteenth century brought significant stylistic changes in architecture, and earlier structures that did not suit the tastes of later generations made way for newer ones. Pennsylvania's success also doomed its earliest buildings. As Philadelphia thrived, and its population doubled over and over again, many of these first houses on their spacious lots were also razed, making way for more densely packed buildings, and later industrial and mercantile structures near the Delaware River.

The Slate Roof House, where Penn and his family lived during his second, final stay from 1699 to 1701, was one of the young town's most impressive spaces. Designed for Samuel Carpenter by architect James Porteus, a Scot whom Penn had sent to the colony "to design and execute his Proprietary buildings," the house may have been one of the first American buildings constructed in the H or U shape that was becoming popular in England during the reign of King James II. It was two stories tall, built of local brick, had two projecting symmetrical wings, and a brick-surfaced court facing Second Street. Alexander Gradon, whose mother ran a boardinghouse in the building in the 1770s when John Adams stayed there, recalled that it was "a singular old fashioned structure, laid out in the style of a fortification, with abundance of angles both salient and re-entering." The alley just north of the house connected it to the busy port of Philadelphia, and the deep garden (a landmark in John Adams's time) remained into the nineteenth century. The most distinguishing feature of Carpenter's mansion gave it its name: a roof made of slate, rather than the more common wooden shingles.

Several efforts were made during the nineteenth century to preserve or move the Slate Roof House because ☞

Top: William Breton, one of the first Philadelphia artists to attempt to preserve this city's heritage through his paintings, sketches, and engravings of historic sites, captured the Slate Roof House, already famous for its association with Pennsylvania's founder when he made the image in the 1820s. The house was noted for both its extravagant roofing material and the two projecting bays that faced Second Street. Bottom: Reconstructed floor plan by Dr. Bernard Herman, University of North Carolina at Chapel Hill.

Philadelphians, still reeling from the loss of the Slate Roof House, adopted the small colonial house on nearby Letitia Court as "probably" being the house built for Penn's daughter. Long after they moved it to Fairmount Park and redubbed it "William Penn's Cottage," historical architects proved that, while the building was one of the oldest in Pennsylvania, it actually dated from years after Penn returned to England.

☞ of its age and connection to William Penn, but these failed and the building was razed to make way for a corn exchange in 1867. Perhaps remorseful over its loss, Philadelphians embraced another, simpler structure and sought to connect it to Penn. The Letitia Street house, originally located on the small lane that runs from Market to Chestnut Street between Front and Second, must have been the home of Penn's daughter Letitia, Philadelphians reasoned. In 1883 the small colonial house—much more typical of the style of the earliest structures in the Delaware Valley than the Slate Roof House—was moved to the newly created Fairmount Park, near the Philadelphia Zoo. Preservationists took the onetime row house and placed it on a bluff overlooking the Schuylkill River, much like the grander, eighteenth-century buildings that became its neighbors. For years, the building housed a museum called "William Penn's Cottage." Modern architectural research later proved that the building was actually built in the 1710s, years after Penn and his family left for Britain. Today, the house that would be the oldest residence in Philadelphia houses offices in Fairmount Park. ☜

Privileges while living in the Slate Roof House. The colony's new one-house legislature would have more power than any other elected body in England's North American colonies, including the right to elect their speaker and to draft legislation. The Council was now just an advisory body for the governor, and the governor could not dissolve the legislature at his will. This system of government would stand until the American Revolution.

William Penn's brief periods of residence did not allow for much stability, and the lieutenant governors appointed first by Penn and then by his second wife Hannah Callowhill Penn and their sons did little to help. The religious diversity of the colony also led to difficulties. Quakers felt that their role in some governing functions, particularly defense, was incompatible with their religious beliefs. Other colonists, particularly Anglicans and Presbyterians, were dissatisfied because they were excluded from political power or felt their beliefs were being ignored. Penn's "peaceable kingdom" was not always peaceful.

When he arrived in 1682, William Penn intended to live in his colony for the rest of his life, but outside forces intervened. In 1684 he was forced to return to England to settle the boundary dispute between Pennsylvania and Maryland's proprietor, Lord Baltimore. Penn intended to return in a short time, but political turmoil erupted in England when King James II was deposed in the Glorious Revolution, and subsequent growing economic problems delayed his return. Penn did

☞ Hannah Callowhill Penn

Hannah Callowhill Penn arrived in Philadelphia on Sunday, December 10, 1699, accompanied by her husband, William Penn, his daughter by his first marriage, and his young secretary, James Logan, an Irish-born Quaker. One month later, Hannah gave birth to her first child, a boy the Penns named John. Quaker colonists were enthusiastic to greet the returning founder and his bride, and saw the arrival of the new baby as a sign that their proprietor would now be a permanent part of colonial life.

Hannah Callowhill was born in Bristol, England, in 1671, the daughter of a wealthy Quaker merchant. By her teenage years, all of her siblings had died, and Hannah became heir to her father's estate. When she was twenty-four, she met William Penn, who was twenty-six years older than she was and a widower, while he was in Bristol attending Quaker meetings. The two corresponded, and married on March 5, 1696. Hannah Penn's residency in Pennsylvania was short, but her influence would be extensive. She ran the households at the Slate Roof House and at Pennsbury, the family's country estate twenty miles up the Delaware River from Philadelphia, overseeing a ☞

Hannah Callowhill Penn served as proprietor of Pennsylvania from her husband's death in 1718 until her own in 1726, the longest and most significant position of authority that a woman took in colonial English history. She preserved her husband's legacy and her sons' inheritance.

On the 14th of this month [October], Anno 1644, was born William Penn, the great founder of this Province; who prudently and benevolently sought success to himself by no other means, than securing the liberty, and endeavouring the happiness of his people. Let no envious mind grudge his posterity those advantages which arise to them from the wisdom and goodness of their ancestor; and to which their own merit, as well as the laws, give them an additional title.

—Benjamin Franklin, *Poor Richard Improved*, 1748

☞ workforce that included both free and enslaved workers. She participated in numerous Quaker activities. And she managed the family's finances, always difficult because her husband proved to have money management problems and colonists often refused to pay the taxes and fees that the proprietor demanded.

After the family returned to England in late 1701, Hannah Penn's roles increased. Her husband suffered a series of strokes in 1712, and it fell to her to manage both her family and the colony. At the time of his first stroke, Penn was negotiating selling both his land and administrative rights in Pennsylvania to Queen Anne. His illness sidetracked those plans, and the queen's death in 1714 and the ascension of her cousin King George I ended the plan to turn Pennsylvania into a royal colony. Instead, Hannah Penn managed the colony's government until she died in 1726. She was the only woman who governed a British colony for that long, and she maintained her family's interests until her sons John, Thomas, and Richard were old enough to inherit and maintain the family's interests. ☜

not come back to Pennsylvania until 1699, and that stay was short, too. The resumption of warfare in Europe put Penn's claim on Pennsylvania in jeopardy, and in 1701 he returned to the mother country to try to restore his increasingly depleted personal wealth. A great lawgiver, Penn was simply not a very good businessman.

Penn's last years were difficult. While his claim to his colony was approved by King William and Queen Mary, his ties to the English government were tenuous at best. In addition, Penn's personal finances were a constant worry. In 1708, he was imprisoned for debts he owed to his former agent.

In 1712, Penn had a stroke that debilitated him for the rest of his life. Penn's second wife, Hannah Callowhill Penn, assumed control of the colony and maintained it until her young sons came of age. William Penn died July 30, 1718. His legacy would continue in the centuries to follow: his religious toleration, encouragement of diversity, and freedoms granted under the Charter of Privileges were all significant. But by the middle of the eighteenth century, Penn's sons came to see the colony as more of a feudal estate than the "Peacable Kingdom" their father had dreamed of. Penn's legacies would lead to many of the struggles that the colony faced in the decades ahead.

After his conversion to Quakerism, Penn's personal qualities, as well as his wealth and legal training, led him to leadership positions in the Society of Friends. Here, Penn sits on the facing bench, showing his high status in the Quaker meeting, surrounded by Friends wearing the plain style that some members adopted to show their faith.

Gloria Dei (Old Swedes) Church, situated in South Philadelphia, is the oldest religious structure in Pennsylvania. The building tells the story of the English craftsmen who constructed it in 1700, as well as the Swedish settlers who came to the Delaware Valley more than half a century earlier.

TWO

Gloria Dei Church
and
Southwark

NESTLED IN A SMALL CHURCHYARD about one mile south of Philadelphia's Market Street, not far from the banks of the Delaware River, and surrounded by humming modern highways, sits Gloria Dei Church, the oldest religious structure in Philadelphia and one of the oldest buildings in Pennsylvania. Today, its brick walls, steep-pitched roof, and quaint surrounding churchyard with centuries of tombstones make a picturesque scene, an idyllic reminder of Philadelphia's earliest settlements and, it is believed, the only surviving building in Pennsylvania that William Penn ever set foot in. But the early history of Gloria Dei, or Old Swedes' Church, was very different. The church grew out of an era of contested empires battling for land and resources in North America. Its

The colony of New Sweden drew Swedish and Finnish settlers to both sides of the Delaware Valley from 1638 through the 1650s, trading with American Indians for furs and other goods. This map, published in 1702 in *Kort beskrifning om provincien Nya Swerige uti America* by Thomas Campanius Holm, showed both the landscape the settlers encountered and the people who greeted them.

location, construction, and survival all speak to the presence of Europeans in what is now Pennsylvania decades before Penn and his fellow Quakers founded their colony.

Gloria Dei Church stands in an area the Lenni Lenape Indians called "Wicaco" or "peaceful place," a land that saw its first European colonization as part of the colony of New Sweden in 1638. In the 1630s, Sweden was one of Europe's most powerful nations, with boundaries that stretched over modern Finland and Norway as well as parts of Russia, Poland, Estonia, Germany, and Latvia. Swedes followed their military victories by seeking new wealth from the New World, and in 1638 carried out plans for a colony. Their goal was to enter the highly profitable trade in beaver furs, the essential raw material for the stylish hats prized by men and women in the era. By founding New Sweden in the Delaware Valley, they were competing directly against the Dutch whose New Netherland colony was located to the north, along the Hudson River. Seeking access to trade routes, Swedes built trading forts in three areas: Christiana, now the site of Wilmington, Delaware; Casimir, now New Castle, Delaware; and Wicaco, the area in South Philadelphia where Gloria Dei now stands.

Peter Minuit, a former director-general of the Dutch New Netherland colony most remembered today as the man who swindled Manhattan Island away from its Native American owners, had grown disgruntled with his own employers, the Dutch West India Company. Minuit convinced Sweden's Queen Christina and her ministers that an outpost in the New World would benefit Sweden, and he led the settlement in the Delaware Valley. Not all of the first settlers who sailed aboard the *Kalmar Nyckel* and *Fogel Grip* for New Sweden were actually Swedes; Finns and Dutch made up the rest of the party. Like other European colonies scattered throughout the Atlantic World, New Sweden was primarily a trading post, with little pretention of being a colony where families would live permanently. No women or children came on the first ships, whose voyagers included trappers and men who could grow highly lucrative colonial crops, like tobacco.

From the start, New Sweden's relations with the Lenni Lenape were strained. Many years later, the Seneca chief Cornplanter recalled the ways the Swedes had acquired land: "The Great man wanted only a little, little, land, on which to raise greens for his soup, just as much as a bullock hide would cover. Here we first might have observed their deceitful spirit. The bullock's hide was cut up into little strips, and did not cover, indeed, but encircled a very large piece of land."

"They were to raise greens on it," Cornplanter said, "instead of which they planted great guns." Relations between Indians and whites grew worse in the years to follow. Johan Printz, the first Swedish royal governor, attempted to frighten the Lenape after his appointment in 1643 by telling them that he expected large numbers of settlers to arrive at any time, but when the settlers failed to show up, Indians attacked Swedish farms south of Wicaco. A treaty followed, but Printz observed that the Lenape "trust us in no wise and we trust them still less." In a report to the government at Stockholm, he requested two hundred soldiers

Swedish colonists entered into trade with the Lenni Lenape people whom they encountered in the Delaware Valley, with both groups discovering strange customs and life ways, all portrayed in this engraving of "Nova Svecia." From *Kort beskrifning om provincien Nya Swerige uti America* by Thomas Campanius Holm (1702).

be sent to help him "break the necks of everyone in the river." The only thing that kept minor clashes from escalating into widespread warfare was that the Swedish forces were weak.

But the colony's time in the area was to be short. In part, this was due to a limited infrastructure of Sweden's empire. Minuit died at sea during his return voyage to Sweden in August 1638, and the colony had no governor for the next two years. New Sweden always suffered from a lack of settlers and supplies; only a dozen ships, carrying few supplies and small numbers of settlers, came to the colony in the sixteen years that it was part of Sweden's empire. And New Sweden was a victim of worldwide imperial battles. In 1655, the administrators of New Netherland sent several hundred troops south from present-day New York to retaliate against the Swedes who had captured one of their outposts the year before. Bowing to superior forces, the Swedes gave up without a fight. For the next nine years, the Delaware Valley would be part of the Dutch Empire, until English forces under the command of James, the Duke of York (King Charles II's younger brother, who would later rule as King James II), captured the area in 1664. In 1681, King Charles granted the territory to William Penn for his "holy experiment."

New Sweden's existence in the new world was short-lived, but Swedes remained a presence centuries after their empire left. In part, this was due to Penn's policy of religious and cultural toleration. After 1681, Swedes were joined by settlers from England, Ireland, Wales, Scotland, and principalities in modern-day Germany, and by enslaved people from a variety of locations on the African continent. The Swedes who wished to remain and to farm land or practice their trades encountered little prejudice from their new government. "I must needs commend their respect to authority, & kind behaviour to the English . . . they are people proper & strong of body," William Penn wrote in August 1683. Other Swedes continued to migrate to the new colony of Pennsylvania in the years that followed.

The Swedish community now living in "Southwark" (a name English colonists had borrowed from the land south of the Thames River in London and applied to the area south of Philadelphia) continued to practice their Lutheran faith, and it held them together as the years passed. Sweden's church leadership continued to encourage and support their congregations in the Delaware Valley, and in 1697 sent two young pastors, Erik Björk and Andreas Rudman, to the area to minister to congrega-

And it was called GLORIA, and in Swedish, Gudz Ähros Huus, and in English, House of God's Glory.
—Pastor Erik Björk, 1700

The church is 60 feet long, 30 feet wide, and 20 feet high. The roof is made of cedar shingles, 18,000 of them. There are six windows, three on each side, twelve feet high. The whole interior is covered with plaster, although the ceiling was first secured with laths. On each side the pews are arranged in two quarters, and in addition there is a lengthwise pew under the windows, with an aisle between this and the quarters.

—Pastor Andreas Rudman, November 1700

tions there. Björk served the church at Christiana; Rudman assumed the pulpit at Wicaco.

When Rudman arrived to minister to the Swedish Lutherans of Southwark, he encountered a church building that looked more like a military building than a house of God. Located in the churchyard just south of the present Gloria Dei, the first Wicaco Church was made of logs, with brick walls and a stone foundation built in the 1670s. On nearby Tinicum Island stood another log blockhouse, a former defensive building, serving as Gloria Dei Church. The accounts Rudman sent back to Sweden in 1700 noted that the two men could still see the church's founding date, 1649, on the canopy above the pulpit.

The construction of a permanent church building for his congregation marked an important moment in the life of Pastor Rudman and for the members of Gloria Dei's congregation. "Now know first that through God's grace I have got my church finished after going through unbelievable hardships. With God's help still, the difficulties accumulating daily are safely overcome," Rudman wrote in one of his rare letters home to Sweden. "When we held our services in the old church, which was a defense, or blockhouse, we had to get along as best we could." The new building represented a physical and social break with the past: the belief in peace and nonviolence that William Penn and his fellow Quakers had brought to the area after 1682 had relieved the need for a blockhouse or fort along the Delaware. The Philadelphia region would not have another fort until just before the American Revolution, seven decades later.

🙠 Architecture: Swedish Buildings and Early America

Gloria Dei Church is an incredible survivor, a rare remnant of the first European community in the Delaware Valley. But the church as it stands today also reflects the cultural diversity that existed in early Pennsylvania.

The "Swedes Church" was constructed by English master mason Joseph Yard and carpenter John Harrison, and the building reflects both ethnic groups. Yard and his workers constructed the church of a Flemish bond brick pattern, alternating long "stretchers" of bricks with "header" bricks laid with the short side facing out, glazed by adding saplings to the kiln process to coat the exposed surface with a shining dark black color. The result became a quintessential pattern of Georgian architecture and extremely popular in early Pennsylvania. On either side of the church's main door, Yard used glazed headers to create a diamond pattern. This decorative element was commonly found in early eighteenth-century English country houses in the Delaware Valley. 🙠

The Swedish church, which is otherwise called the Church of Wicaco, is in the south part of the town, almost outside of it on the riverside, and its location is therefore more agreeable than that of any other.

—Swedish Traveler Peter Kalm in 1748

Gloria Dei Church's chancel (1700) included a three-sided bay, with windows facing the nearby Delaware River and the Atlantic World that had drawn the first Swedish settlers to what later became Philadelphia. Colonists remembered their history by this architectural feature, which was based on the Lutheran cathedral at Uppsala, Sweden.

☞ The church's chancel–the area immediately behind its altar–is likely a result of the desire of its first pastor to reflect the congregation's heritage. "The east end of the church is angular," Rudman wrote in 1700. The three-sided space–a landmark for Philadelphians from the eighteenth century onward—copies similar architecture in Swedish Lutheran churches, including the Uppsala Cathedral where Rudman was ordained, and other colonial Lutheran churches in America at that time. The pastor wrote of the severe lack of printed materials—Bibles, hymn books, and sermons–that could perpetuate Swedish faith and identity to his church members. Just as he attempted to maintain those connections through his small library and through the ideas he carried in his head, so he probably instructed the English men who were building the church to use an unusual building style to embody Swedish ideas and traditions. Aside from this church, few remnants of Pennsylvania's time as an outpost of the Swedish Empire survive. The Swedes and Finns who settled in the colony built houses of impermanent materials, and style changes in the eighteenth and nineteenth centuries, long before ideas of historic preservation began, doomed these buildings.

But one architectural innovation of these settlers of a long-lost colony became the quintessential American building. Log cabins, first introduced to the Delaware Valley in the 1600s, spread throughout the area and the idea was later carried west by English, Scots, and German settlers. A few of these buildings survive from the area's days as New Sweden, physical reminders of the empires, settlements, and cultures that have shaped the area. ⌫

While Sweden's time as a colonial power in North America was short, the architectural innovation Finnish and Swedish colonists brought to the Delaware Valley became a quintessential American building: the log cabin. This surviving Swedish cabin is located in Delaware County, Pennsylvania.

The minister gave an account of the church's dedication in a report to his Lutheran superiors in Sweden: "This year, on the first Sunday after Trinity Sunday, it was consecrated by me with the text 2 Sam. 7:29 ["Therefore now let it please thee to bless the house of thy servant, that it may continue for ever before thee: for thou, O Lord GOD, hast spoken it: and with thy blessing let the house of thy servant be blessed for ever"] . . . and called, for several reasons, by the former one's name, GLORIA," Björk wrote in November 1700. Perhaps the use of the earlier church's name signified a connection to the earliest Swedish tradition in the area. Perhaps congregation members who saw the main church move from Tinicum Island–a location near the trading post colony–to the area closer to the emerging colonial capital of Philadelphia were placated by the retention of the old name. Whatever the reason, the "official" name was often forgotten in favor of calling the congregation "The Swedes' Church" from its earliest days.

At its consecration, Rudman wrote, "The church was as full as it could possibly be, for it is no farther than two musket shots from the south side of the town. The people stayed from beginning to end." Indeed, the ceremony must have been one of early America's first ecumenical celebrations: in addition to Rudman and his "faithful colleague" Pastor Björk, the "English priest" delivered a sermon at noon that day.

Sweden's hold on the Delaware Valley ended in 1664, and while the Swedish community remained, the area immediately around it devel-

Artist William Birch captured the first image of Old Swedes' Church in 1799 in his print "Preparing for War to defend Commerce." With the historic church in the background, Philadelphia shipbuilders construct a U.S. naval ship. The former Swedish colony, subsequently known as Southwark and then South Philadelphia, was closely associated with the maritime trades well into the twentieth century.

oped with a mix of residents and cultures in the years that followed. By the era of American independence, Southwark had become closely affiliated with the maritime economy of the British Atlantic world and the trades and tradespeople who were a part of that economy.

The decades that the Rev. Nicholas Collin served "Old Swedes" saw his neighborhood transform from a half-forgotten remnant of the Swedish colony to a bustling, urban, industrializing neighborhood in the new United States. In addition to recording births and deaths, Collin paid witness to a changing world from the windows of Gloria Dei Church. The expanding American economy and the diplomatic challenges facing the new nation were evident just

⮞ Rev. Nicholas Collin

Long after New Sweden's control of the Delaware Valley ended, Swedish interests and culture in the area continued, and perhaps no Swede had a greater impact on the area for a longer period than Nicholas Collin, the minister at Gloria Dei Church from 1786 to 1831.

Rev. Nicholas Collin

Nils Collin was born in Sweden, graduated from the University of Uppsala, and arrived in America on May 12, 1770, as missionary pastor to the Swedish Lutheran parishes at Racoon and Pennsneck, New Jersey. His time at that post would see the coming of the revolution and a decided split in New Jersey communities over support for the Tory and Patriot causes. By 1778, Collin was ready to go home. He wrote pleading letters to the archbishop of Uppsala, relating the "pressing terms for my recall." He had served his mission for eight years, he said, and "was consequently entitled to preferment at home."

Sweden's king chose instead to keep all missionaries in place for the time being, as travel during the war was almost impossible. Collin found himself in an increasingly unpleasant situation. He could not draw his commissary salary from Sweden, and his congregants could not or would not contribute to church funds. Moreover, income from church properties declined to one-tenth of their pre-war value. Collin spent the rest of the war impoverished at his post in New Jersey.

The strife and poverty did have a positive outcome, as it turned out. Collin found "considerable time to amuse myself with my dear mathematics and philosophy," and when he moved from New Jersey to Philadelphia in 1786 he joined a circle of men who met regularly to discuss the natural world and other topics that eighteenth-century vocabulary lumped together under the term "philosophy."

One of Collin's new friends was Benjamin Franklin, who had returned from Paris in 1785 and who hosted regular meetings of the American Philosophical Society in his dining room at Franklin Court. Franklin declined Collin's own dinner invitation in December 1788, writing, "my Malady . . . makes it so extreamly inconvenient to me to dine abroad, that I have not once done it since my Return to America." But the two men met regularly to discuss a host of topics. Like other men of the cloth, Collin ⮞

On Monday last the Rev. Dr. Colin, delivered a sermon in the Swedish Church. . . . In this discourse the Doctor enforced the duty, and displayed the advantages of patriotism in a most elegant and original manner, and concluded by taking notice of the present happy situation of the United States in the adoption of the Fœderal government.

Opposite: Reverend Jehu Curtis Clay standing among the gravestones at Gloria Dei Church, c. 1860.

sought to draw the famous deist into discussions of religion, talks that may have been one-sided. After Franklin's death in 1790, Collin wrote to Franklin's grandson, remembering, "I often had the satisfaction of conversing with this immortal sage in his last illness." Five years after Franklin died, Moreau de St. Mery, an exile from the French Revolution, recorded traveling to South Philadelphia where he "viewed the Swedish church and saw its philosopher and philanthropist pastor, Dr. Collin, my colleague at the Philosophical Society of Philadelphia."

Inspired by the Enlightenment, Collin was a careful observer, correspondent, and recorder of information. That, combined with the financial struggles he had experienced during the revolution, inspired him to leave a wealth of information about his congregation and the Southwark community in the early national period. Collin kept careful account books of births, deaths, and marriages, recording "remarkable occurences" related to weddings—as when one prospective groom insisted he had to be married that very day because "his love was so violent that he might suffer if he refrained from bedding with her that night"—and detailing the often gripping poverty and related poor health that many of the working people of his community experienced.

Many of these records explained how the person who sought a marriage or a burial spot was related to the Gloria Dei Parish through family ties. But Collin's records also showed a demographic shift in the community as "the Swedish language decreased continually by decease of the ancient people." Collin preached periodically from the English Book of Common Prayer as the years went on, and helped his congregants transform the former missionary churches in America to parishes that were to choose their own ministers, now native born and English speaking. Collin died in 1831 and was buried near his pulpit in Gloria Dei Church. In 1845, the church became a part of the Episcopal Church of the United States.

across Front Street. Shipbuilders there were building the *United States,* one of the American Navy's first frigates and a sign of the growing tensions between the country and its former French allies. The Quaker diarist Elizabeth Drinker's pacifist religious beliefs made her shudder to see a newly created weapon of war when she recorded on May 9, 1797, "'Tis a long time since I have seen such a concourse of people as passed by . . . going to and returning from the Frigate, which was launched about one o'clock, a little below the Swedes Church. The first vessel that was ever built here, and I wish I could say, it was the last that ever will be."

Before and after the sermon several fœderal odes, which had been previously set to music, were performed by a band, accompanied by voices. The whole of this sacred and patriotic entertainment was conducted in such a manner as to give the highest pleasure to a crouded and respectable audience. Too much praise cannot be given to the Rev. Dr. Colin, for this contribution to the order and happiness of the United States, in addition to many others which he has given during the late controversy upon the subject of the fœderal government.

—*Pennsylvania Gazette,* August 6, 1788

The intersection of Second and High (Market) streets was the epicenter of power and commerce in Philadelphia until the mid-eighteenth century, with the Friends Great Meeting House at left, and the Town House, which held the colony's courts and assembly, meeting on the second floor. Directly behind that building, the market sheds stretched, supplying food and entertainment to citizens and visitors. The town's Presbyterian and Anglican churches were located nearby. William Breton, an early nineteenth-century artist, made this drawing and others of the scene, long after Philadelphia's court had moved to Independence Square.

THREE

Market Street and *Christ Church*

PENNSYLVANIA'S FIRST SETTLERS followed William Penn to the new world for religious reasons, crossing the Atlantic on an eight- or twelve-week voyage to live in a colony where they could follow their individual consciences, join communities with other like-minded members of their own faiths, and live peacefully alongside people of other faiths. But those first settlers were also practical men and women, people who realized the importance of commerce in the Atlantic World as well as the necessity of providing food and supplies for the colony in which they would now live. As quickly as they began to build houses of worship, they built wharves jutting into the Delaware River to welcome ships from around the world, and a market to sell locally grown produce to fill colonists' tables and stomachs.

By 1685, William Penn would report: "There are Two Markets every Week, and Two Fairs every year." The first market days were held very close to the river, "on the west side of Delaware front street, within the High street," and in 1693 the twice-weekly sales moved one block west, "where the Second Street crosses the High street." That August, Philadelphia's council voted "that after the 12th instant, the market & stalls be for the present removed to market-hill, & be there keept until such time only, and no Longer, as the Lt. Gor. shall cause the place wher the second street crosses the High-street, to be staked out for the market place, & till a Bell-house be built & erected, & the bell hung in the sd place." By the early 1700s, the Philadelphia market was bustling, with the newly built market stalls stretching west from the Court House at Second along the middle of High Street—already gaining the nickname "the market street." It was this scene that greeted a seventeen-year-old runaway from Boston one Sunday morning in October 1723.

Benjamin Franklin had just arrived in a rowboat that had carried him down the Delaware. The city that he entered that morning as he walked up the hill from Market Street Wharf to the Court House was vastly different from his native town, in both the look of the streetscape and backgrounds of its citizens. His native Boston, fifty years older than Philadelphia, was noted for its narrow, meandering streets, connecting the homes, shops, and meetinghouses of the Puritan colonists who had fled to that "city on a hill" to escape religious persecution in England. After Franklin bought breakfast from a baker and drank a few tankards of water from the river, he began to stroll Market Street as the city awakened on that Sunday morning. "I walk'd again up the Street," he remembered, "which by this time had many clean dress'd People in it who were all walking the same Way; I join'd them, and thereby was led into the great Meeting House of the Quakers near the Market. I sat down among them, and after looking round a while and hearing nothing said, being very drowzy thro' Labour and want of Rest the preceding Night, I fell fast asleep, and continu'd so till the Meeting broke up, when one was kind enough to rouse me. This was therefore the first House I was in or slept in, in Philadelphia."

Franklin delighted in telling the story of his ridiculous appearance for decades afterward, comparing the dirty, tired teenager who fell asleep in a silent Quaker meeting with the man of intelligence and connections that he later became. The stories he told of his youth were inextricably connected to the colony that became his home at the age of seventeen, just as his name would be forever afterward associated with Philadelphia.

That the market was clear in Franklin's memory almost fifty years later should come as no surprise. Eighteenth-century visitors marveled at the diversity and quality of foods that they could purchase at Philadelphia's market, which welcomed farmers to sell their goods every Wednesday and Saturday. Reflecting on the abundance of the fields, one of Pennsylvania's earliest settlers called the area "the best poor man's country in the world." In 1744, William Black wrote "you may be supply'd with every necessary for the support of life thro'ut the whole year, both extraordinary good and reasonably cheap, it is allow'd by Foreigners to be the best of its bigness in the known World, and undoubtedly the largest in America." By mid-century, Christ Church would treat market-going farmers to a bell concert on the evenings before market day, which often resulted in the rural visitors coming to the church to see the bells they heard. The sight the next morning was no less clamorous. "The Philadelphia market deserves a visit from every foreigner," J. D. Schoepf recorded in 1783. "Astonishment is excited not only by the extraordinary store of provisions but also by the cleanliness and good order in which the stock is exposed for sale." Schoepf described the market sheds, stretching between Front and Second streets, then Second and Third, and the way the area "swarms with buyers and sellers." Four years later, the Rev. Manasseh Cutler noted, "The market is considered by many as the greatest curiosity in the city. It is a building of near half a mile in length, of one story high, supported by brick pillars at a small distance, the distance between them being open; but a vacancy is left for the cross streets, of equal width with the streets. The floor is raised about two feet above the level of the street." But beyond the food, it was the people who presented the greatest show, the minister reported: "The stalls were furnished with excellent meat, and there was every kind of vegetable and fruit which the season afforded. The crowds of people seemed like the collection at the last day, for there was of every rank and condition in life, from the highest to the lowest, male and female, of every age and every color. Several of the market women who sold fruit, I observed, had their infants in their arms and their children about

them, and there seemed to be some of every nation under Heaven."

"The market-house . . . is perhaps exceeded by none in the world, in the abundance, neatness, and variety, which are exposed for sale every Wednesday and Saturday," the *American Gazetteer* recorded in 1797, and the following year French resident Moreau de St. Mery noted, "For beef, veal and mutton the big market of Philadelphia is only second to that of London-hall."

The market stalls Franklin saw on his first day were probably quiet—the colony's Quaker leaders strictly banned sales on Sundays, just as they regulated behavior in the sheds. Air quality was one serious issue. While a 1722 regulation "Ordered That no Person, Butcher or Others, be

William Birch's print of the High Street Market, looking west from the Jersey Market between Front and Second streets, captured a quiet moment. On Wednesdays and Saturdays, the spaces were crammed with farmers, butchers, and a variety of other salespeople supplying the foods that Philadelphians ate.

At Delaware's broad
Stream, the View
begin,
Where jutting
Wharfs, Food-freight-
ed Boats take in.
Then with th' advanc-
ing Sun, direct your
Eye;
Wide opes the Street,
with firm Brick
Buildings high:
Step, gently rising, o'er
the Pebbly Way,
And see the Shops
their tempting Wares
display;
(Chief on the Right,
screen'd from rude
Winds and blest,
In Frost with
Sunshine) Here, if Ails
molest,
Plain surfac'd Flags,
and smooth laid Bricks
invite
Your tender Feet to
Travel with Delight.
An Yew-Bow,
Distance, from the
Key built Strand,
Our Court-house
fronts Caesarea's Pine
tree Land.

suffered to Smoak Tobacco in the Market or Market house, or in any stalls, under the penalty of one Shilling for every offense, as the same is Inflicted by an Act of Assembly of this province, now in force Against Smoaking in the Streets," kept one smell in check, others must have abounded. The same regulation said that no person "shall Kill or Slay any Beast, or lay any Garbage, Gutts, Dung or Offals, in or at the stalls or Shambles, or in the Market, under the penalty of one Shilling for every offense."

Franklin immediately became a part of the community whose homes and shops surrounded the market sheds. As he remembered that morning fifty years later, he asked a nearby baker for "bisket," but the baker didn't know what "bisket" was, that cheap, working-man's meal not being available in Philadelphia. The young printer then asked for a three-penny loaf of bread, the cheap, unappetizing if nourishing food that he'd often eaten in Boston. Again, the baker didn't know what he meant. So the temperamental Franklin asked him for three pence worth of whatever kind of bread he did have, and he was shocked when the baker handed him three, large, loaves of white bread, the food of the wealthy "upper crust" of Massachusetts. What Franklin experienced (but could not have been able to explain, at the time) was that his native New England was suffering from a wheat blight that had been damaging crops for years. That, plus the damages and fatalities from near-constant warfare between British colonists and the New France colony to their north, had caused inflationary prices and a limited diet. Neither factor had affected Pennsylvania, however. The abundance Franklin experienced in

1723 still held true when John Adams arrived fifty-one years later: food was more plentiful (and better, some observed) in Philadelphia. Little wonder that after a few weeks of eating the lavish meals Philadelphians served him, Adams wrote to his wife, Abigail, "I shall be kill'd with Kindness, in this Place."

The market sheds set the tone for the busy, often crowded, and sometimes prosperous city scene that spread out as new arrivals walked up the hill from the river. The market drew shoppers from around the city, and the buildings that housed many of Philadelphia's governmental and social institutions were nearby in the town's center.

At the heart of Philadelphia's political and economic life was the court house, the building Franklin's friend Joseph Breintnall said "fronts Caesarea's Pine tree Land" (meaning New Jersey, just across the Delaware River). The court house was a brick structure, built in 1710 between the two sections of the original market sheds. From

A detail from Scull and Heap's "Prospect." The Town House (6), at Second Street, sat atop a steep rise that led to Philadelphia's docks and the Atlantic World beyond. Christ Church's steeple, to the right, was the tallest building in the American colonies, greeting visitors with both its grandeur and the sound of its eight bells.

Thro' the arched Dome, and on each Side, the Street Divided runs, remote again to meet.

—from Joseph Breintnall's "A plain Description of one single Street in this City," January 1729

the time of its construction, the court house drew men to climb its two exterior staircases to vote in annual elections. It served as the center of protests and celebrations, and even stood in the middle of religious controversy. Benjamin Franklin's *Pennsylvania Gazette* of November 15, 1739, reported, "On Thursday last, the Rev. Mr. Whitefield began to preach from the Court-House-Gallery in this City, about six at Night, to near 6000 People before him in the Street, who stood in an awful Silence to hear him; and this continued every Night, 'till Sunday. . . . Before he returns to England he designs (God willing) to preach the Gospel in every Province in America, belonging to the English." Whitefield was an Anglican preacher who advocated a more personal, emotional Christianity, and while supporters called his religious movement the Great Awakening, his detractors throughout the British Empire barred his use of their pulpits, including the one in nearby Christ Church.

Whitefield's powerful speaking drew in followers, even ones who didn't necessarily share his evangelical beliefs. One of the minister's goals became creating an orphanage in Georgia. When he proposed the idea to Franklin, the printer liked the concept, but not the location, thinking that Philadelphia would be better. The two men continued to disagree, and Franklin refused to give funds for the project:

> I happened soon after to attend one of his Sermons, in the Course of which I perceived he intended to finish with a Collection, and I silently resolved he should get nothing from me. I had in my Pocket a Handful of Copper Money, three or four silver Dollars,

and five Pistoles in Gold. As he proceeded I began to soften, and concluded to give the Coppers. Another Stroke of his Oratory made me asham'd of that, and determin'd me to give the Silver; and he finish'd so admirably, that I empty'd my Pocket wholly into the Collector's Dish, Gold and all.

Whitefield may have persuaded Benjamin Franklin, but his fellow Anglican clergymen were less receptive to his ideas, which they saw as challenging the traditional authority of the church leadership and its practices, spelled out in the Book of Common Prayer. In Philadelphia, the center of Anglican orthodoxy was Christ Church, a Church of England parish founded by colonists in 1695. A provision in King Charles II's 1681 charter to William Penn required that

George Whitefield from a biography published in 1774.

> if any of the inhabitants of the said province, to the number of Twenty, shall att any time hereafter be desirous, and shall by any writeing or by any p[er]son deputed for them, signify such their desire to the Bishop of London, that any preacher or preachers to be approved of by the said Bishop, may be sent unto them for their instruccon, that then such preacher or preachers, shall and may be and reside within the said province, without any deniall or molestacon whatsoever.

William Penn's policy of toleration allowed every religion to co-exist in his colony, but Penn had always envisioned a city populated by and under the control of members of the Society of Friends. He planned for that idea to be made visually evident by placing the central Quaker meetinghouse at Center Square, surrounded by

Christ Church, Philadelphia, widely regarded as one of the grandest Georgian buildings in the American colonies.

public buildings (including his own house). But Penn's plans never came to fruition, and the Friends built their "great" (but plain) meetinghouse in the center of the city's commercial district on Second Street at Market, close to the homes of the Quaker merchants who led the meeting.

Religious liberty existed, and toleration was the rule, in eighteenth-century Pennsylvania, but that did not mean that everyone always got along very well. The Anglicans completed their original small church building in 1696. Whether the clergy would serve "without any deniall or molestacon" was still up for debate.

One Sunday morning in July 1715, the congregants arrived for services to find the church locked up tight. The previous night, the sheriff of Philadelphia had arrested Christ Church's acting rector, the Rev. Mr. Francis Phillips, leading him bare-legged through the streets of town in his nightshirt and putting him in the town's prison. Phillips was charged with slander; allegedly, he had said that he had slept with three women, including the wife of Anglican leader William Trent and the daughter of John Moore, one of the congregation's founders, as well as propositioning Elizabeth Starkey, the indentured servant of John Humphreys, clergyman at the Anglican parish in Chester, Pennsylvania. Sheriff Peter Evans, who was a member of Christ Church, was courting Miss Moore, and refused to allow the minister to send for his bail or to be housed in the undersheriff's house rather than the jail, as was the custom for prisoners of high rank.

Were the charges against the minister true? Probably not, but proving that someone had gossiped or not was almost impossible. That Sunday, two hundred men and boys from Christ Church marched to the jail, demanding that the popular clergyman be released. When that was accomplished a few days later, the crowd turned to mob violence, attacking the house of John Smith, one of the men who had accused Phillips. Sheriff Evans then challenged Phillips to a duel, to defend his fiancée's honor. The minister ignored the challenge. In the trial that followed, the jury found Rev. Phillips guilty of slander and fined him £20, but the minister denied the legitimacy of a trial and fine, and Governor Charles Gookin forgave Phillips's fine. That October, the bishop of London ordered the minister to return to England, eight months after the controversy had begun, and Phillips left Philadelphia.

The Phillips conflict probably resulted from the controversies between the church laity, the clergy, and the laws and customs of the established Church of England, which contrasted with the laws in colonial Philadelphia. The Church of England was the official church of the mother country, where it had legal rights and protections; but its regulation was left up to local laws and enforcement in the colonies, where there was no bishop to head the church. Each colony dealt with this in different ways, in some cases, such as Virginia, taxing the local population to support the church. But in Pennsylvania, with its religiously diverse population and Quaker leadership, the Church of England was left in an unusual limbo. Conflicts between factions within the congregation, vying to support one clergyman or another or to exert their own authority, led to or exacerbated tensions in the small Anglican congregation.

By the 1720s, however, parish life had lost its frontier-town atmosphere, and the wealthy merchants who now led Christ Church had the resources to build a brick addition to the wood frame building in 1727, and then began to rebuild the church's eastern end in 1735. The building's architect is unknown, but Dr. John Kearsley, a local physician and member of the church, played in integral part in the building's construction. His 1772 obituary stated "He was well acquainted with the Principals of Archi-tecture, a Monument of which we have in *Christ-Church*—a building which (in the Opinion of Strangers) in Point of Elegance and Taste, surpasses every Thing of the Kind in America."

Adding to the elegance of the main structure, which boasted one of the first Palladian windows in the colonies, trompe l'oeil painted decorations on the ceiling of the chancel, and an

This 1785 engraving of Christ Church's interior shows the splendor that welcomed worshippers in the eighteenth century. The building's Palladian window, with a central curved window flanked by two smaller rectangular ones, featured clear glass panes that caught the morning sunlight streaming from the east.

elegantly carved pulpit and sounding board, was the tower and steeple, constructed between 1753 and 1754. Christ Church hired master builder Robert Smith to construct the steeple on the building's west side, funded in part by a lottery organized by Benjamin Franklin (whose wife and daughter were members of the congregation), and atop the tower was an eight-bell chime cast by the Whitechapel Bell Foundry, the same foundry that had provided the original, ill-fated bell (now known as the Liberty Bell) for the State House's tower. Christ Church's 196 foot steeple was the tallest building in the

American colonies, a landmark for visitors traveling by land or water to Philadelphia, the largest town in British North America, disclosing the power and success of the empire by the 1760s.

Assistant Rector Jacob Duché's comment that the church where he served looked like a London building was an observation shared by many who visited in the 1770s. Indeed, the Anglican community of Philadelphia could look on the previous few years as a time of peace and tranquility, with less dividing them from Philadelphians of other faiths, and enough clergymen to see to their ecclesiastical needs.

Among the many notable aspects inside Christ Church are the grave tablets set into its floor, marking the final resting place of early congregants. One of the most prominent of these is the Reverend Richard Peters's marble slab in the center aisle, which greets worshipers as they approach the communion rail to take the Lord's Supper, or tourists as they walk to the church's east end to view the eighteenth-century pulpit. Peters was rector of Christ Church from 1762 to 1775, the culmination of a long career in Philadelphia in an era marked by challenges for the church. In many respects, Peters's life reads like a Jane Austen novel, interrupted at the end by the American Revolution.

Richard Peters arrived in Philadelphia in 1735, trying to escape scandal in the new world. While studying in Holland, he had married a woman only to discover that the servant girl he had married earlier was not dead, as he believed. Guilty of bigamy, Peters and his second wife separated, and he departed for Pennsylvania.

Controversy continued to dog Peters in the years that followed. Christ Church's vestry elected him assistant rector in 1736, but the church's rector opposed him on both moral and theological grounds, and Peters gave up preaching to serve the proprietors as their colonial land agent. His close connection with the Penns, to whom he wrote that "in any station you may depend on my Services your Interests being as dear to me as my own," and their friends made him an increasingly controversial figure in local affairs. In the 1740s, Benjamin Franklin thought of Peters as a good candidate to head the newly established Academy of Philadelphia, but "Peters, who was out of Employ" declined, "He having more profitable Views in the Service of the Proprietors." The animosity born then between Franklin and Peters increased in the years to follow, as the two men became leaders of the opposing Anti-proprietary (Quaker) and Proprietary political factions.

When Peters became rector of the parish in 1762 following his predecessor's death, he fulfilled a lifelong dream. He had carefully preserved his British ordination certificates, showing that he was a fully recognized clergyman of the Church of England. Philadelphia's Anglican community now included a thriving, prosperous congregation and two elegant churches in Christ Church and St. Peter's; it also controlled the Academy and College of Philadelphia, which Peters served as board president and his close friend the Reverend William Smith headed as provost, much to the disgust of Benjamin Franklin, who had founded it, and of the college's Presbyterian supporters and faculty, whose opinions were largely ignored.

Christ Church's wineglass pulpit, created by Philadelphia cabinetmaker John Folwell in 1769, where Christ Church's congregants heard sermons praising the royal family and later the newly created United States. At the pulpit's base is the grave marker of John Penn, William Penn's grandson and one of the colony's last proprietors.

Reverend Richard Peters.

Richard Peters was a popular leader of his parish, and he might have hoped that his last years would be carefree, but this would not be the case. By the time that transatlantic strife brought the Continental Congress to Philadelphia, Christ Church's intimate ties to the British Empire would lead to much discord for the congregation. Soon after finally assuming leadership in Christ Church, Peters was faced with difficult decisions about loyalty and duty as the empire was torn apart. It was the bells of Christ Church that rang to gather the people of Philadelphia to protest the Stamp Act in 1765, when the ship carrying the unpopular stamped paper landed at the town's wharf, accompanied by a warship to protect its highly controversial cargo.

Peters increasingly saw himself as a man in the middle, tugged by both his adopted home and his mother country. Every Anglican clergyman was required to swear allegiance to the monarch during his ordination, and Peters took the vow seriously. When Christ Church's bells tolled to mourn the closing of Boston Harbor in 1774 to punish Massachusetts for the Boston Tea Party, Peters went public. "We are desired, by the Rector of that Church, to acquaint the Public, that the Bells were not rung with his Knowledge or Approbation, and that, by his express Direction, there was no particular observance of that Day, in either of the Churches under his Care.—It is well known, that the established Church is restrained from any religious Observance of Days, except those appointed by the Church, and the public authority of the Government," the *Pennsylvania Gazette* reported on June 8. Thus, Peters was announcing that he had not protested the actions of the British government, because he had not received permission *from* the British government to do so.

By the next year, the situation in the empire grew worse, and Peters's consternation increased. In June, the Continental Congress asked the minister to participate in a "Day of General Humiliation, Fasting and Prayer" on July 20. The church's vestry agreed to participate, and the Congress processed solemnly from the State House to Christ Church at 9 o'clock that morning to hear the assistant rector, Jacob Duché, preach. That fall, Peters retired, leaving Duché rector with Thomas Coombe and William White as his assistants.

Christ Church's clergymen were about to witness the arrival of the American Revolution firsthand. As twilight fell on September 8, 1774, a group of prominent Philadelphians took their distinguished visitors to view the prospect of the city from its highest point: Christ Church's celebrated steeple. For John Adams, who had attended services there on the previous Sunday, the view was remarkable: "At Evening We climbed up the Steeple of Christ Church, with Mr. Reed, from whence We had a clear and full View of the whole City and of Delaware River," Adams recorded. Just above the men's heads that evening, a copy of the king of England's crown adorned the steeple's weather vane.

As Adams looked down from Christ Church's steeple, the setting sunlight would have revealed a crowded village lying alongside the Delaware River. Second Street, at the edge of Philadelphia when Christ Church was established there in 1695, was now in the city's center. As the congregation had grown, and had built a larger edi-

June 1. This being the day when the cruel act for blocking up the harbor of Boston took effect, many of the inhabitants of this city, to express their sympathy and show their concern for their suffering brethren in the common cause of liberty, had their shops shut up, their houses kept close from hurry and business; also the ring of bells at Christ Church were muffled, and rung in solemn peel at intervals, from morning till night; the colors of the vessels in the harbor were hoisted half-mast, the several houses of different worship were crowded.

—Diary of Christopher Marshall, 1774

fice to house its growing, prospering congregation, its neighboring houses of worship had
grown, too. Just a block away, at High Street,
stood the Friends Meetinghouse, and a few yards
west of it stood the Presbyterian Church where
Adams had heard "Mr. Sprout" preach, using
"no Notes—dont appear to have any. Opens his
Bible and talks away. Not a very numerous, nor
very polite Assembly," Adams recorded. In the
space between these buildings and his perch,
Adams would have been able to observe Market
Street, and the market sheds that gave
Philadelphia's largest and busiest street its name.

Richard Peters died on July 10, 1776, just
two days after the bells of his church had rung
the news that the congress had approved the
Declaration of Independence. Now, each of the
church's clergy was faced with a dilemma, and
each took a different path. Coombe packed up
and returned to Britain, eventually taking a post
as a minister there. Duché supported the American cause at first, then changed his mind and
also returned to England after asking George
Washington to give up the revolutionary struggle. He returned to Philadelphia, very unpopular, years after the war. When lightning struck
the church's steeple on June 9, 1777, destroying
the copy of England's crown, some took it as a
sign of the end of English control of an
American church.

Christ Church's future eventually rested with
William White, one of Peters's former assistants.
He was not a very political person, and he alone
remained to lead his congregation through the
revolution and into the years that followed.
White was so popular in Philadelphia that
Quakers and Presbyterians referred to him as

"our bishop" after he was consecrated in 1787. Today, a golden bishop's miter adorns the top of Christ Church's tower, celebrating White's role and leadership in the parish.

☞ Alice

None of the famous visitors to Christ Church in Philadelphia ever mentioned Alice. No noteworthy Continental Congressman or member of the first federal government left a record of seeing her, or members of the congregation who looked like her, when they attended services at "America's Church." Yet it is very likely that, when these visitors lifted their heads in prayer, they saw the faces of the African Americans of the congregation, seated above them in the church's loft, praying in the seats reserved for servants and slaves.

Alice, from a nineteenth-century print.

What separated Alice (like many enslaved people, she seems to have been known only by a first name) from her fellow black congregants in colonial Christ Church was longevity. When she died in 1802, she was acknowledged to have been one of the oldest people in the new nation, with some estimates giving her age as 116. Her survival, and her keen memory that recalled the origins of the colony and the country, drew her fellow Americans white and black to her in the last years of her life.

She "was born in Philadelphia, of parents who came from Barbados, and lived in that city until she was ten years old, when her master removed her to Dunks's Ferry," north of Philadelphia, along the Delaware River, "in which neighbourhood she continued to the end of her days," Poulson's *American Daily Advertiser* reported upon her death. Like many Americans of African descent, her family had come to the British continental colonies by way of the Caribbean, living lives that were both cosmopolitan and exemplary of the denial of human freedom that slavery represented.

An enslaved woman without a political voice, Alice's memory of the first settlement of Philadelphia became more and more valuable as decades passed. "Being a sensible, intelligent woman, and having a good ☞

William Breton used colonial reminiscences to recreate this view of the first Christ Church building, a small wooden building that sat along Second Street near the market.

☞ memory, which she retained to the last, she would often make judicious remarks on the population and improvement of the city and country; hence, her conversation became peculiarly interesting, especially to the immediate descendants of the first settlers, of whose ancestors she often related acceptable anecdotes," the *Daily Advertiser* reported.

"She remembered William Penn, the proprietor of Pennsylvania, Thomas Story, James Logan, and several other distinguished characters of that day," her obituary recalled. Yet Alice, who knew the founder well enough to remember lighting his pipe for him in her youth, also remembered the beginnings of human slavery in Pennsylvania. In 1684—two years after Penn had founded Pennsylvania—the ship *Isabella* landed at Philadelphia, transporting the first 150 enslaved Africans to the colony, which then had a population of 1,000. If Alice's age in 1802 was indeed 116, then she was almost certainly the child of two of these enslaved people. Her early years coincided with slavery's permanent establishment in the colony. In October 1689, Penn wrote to his agent, "I both desire and empower thee to be supervisor of my plantations, houses, servants, stock, growth, and emprovements, and to direct my people what to doe therein . . . I wou'd have but a little family [servants], indeed none but the blacks."

Alice's recollections painted a historical portrait for the people of nineteenth-century Philadelphia, as she "remembered the ground on which Philadelphia stands, when it was a wilderness, and when the Indians (its chief inhabitants) hunted wild game in the woods, while the panther, the wolf, and beasts of the forest, were prowling about the wig wams and cabins in which they lived."

And she remembered Christ Church, her spiritual home for her entire adult life. Through interviews, she left one of the best accounts we have of the early appearance of the church. "The first church she said was a small frame that stood where the present building stands, the ceiling of which she could reach with her hands from the floor," her obituary reported. "She was a worthy member of the Episcopal society, and attended their public worship as long as she lived. Indeed, she was so zealous to perform this duty, in proper season, that she has often been met on horseback, in a full gallop, to church, at the age of 95 years. . . . The veneration she had for the bible, induced her to lament, that she was not able to read it."

Alice could remember the earliest days of her church, a Church of England parish in a Quaker town. She could recall the building of the church's grand edifice that began as an addition to the first church, then eventually sur-rounded and replaced that little building. And she could remember the building of the parish's magnificent church steeple, completed in 1754. The sight of the church's spire, and the songs that its eight bells rang out on Sunday mornings, likely guided her as she galloped to services.

But Alice could also remember that the leaders of the parish exiled her to the distant parts of God's house. When Christ Church's chimes rang a message of freedom in the 1770s, they did not toll for the enslaved members of their own congregation who sat in the loft. ⌐<

Christ Church's interior today, showing the Palladian window facing east, and the church's bal-cony (altered in the 1830s), where it is believed enslaved African Americans sat during the eighteenth century.

Franklin Court's Market Street Houses, constructed as rental properties after Benjamin Franklin returned from Paris in 1785, revealed their owner's fascination with civic improvement and modern inventions, including extended brick party walls that could stop a house fire from spreading from roof-to-roof, hatches to reach the roofs to put out fires, and other innovations. The court's original arched carriageway witnessed Franklin's departure for the Constitutional Convention in 1787, and his funeral procession in 1790.

FOUR

Franklin Court

FROM THE DAY HE ARRIVED, a seventeen-year-old runaway, cold and hungry from traveling overnight by rowboat, until the day that the people of Philadelphia mournfully lined the streets to watch his coffin pass sixty-seven years later, the block surrounded by Third and Fourth streets on Market was intimately connected with Benjamin Franklin. His life there saw his transformation from a poor boy to one of the most famous men in the new country. This block saw him rise in talent and power, saw his mind develop, and witnessed the fruition of his talents as a scientist, community leader, and politician.

Franklin's life was not a rags-to-riches tale, even though he arrived in Philadelphia with just a few coins in 1723. What separated him from

I live in a good House
. . . contriv'd to my
Mind, and made still
more convenient by an
Addition since my
Return.

—Benjamin Franklin
to Madame Brillion,
April 19, 1788

the wandering poor whom he may have met on the docks on that Sunday morning was the artisan skill that he carried in his head. Writing decades later, he could still feel the disappointment of being denied a Harvard education because his father could not afford the tuition. Instead, Franklin had been apprenticed to one of his sixteen siblings and learned the printing trade. He loved reading and loved words, and his talents matched the skills of the printing house. But he bucked at the demands of his brother. After James Franklin got into trouble with the authorities in Boston for speaking out against them (freedom of the press was still more than a half century away), Benjamin Franklin bolted. Friends helped him sneak out of town and escape the contract that bound him to his brother. He sought work in New York first, failed, then turned south. He walked across New Jersey, boarded a rowboat heading down the Delaware River, and arrived in Philadelphia on October 6, 1723.

Almost fifty years later, Franklin remembered in detail his first hours in Philadelphia, showing the important role the city played in his life. The differences between Boston and Philadelphia were immediately striking: wide streets met at right angles, brick buildings lined the thoroughfares, and diverse religious meetings gathered on that morning.

Franklin quickly found work in Samuel Keimer's printing house, located in a small wood-frame building on land that is now part of Franklin Court. Keimer had no family, so Franklin did not live with his employer, as was often the custom, but instead found lodging in the home of John and Sarah Read. While living there, he began to court their daughter, Deborah.

Benjamin and Deborah wanted to get engaged, Franklin later wrote, but her family discouraged the marriage because of his limited funds and prospects. The courtship then took an odd turn. A short time after he arrived in Philadelphia, Franklin met Sir William Keith, the English baronet the widowed Hannah Callowhill Penn had appointed lieutenant governor. Sir William was in the middle of a power play at the time, attempting to gain the support of the electorate to wrest control of the colony from the Penn family proprietors and their supporters. Keith encouraged Franklin, telling him to go to London to purchase printing equipment, and saying that he would give him government printing jobs when he returned. But when Franklin arrived in Britain he learned that Keith's promises of financial support were worthless. The governor had either overextended himself or Franklin's enthusiasm for a bright future had made him hear what he wanted to hear. In any case, the eighteen-year-old was now three thousand miles from home with no money to pay for his return trip, much less the equipment needed to open his own printing house.

But the time in London turned out to be a great advantage for Franklin. He once again relied on his printing skills to get work, and he learned that London held a wealth of riches for a young man with an expansive mind. He thrived in the clubs and coffeehouses where men gathered to discuss ideas, and he haunted the bookshops that lined London's streets. He also learned that girls in London were very friendly

Deborah Read Franklin was one of the people who witnessed the runaway apprentice's arrival in Philadelphia in 1723, and remained his friend, partner, and substitute manager until her death in 1774. Portrait by Benjamin Wilson, after an unknown American artist, c. 1758–1759.

to young Americans. He wrote to Deborah, freeing her from her promise to marry him.

By the time Benjamin Franklin returned to Philadelphia in October 1726, Deborah was in a strange limbo between marriage and widowhood. Encouraged by her parents, she had wed John Rogers, a potter whose shop was on Market Street, on land that is now part of Franklin Court. But Rogers soon disappeared, and rumors began to circulate that he was a bigamist, with another wife in the Caribbean. Women had no right to divorce in the colonies without proof of abuse or bigamy, and Deborah could not even produce her missing husband. Should she remarry, the laws of the time called for her to be publicly whipped if her first husband returned. Also, second husbands were legally responsible for any debt their predecessor had run up.

Benjamin and Deborah rekindled their relationship, despite these hurdles. He wrote,

> We ventured however, over all these Difficulties, and I [took] her to Wife Sept. 1. 1730. None of the Inconveniencies happened that we had apprehended, she prov'd a good and faithful Helpmate, assisted me much by attending the Shop, we throve together, and have ever mutually endeavour'd to make each other happy.

Franklin's career was prospering by the time his married life began. In 1727, he had set up his own printing office in partnership with Hugh Meredith, another of Samuel Keimer's former journeyman printers. While that partnership did not last, Franklin showed himself to be a hardworking, successful artisan, and friends and neighbors loaned him money to buy Meredith out of the business. Two years after opening his shop, Franklin purchased Keimer's failing newspaper, renaming it the *Pennsylvania Gazette*, and turning it into the most successful paper in the colonies. The shop's business expanded in late 1730, when Franklin published his first edition of *Poor Richard's Almanack*, a source of both local information and commonsense wisdom that celebrated the middling sort—artisans, farmers, shopkeepers, and their wives.

Deborah Franklin would prove to be one of the most important people in Franklin's life during these years. She thrived as an artisan's wife, managing the shop, keeping stock, and leaving a detailed record in their shop books that reveals the everyday lives of a family in a rising city. Their common-law marriage produced two children: Francis (1732–1736), who died of smallpox while still a young child, and Sarah, who was familiarly called Sally, born in 1743. From the start, they also raised William, the boy born about 1731 whom Franklin fathered with a woman whose name he never publicly revealed.

The partnership that Benjamin and Deborah Franklin experienced early in their marriage changed over time. By the late 1740s, Franklin became tremendously successful as a printer, and in 1748 he turned active control of his printing office over to his partner David Hall, so in "retirement" he could devote himself to scientific research and public affairs. The change was a welcome relief to a man who always had new, exciting ideas to try out. But Deborah, removed from her part of their business activities, found herself cut off from both her former work and sharing the life of her husband, in many ways.

This engraving of Benjamin Franklin by Edward Fisher, after an oil painting by Mason Chamberlin, showed Franklin at the height of his powers as a natural philosopher in 1762. As lightning strikes a building in the distance, Franklin observes two small bells that he had hung in his home, an early warning device that rang when the lightning rod attached to one of the bells became electrically charged.

Other, bigger changes that took place in the 1750s also affected the Franklins' home life. In the parlor of their home, Benjamin Franklin began to experiment with static electricity equipment, and in 1752 he conducted his experiments that proved lightning was electricity, one of the eighteenth century's most significant and startling discoveries. Fame and awards soon followed. His political star was rising at the same time. In 1757, the Pennsylvania Assembly sent Franklin to London to petition the Penn family to pay taxes on their lands to help protect Pennsylvania's frontier settlements. Deborah refused to accompany him, perhaps because she detested ocean travel. In any event, the assignment kept Franklin in England for five years. During that era he became one of the most celebrated intellectuals in the Euro-American world, and received an honorary degree from the University of St. Andrews in Scotland that forever after gave him the name "Doctor Franklin."

Dr. Franklin returned to Pennsylvania in 1762 and received the thanks of the Assembly, along with five years' back pay. He and Deborah began making plans to finally build their own home in a center court along Market Street between Third and Fourth, behind the small house that her parents had owned. Some of the land on which they built was from Deborah's inheritance, some was parcels of land Franklin had been purchasing for years. But Franklin would have little chance to participate in the building. In 1764, he lost his reelection bid to the Assembly in a nasty campaign. His anti-proprietary group, known as the Quaker Party even though many of its members were not Friends, maintained their control of the Assembly, and

The German bleats & bears y.^e Furs | Th. Hibernian frets with new Disaster | But help at hand Resolves to hold down
Of Quaker Lords & Savage Curs | And kicks to fling his broad trim.^d Master | Th. Hibernian's Head or tumble all down

sent Franklin to the mother country to either get the Penns to help defend their colony or get the king's ministers to take it over. Franklin was adamantly pro-British and pro-monarch, and he relished the opportunity to return to his rented rooms near the Thames River and his conversations with politicians, scientists, and men of letters.

Once again, Deborah refused to travel with her husband. When they parted on November 7, 1764, it would be the last time that Deborah and Benjamin Franklin ever saw each other.

Work on their new home had begun in the spring of 1763, with Franklin's friend Samuel Rhoads supervising the construction and Robert Smith serving as master carpenter. Philadelphia was experiencing a building boom at the end of the Seven Years' War, and lack of workers and materials slowed the Franklins' construction

Franklin's business acumen and scientific fame led to new political power by the 1760s, making him extremely unpopular with the Proprietary Party leaders, who supported the Penn family. This 1764 cartoon shows Franklin (whom his detractors ridicule by placing a fox between his knees) looking on as Quakers and American Indians ride on the backs of Scots-Irish from the frontier, stepping over the slain bodies of English settlers.

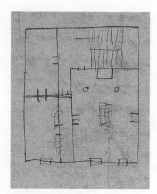

Living in London as Pennsylvania's colonial agent, Franklin sketched this floor plan of the house near Market Street that Deborah was overseeing in his absence.

project. Deborah Franklin moved into the still-unfinished house in May 1765, keeping her husband well informed of current events as well as the everyday bits of domestic life around the house, including placement of wallpaper and furniture, and the benefits of new equipment in their cellar kitchen.

When completed, the house was a three-story Flemish-bond brick structure, thirty-four feet square. Each floor had three rooms, and while no image of the house survives, it is possible to paint a mental picture of the home that Deborah completed while her husband—anxious to be involved in finishing this "modern" structure—was an ocean away. Like many women of the middling sort, Deborah had learned to read, but her writing was limited. She sounded out the words to describe their new home's arrangements: "The Southeroome I sleep in with my Susanah a bead with ought [without] Curtins a Cheste of Drowers a tabel a Glase and old black wolnot chairs sum books in my Closet and sume of our famely pickters," Deborah explained, describing the room she lived in with her maid, an enslaved woman, in attendance. "Now for the room we Cale yours thair is in it your Deske the armonekey maid like a Deske a large Cheste with all the writeings that was in your room down stairs the boxes of glases for musick and for the Elicktresatecy and all your close and the pickters as I donte drive nailes leste it shold not be write," she wrote.

Benjamin Franklin's time in London continued in the years that followed, and the letters between the couple detail the importance of décor for a prosperous family in the British Empire.

The Blewroom has the Armoneyca and the Harpseycord in it the Gilte Sconse a Carde tabel a seet of tee Chaney [china] I bought sens you wente from home the worked Chairs and Screen a verey hansom mohoganey Stand for the tee kittel to stand on and the orney mental Chaney but the room is not as yit finished for I think the paper has loste much of the blume by paisteing of it up thair-fore I thought beste to leve it tell you Cume home[. T]he Curtins is not maid nor did I pres for them as we had a verey graite number of fleys as it is observed thay air verey fond of new painte.

When he received her letter, Benjamin Franklin replied,

I suppose the blue Room is too blue, the Wood being of the same Colour with the Paper, and so looks too dark. I would have you finish it as soon as you can, thus. Paint the Wainscot a dead white; Paper the Walls blue, and tack the gilt Border round just above the Surbase and under the Cornish. If the Paper is not equal Coloured when pasted on, let it be brush'd over again with the same Colour: and let the Papier machée musical Figures be tack'd to the middle of the Cieling; when this is done, I think it will look very well.

Various forms of scientific study two centuries later would explain what the Franklins were describing: archaeologists discovered plaster fragments in the Franklin Court site that were painted with sour milk paint, a common wall covering of the eighteenth century, but one that drew many flies. The decorations Franklin

I honour much the Spirit and Courage you show'd, and the prudent Preparations you made in that [Time] of Danger. The [Woman?] deserves a good [House] that [is?] determined [torn] to defend it.

—Benjamin Franklin to Deborah Franklin, London, November 9, 1765

called for—white paneling, glazed or painted wallpaper coving the lime-filled plaster, and tacked-on gilded papier-mâché decorative elements or border—were found to be at the height of fashion in both Philadelphia and among his new neighbors in the mother country.

Deborah's letters full of news and packages of favorite foods from home reached her husband as he struggled with the increasingly difficult problems of the British Empire. His central mission of getting Thomas Penn, the proprietor, to support the colony was quickly brushed aside by bigger issues. Franklin arrived in London just as Parliament passed the 1765 Stamp Act, a law colonists detested because it taxed their internal commerce without allowing them a voice. Some in Philadelphia blamed Franklin for the new tax, and mob violence threatened to destroy the Franklin house as revenge. Deborah refused to leave the house that she had now worked on so hard, and her husband's friends surrounded the building to protect her and it.

The years that followed were wonderful ones for Franklin, whose fame and prestige in England grew. He traveled in England, Scotland, Ireland, and France and was received with acclaim by the leading lights of the Enlightenment, including Joseph Priestley, Erasmus Darwin, Thomas Percival, and David Hume. He also became an outspoken advocate for American interests in England. But over and over again, as Deborah repeatedly stated her hopes that her husband would return soon, events in London continued to detain him. In December 1773, Franklin was called before Parliament after he revealed private correspondence from Thomas Hutchinson, the governor of Massachusetts Bay, which urged members of the government in London to suspend civil rights in Boston as a way to quell the rebellion there. Franklin and others in America saw the plan as reckless and a direct violation of their rights as Englishmen. Alexander Wedderburn, the king's solicitor general, turned his full fury on Franklin for releasing the information. He called Franklin a liar and thief, fired him from his lucrative job as postmaster general of the colonies, and informed him that he was no longer welcome in the capital. Furious, Franklin stood in stony silence as the charges were hurled at him for over an hour. As he left Parliament that day, he turned to Wedderburn and muttered, "I shall make your king a little man for this."

As Franklin's relationship with the empire disintegrated, Deborah Franklin grew ill in Philadelphia and died at her home on December 19, 1774. She was buried in Christ Church Burial Ground.

Benjamin Franklin finally returned to Philadelphia on May 5, 1775. He arrived at almost the same spot where he had entered the city from the docks on the Delaware fifty-two years earlier, but what he saw was much different. Now far larger, more populous, and more cosmopolitan, the city was also full of newcomers and news, including the stories of the Battle of Lexington and Concord just a few weeks earlier. Benjamin Franklin immediately returned to work as a member of the Pennsylvania Assembly and the Second Continental Congress.

I came here on Thursday last to attend the Funeral of my poor old Mother who died the Monday Noon preceeding. . . . She told me, when I took Leave of her, on my Removal to Amboy, that she never expected to see you unless you returned this Winter, for that she was sure she should not live till next Summer. I heartily wish you had happened to have come over in the Fall, as I think her Disappointment in that respect preyed a good deal on her Spirits.

—William Franklin, Royal Governor of New Jersey, to Benjamin Franklin in London, December 25, 1774

Benjamin Franklin carefully chose the way popular prints portrayed him when he arrived in Paris as America's first minister there in 1776. Wearing a plain, Quaker-style suit and shirt, his spectacles, and a marten pelt hat, he seemed to embody the French image of a man of the Enlightenment.

I found your house and furniture upon my return to Town, in much better order than I had any reason to expect from the hands of such a rapacious crew; they stole and carried off with them some of your musical Instruments. . . . Your armonica is safe. They took likewise the few books that were left behind.

Franklin was never destined to live in the house he and Deborah had built for very long. Historians estimate that he worked eighteen-hour days by the spring and summer of 1776, negotiating his conservative colony's path to revolution. After signing the Declaration, Franklin traveled to Canada to try to convince colonists there to join in the War for Independence. Finally, late in the year he sailed for France, accompanied by his grandsons William Temple Franklin and Benjamin Franklin Bache, to lay the cause of revolutionary America before "a candid world."

Benjamin Franklin left, but the house was far from empty. His daughter, Sarah (Sally) Franklin, and her husband, Richard Bache, resided there during the war, filling the house with children and working to support the American cause, until they were forced to flee when the British invaded after American defeat at the Battle of Brandywine on September 11, 1777. In 1778, the Bache family returned to find the house damaged and furniture and art missing. Fortunately, they had taken the precaution of asking friends to hide Benjamin Franklin's papers outside the city.

But the Franklin family's most startling transformation during the American Revolution was the break that occurred between Benjamin Franklin, the revolutionary father, and his only surviving son, William, who remained a Loyalist. The revolution would also be a civil war, tearing friendships, communities, and even families apart. William was imprisoned by Patriots in New Jersey and eventually fled to England. Trying to mend the break after hostilities had ended, William Franklin wrote from

England to his father in Paris in August 1784 suggesting they reconcile. The response he received was one of the angriest letters Benjamin Franklin ever mailed:

> Indeed nothing has ever hurt me so much and affected me with such keen Sensations, as to find myself deserted in my old Age by my only Son; and not only deserted, but to find him taking up Arms against me, in a Cause wherein my good Fame, Fortune and Life were all at Stake. You conceived, you say, that your Duty to your King and Regard for your Country requir'd this. I ought not to blame you for differing in Sentiment with me in Public Affairs. We are Men, all subject to Errors. Our Opinions are not in our Power; they are form'd and govern'd much by Circumstances that are often as inexplicable as they are irresistible. Your Situation was such that few would have censured your remaining Neuter, tho' *there are Natural Duties Which precede political Ones, and cannot be extinguish'd by them*. This is a disagreeable Subject. I drop it.

When Benjamin Franklin composed his last will and testament in 1788, he left his son only the funds that William had borrowed and never returned, the books and papers he had likewise borrowed and not brought back, and lands in Nova Scotia that the crown had confiscated, adding, "The part he acted against me in the late war, which is of public notoriety, will account for my leaving him no more of an estate he endeavoured to deprive me of."

When Franklin and his grandsons returned from Europe in 1785, he immediately began fit-

. . . Some of your electric Aparatus is missing also. A Captain Andre also took with him the picture of you, which hung in the dining room, the rest of the pictures are safe, and met with no damage except the frame of Alfred, which is broken to pieces. In short considering the hurry in which we were obliged to leave the Town, Sally's then situation, and the number of things we consequently left behind, we are much better off than I had any reason to expect.

—Richard Bache to
Benjamin Franklin,
July 14, 1778

William Franklin,
Franklin's illegitimate child
whom he and Deborah
raised, was one of his
father's closest companions
and had risen in prestige
to serve as New Jersey's last
colonial governor. His
decision to remain loyal to
the British government led
to a break with his father
that continued even after
the Revolution. Portrait by
Mather Brown, c. 1790.

I must not omit
informing thee that
yesterday arrived . . .
that great Patriot and
experienced
Statesman, to which I
may add that eminent
Philosopher Benjamin
Franklin. He was
received in the City
with all possible
Demonstrations of Joy

ting up Franklin Court to suit him for his final years. He tore down the small, dilapidated houses along Market Street to make way for larger rental properties. He added a wing along the east side of the house for a large dining room, a library, and bedrooms on the third floor. And he built a building to the north of his house for his grandson's printing business.

In the spring of 1790, Thomas Jefferson visited Franklin Court. Traveling from Monticello to New York to become America's first secretary of state, Jefferson stopped along the way to visit his old friend. "At Philadelphia," Jefferson wrote in his autobiography, "I called on the venerable and beloved Franklin." There, he found Franklin in bed, struggling with the illness that would soon end his life.

After a long discussion about the affairs taking place in France, Jefferson asked Franklin about the autobiography that he had heard Franklin was writing. Standing at his grandfather's bed was young William Bache, Sally's son. The grandfather directed William to fetch part of the manuscript from a nearby cabinet. There, Franklin entrusted Jefferson with his only copy of part of the famous document.

The statesmen who journeyed to Franklin Court during the five years that Franklin lived there after returning from France frequently recorded such scenes: grandchildren scurrying about or doing their lessons for their "grandpapa's" approval, a pleasant domestic scene where Sally Franklin, who inherited both her father's looks and tenacity, maintained the home.

The last five years of Benjamin Franklin's life proved to be pleasant if busy ones, years when he could finally spend some time in his house.

Franklin was elected president of the Commonwealth of Pennsylvania, revived the American Philosophical Society, attended every day's meetings of the Constitutional Convention, and in his last days, tackled one final controversy: slavery.

Visitors who stroll the flagstones of Franklin Court or visit the Underground Museum are often amazed that Benjamin Franklin was a slaveholder. Indeed, the young printer who advertised "A Likely Negroe Woman to be Sold. Enquire at the Widow Read's in Market Street, Philadelphia," in April 1730 was a slave merchant as well, selling an enslaved woman—owned by his mother-in-law—whom he likely knew well. The decades that followed saw the Franklin family grow wealthy, and some of that wealth went to buying people. Deborah and Sally Franklin's burden of housework was lightened by the labor of men and women held in bondage including Susanna, the maid who slept near Deborah's bed on the house's second floor, and George, the enslaved man who prepared the house and garden for them. Franklin himself took an enslaved man with him to London and took no part in the newborn British abolition movement. As a member of the Continental Congress and Constitutional Convention, Franklin negotiated compromises so southern slaveholders would support plans for a new nation.

All of that made Franklin's actions in the last months of his life more remarkable. In February 1790 the Pennsylvania Society for Promoting the Abolition of Slavery drafted a petition to Congress, calling for an end to slavery in the United States. Franklin signed the document as

by the Citizens who accompanied him from Market Street Wharf to his own house and he was welcomed by the Commonalty with repeated Huzza's of "long life the venerable Franklin!"

—John Todd, September 15, 1785

'Tis a very good house that I built so long ago to retire into, without being able till now to enjoy it. I am again surrounded by my friends, with a fine family of grand children about my knees, and an affectionate good daughter and son-in-law to take care of me. And after fifty years public service, I have the pleasure to find the esteem of my country with regard to me undiminished.

—Benjamin Franklin to John Hunter, November 24, 1786

Benjamin Franklin owned this medallion, created by famed English porcelain artist Josiah Wedgwood, showing the antislavery image and motto that asked "Am I not a Man and a Brother?"

Can sweetening our tea, &c. with sugar, be a circumstance of such absolute necessity? Can the petty pleasure thence arising to the taste, compensate for so much misery produced among our

the group's president, and southern Congressmen were furious. Rep. James Jackson of Georgia railed that Franklin must be senile if he had put his name to such a document, and shouted that slavery was actually good for the country, an argument that would be echoed many times in the seven decades leading to the Civil War. Unflustered, Franklin took pen in hand one last time and published an anonymous essay in which he took on the persona of an Algerian leader who argued that capturing Christian sailors and enslaving them was actually good for them. Franklin's literary skills and his biting wit had not been diminished by the illnesses that were plaguing him in the last weeks of his life.

When Benjamin Franklin died at Franklin Court in the early morning hours of April 17, 1790, the nation mourned, but the United States Senate did not. Representative James Madison led the House chamber in going into mourning, but when Senator William Maclay made the motion that the Senate also publicly mourn Dr. Franklin, pro-slavery southern senators opposed the suggestion, still bitter that Franklin "betrayed" them by speaking out against slavery. In the end, the Senate's reaction did not matter much. As Sally and Richard Bache led the procession out of Franklin Court's covered carriage way, the sight they encountered was amazing. Thousands of Americans crowded the streets, roofs, and even chimneys to get one last look at the coffin as it traveled to Christ Church Burial Ground to join Deborah in a corner near Arch and Fifth streets. Franklin, ever a believer in freedom of religion, requested that each clergyman in his diverse city be invited to accompany his body to the gravesite, including the rabbi of Mikveh Israel Synagogue. As Franklin's body was lowered into the soil of his adopted city, the Pennsylvania Militia—the group that he had founded in 1747 to protect the city from French attack—fired a salute, echoed moments later by the ships sitting in Philadelphia's port.

Sally Franklin Bache and her husband Richard continued to live in her parents' house for a time after her father's death. There, Judith Sargent Murray, whose letters provide an intimate glimpse into life in Philadelphia, met them at Sally's party, or "levee," on July 3, 1790. She described Richard having a "manly expression . . . tempered by a prepossessing sweetness." Sally was "a most amiable Woman, easy of access, affable, and perfectly engaging . . . she hath been well educated and consequently is descriptive of a woman thoroughly well bred." Murray likewise observed: "Her eldest Son hath completed his apprenticeship to a Printer. . . . The descendant of Franklin exhibited the marks of a gentlemen." Murray also recorded an anecdote about Benjamin Franklin Bache: he had recently traveled by coach to a neighboring city when he caught the attention, and ire, of a arrogant young man, or "fop." "The Fop inquired into the nature of his pursuits—'I am a Printer Sir.' What Sir, a Printer! And he instantly ordered into his features, the most contemptuous expression—observing during the remainder of the journey, the most obstinate taciturnity." The new American republic's democracy was sometimes a thin veneer over old class prejudices.

After her father's death, Sally and Richard Bache traveled to England to see her brother,

Sarah (Sally) Franklin Bache shared her father's commitment to the American cause, leading Philadelphia women to raise money and make shirts for Washington's army during the Revolution. This portrait by John Hoppner from 1793 shows her in the style of "republican simplicity" that gained popularity during the French and American Revolutions.

fellow creatures, and such a constant butchery of the human species by this pestilential detestable traffic in the bodies and souls of men?

—Benjamin Franklin, 1772

> Bache has the malice & falsehood of Satan. ... But the wretched will provoke measure which will silence them e'er long. An abused and insulted publick cannot tollerate them much longer. In short they are so criminal that they ought to be Presented by grand jurors.
>
> —First Lady Abigail Adams

> Benjamin Franklin Bache

When the first issue of the *General Advertiser* emerged from the printing office of "Benj. Franklin Bache, at No. 112 Market Street, between Third and Fourth Streets, Philadelphia," in October 1790, its readers must have remarked the pedigree of its publisher. Bache was born in 1769 and was much adored by his grandmother, Deborah, who recorded his early years in great detail in the letters she sent to her husband. "Benny" accompanied his grandfather to France when Franklin was America's first ambassador. His formal education consisted of schooling at an academy in Switzerland, followed by studies at the University of Pennsylvania and then formal training as a printer. While Franklin had many offspring, Benny was the one who followed him into his craft and inherited his talent for raising controversy with his press. "I have determined to give him a trade, that he may have something to depend on and not be obliged to ask favours or office of anybody," Franklin wrote as he oversaw his grandson's education. Perhaps he still smarted that his son and protégé, the appointed royal governor of New Jersey, had remained loyal to the king rather than his father when the revolution broke out. Benny Bache and William's son Temple Franklin were standing at their grandfather's bedside when he died in 1790.

Bache inherited his grandfather's liberalism, and had seen firsthand the destructive ways of an old regime in Paris in the years before the French Revolution. He was a keen student of Enlightenment political writers who preached the rights of the people in government. Unlike most American printers, Bache was multilingual. He read and reprinted news from Europe without a translator.

Benjamin Franklin Bache followed his grandfather into printing and the newspaper business, publishing the *General Advertiser/American Aurora*, noted for its anti-monarchical beliefs and heated rhetoric. The National Park Service has recreated Bache's printing office in one of the Market Street Houses that Franklin built.

Bache first called his newspaper the *General Advertiser, and Political, Commercial, Agricultural and Literary Journal* when it appeared in October 1790, later changing the name to the *American Aurora*. It was an auspicious time. The federal government moved to Philadelphia that fall. The first two American presidents came to wish that they lived farther away from Benjamin Bache. Bache, and many others, found George Washington to be too aristocratic. The president's salons, levees, and especially the grand balls held every year in honor of his birthday stunk in the noses of those democratic-leaning politicos who thought that any such worship of one man was an affront to the ideals of the American republic.

Almost immediately, Bache became a critic of the federal government. He was a leading voice among the Jeffersonian Republicans who opposed Washington's policies, including his neutrality in the wars that erupted between Britain and France, and in the Jay Treaty with Great Britain that made many concessions but gained little for the United States. Bache continued his vehemence when John Adams was elected president by a close vote in 1796, and he was one of the government's main targets when it passed the Sedition Act in 1798, a law that blatantly violated the First Amendment's protection of freedom of the press. Bache was arrested and was awaiting trial when he died in 1798 of yellow fever.

The Children are all promising, and even the youngest, who is but four Years old, contributes to my Amusement. The oldest, Benjamin, you may remember. He has finish'd his Studies at our University, and is preparing to enter into Business as a Printer, the original Occupation of his Grand-father.

—Benjamin Franklin
to Madame Brillion,
April 19, 1788

and then settled in a rural house up the Delaware River near Bristol, Pennsylvania, for a time, away from the bustle and noise of Market Street. They later returned to the family home, and Sally died there on October 5, 1808. Her husband continued to live there, sharing part of the house with the Free African School, until he

By the time the National Park Service began work to create Independence National Historical Park in 1948, Franklin's Market Street houses were barely recognizable, with extra floors and new facades added in the centuries since his death. NPS architects and curators were able to tell the date of the original buildings, based on the styles of nails used to construct them, chemical composition of paints used, and extensive documentary research. Franklin's carriageway is clearly visible.

We enter through an arched avenue, which immediately produces us in a square, seemingly detached from the noise, and confusion of the Town, although, in fact it is but a few paces from Market street—The building is in the Philadelphia manner, lofty and commodious.

—Judith Sargent Murray, July 3, 1790

died in 1812. Their heirs sold the house to settle his estate, and it was torn down later that year, the land now being more valuable than the house.

The view down Orianna Street in 1948, the year Congress created Independence National Historical Park, was an unremarkable one. Like so many narrow alleys in Philadelphia, it was lined with nineteenth-century brick commercial and residential buildings. The only unusual feature was the street's vaulted access to Market Street, but this appeared to be just the previous century's use of precious commercial space in an urban area. Everyone knew that this was once

National Park Service staff members pioneered the field of historical archaeology, combining traditional digging techniques with documentary research, to discover the Franklin family's life. At right is the covered carriageway. Workers uncover eighteenth- and nineteenth-century foundations, privy pits, and wells, which contained a wealth of information about early America. These objects are now on display in the Fragments of Franklin Court exhibit, in one of the Market Street houses.

the site of Benjamin Franklin's home, but the house had been razed in 1812. There was little evidence of the Franklin family.

What the little street revealed during archaeological digs in the 1960s and 1970s was remarkable. National Park Service employees soon found that daily life at Franklin Court—the construction, the commercial activity, the precious items purchased and later broken—had all left their imprint on the space. Architectural historians found eighteenth-century building materials and styles behind the Victorian façades of the Market Street buildings. These much-altered structures were the buildings that Dr. Franklin had built as investment properties late in his life.

Today, the Market Street houses offer a glimpse into the world of Benjamin Franklin. The National Park Service has meticulously

He amuses himself daily in superintending two or three houses which he is building in the neighborhood of his dwelling house.

—Dr. Benjamin Rush, October 27, 1786

☞ Architecture: The "Ghost House"

We know a great deal about the Franklin family's home at Franklin Court, but many aspects of the long-destroyed house remain mysteries. Those mysteries left the National Park Service with a perplexing question: how should they tell the story of the house, without incorporating incorrect guesses into the process?

While several buildings in Independence National Historical Park, including the Graff House, City Tavern, the Pemberton House, and Library Hall were re-created, historians and park officials proceeded carefully, and only with high standards of research. Photographs or mezzotints of each of those original buildings exist. Surviving documents explain the layout of rooms within them.

When the NPS first proposed interpreting Franklin Court, similar plans to rebuild the house were considered. But even though Benjamin Franklin was one of the most famous people in the world, even though his home was the site of countless meetings of government, intellectual, social, and artistic leaders, no one had ever sketched the structure before it was torn down to make way for commercial properties in 1812, years before the invention of the camera.

restored the outsides of these buildings, providing a view that was undoubtedly very familiar to Dr. Franklin during the last years of his life. Inside, the collection preserves a great deal of unwritten information about an era that might otherwise have been forgotten. Remnants of building materials are displayed in the spaces where Franklin's builders originally placed them. Benjamin Franklin's scientific interest is revealed in the exposed walls of Franklin Court, as he innovated a style of separating wooden joists with masonry and plaster to secure the house from fire and make its residents more comfortable. Archaeological digs on the Franklin Court

We know a great deal about Franklin's house, but not enough to accurately recon-struct the building. Instead, noted modern architect Robert Venturi created the "Ghost House" in the 1970s, a steel structure that reveals the location, size, and layout of the original building.

The NPS opted to show the house's size and shape (which were recorded in fire insurance surveys of Franklin's time) but not to fill in the missing details of the building by conjecture. Noted architect Robert Venturi designed the Ghost House, a steel framework that indicates only the outline of Franklin's home and the position of the chimneys. Portals on the ground allow visitors to see the remains of the Franklin family's basement walls and cellar. Quotations from Benjamin and Deborah Franklin are carved into the flagstones around the building. ⌦

block show us that some scientific knowledge was still a long way off: water wells were dug just a few feet from outhouses; both were later filled in with household garbage that would prove to be a treasure trove of information for archaeolo-gists.

The Parthenon-like façade of the Second Bank of the United States, William Strickland's Greek Revival masterpiece, was once the center of nineteenth-century America's economy. Today, the building houses many of Independence National Historical Park's artistic treasures.

FIVE

The Second Bank Area

From its founding, Philadelphia was meant to embody the ideals of the Enlightenment, the transatlantic cultural movement that sought to embrace reason and science, encourage human improvement and liberty, and banish religion-based prejudice. Pennsylvania's founder, William Penn, was a member of the Royal Society of London and saw no contradiction between his devout religious beliefs and an interest in natural philosophy, as the newborn discipline of science was then known.

But it was Benjamin Franklin, the Puritan-born printer who had only a scant year of formal education, who truly placed Philadelphia before the world as a center of intellectual pursuit and scientific discovery. The buildings that surround the Second Bank of the United States today ful-

Philosophical Hall and the re-created Library Hall, as seen from Independence Square. These institutions, and others like them, gave early Philadelphia the nickname "the Athens of America."

fill Franklin's lifelong passion to bring new learning to the people, each structure embracing Enlightenment ideas of reading, philosophy, science, and the arts and architecture, just as the government buildings to the west were at the center of the Enlightenment's concept of political reform.

Philadelphia's role as a leader of learning began soon after Franklin arrived, while this block was still the rural outskirts of town. Returning from his ill-fated but valuable trip to London in 1726 the ever-sociable twenty-one-year-old Franklin began to meet with other young artisans to discuss ideas, write verse, and contemplate plans for their future lives and careers. By 1727, this group of "leather apron men" (a reference to the artisans' work-wear) was meeting every week in a tavern on Pewter Platter Alley, just across Second Street from Christ Church. This mutual-improvement club, which the members named the Junto, grew to be one of the most important groups in Franklin's life.

Committed to the Enlightenment idea of religious toleration (which was a good idea, as its members belonged to a wide spectrum of the churches and sects in town), they discussed history, philosophy, business, and government in a friendly but intellectually serious atmosphere. They even met regularly in the countryside to exercise together, following English Enlightenment writer John Locke's theory that a healthy mind required a healthy body.

In 1731, Franklin came up with what would prove to be one of his most brilliant and long-lasting contributions to society. At the time, he and his fellow colonists' intellectual aspirations were limited by the funds they had to spend on books. A few wealthy colonists like James Logan, the Irish Quaker who had accompanied Penn to Philadelphia in 1699 as the proprietor's personal secretary and gone on to amass a large fortune, had bought huge personal libraries, and organizations like Christ Church and the Carpenters' Company had collected books on topics of interest to their members. But for artisans like Franklin, who longed for a deeper understanding of the science, history, and philosophy that people in the eighteenth century collected together in the term "useful knowledge," literary resources were as limited as their money. Philadelphia didn't even have a good bookshop at the time, Franklin would later recall. He suggested that members of the Junto pool their books together in the tavern room where they met each Friday night, but members damaged one another's books, and tempers rose.

Franklin then proposed his idea: his *Pennsylvania Gazette* announced that a group of "worthy gentlemen" were founding a public

Be it remembered,
In honor of the
Philadelphia Youth,
Then chiefly Artificers
That in MDCCXXXI
They cheerfully
Instituted the
Philadelphia Library;
which, tho' small at
first,
Is become highly valu-
able & extensively use-
ful

—Benjamin Franklin's
inscription for Library
Hall's cornerstone,
1789

library. In reality, it was all public relations; no group existed, yet. But his announcement generated interest and soon the Library Company of Philadelphia formed, selling shares for forty shillings to join and ten shillings per year, consulting with Logan to select titles, and arranging with an agent in London for their first shipment of books. Thus the American lending library was born.

The advantages the library brought to Philadelphia were soon apparent. The twelve members of the Junto and the other shareholders had access to the latest ideas in politics, philosophy, and other branches of learning. Perhaps most important—as it would turn out—they began to explore scientific topics. The Enlightenment was the era of the knowledgeable amateur, and Franklin and his friends fit that description. Peter Collinson, the library's book agent in London as well as a botanist and member of the Royal Society, began to send questions as well as books, beginning a scientific correspondence that connected thinkers in the New World and the Old. In the spring of 1752, colleagues helped Franklin as he began to develop and test his theory that lightning was simply a form of static electricity. The Library Company's collection still contains a glass tube which the men would rub with a piece of fabric to produce static electricity for their experiments. Peter Collinson helped publicize Franklin's theories and his "Philadelphia Experiment" in England—actions that would transform him from a popular local printer into one of the foremost men of science in the eighteenth century.

As the library gained more members and more books in its first decades, it moved several

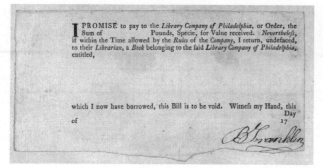

I PROMISE to pay to the *Library Company of Philadelphia*, or Order, the Sum of Pounds, Specie, for Value received. *Nevertheless*, if within the Time allowed by the *Rules* of the *Company*, I return, undefaced, to their *Librarian*, a *Book* belonging to the said *Library Company of Philadelphia*, entitled,

which I now have borrowed, this Bill is to be void. Witnefs my Hand, this Day
of 17

Benjamin Franklin, founder and supporter of the Library Company of Philadelphia in 1731, signed this never-completed loan form.

times. From space in a private house, it moved to the still-new Pennsylvania State House's East Wing in 1739 and then to the second floor of Carpenters' Hall in 1772. In 1775 the directors announced: "The Librarian is directed to furnish the several Members of the said [Continental] Congress with whatever Books they may respectively apply for during their present Session taking Receipt for such Books as he may deliver out." Thus, the Library Company served as the first Library of Congress. The Congress' actions would influence the library in the tumultuous years to come: On March 11, 1777, the librarian published an announcement that "The Members of the Library Company of Philadelphia are hereby notified that Books may be procured from the said Library by Application at the House of the Librarian. . . . The lower part of the Library being at present used as an Infirmary for the sick Soldiery render it inconvenient for the Librarian to attend at the Library Room as usual."

The Company finally had its own building with the construction of Library Hall, designed by an amateur architect Dr. William Thornton in 1789. The building was Palladian in style, red brick with white pilasters and balustrades, with urns at the top. The dual curved staircase led to

Birch's 1799 view of the original Library Hall revealed the neoclassical splendor of the building, with its column-like pilasters, carved urns on the roof, and twin winding staircases leading to the front door. Senator William Bingham paid for the statue of Benjamin Franklin that greeted visitors as it gazed out at the State House Square.

the library's front door, above which stood a statue of Benjamin Franklin, the first in what would prove an often-repeated way of honoring Philadelphia's most famous citizen. Senator William Bingham donated the sculpture of Franklin, who appears in the robes of a Roman senator standing next to a stack of books. In Franklin's hand is the scepter of the English monarch, which he holds upside down, recalling the moment in 1776 when he arrived in Paris to the introduction "he stole lightning from the skies, and the scepter from the hand of a tyrant." Franklin himself approved the style of the sculpture, which had not yet arrived from Italy at the time of his death in April 1790.

Library Hall served as the home of the Library Company of Philadelphia until the 1870s, when a new building was completed on south Broad Street. The Company sold the hall, which was razed a short time later. In the 1960s, the Library Company moved to a modern building in the 1300 block of Locust Street, and it is now one of America's outstanding rare book libraries.

The modern reproduction of Library Hall was built by the American Philosophical Society in 1959, during the rehabilitation of the neighborhood that accompanied the founding of Independence National Historical Park, to hold its massive collection of rare books and manuscripts. The APS is America's oldest "think tank," an organization Benjamin Franklin first envisioned in 1743. "The first Drudgery of Settling new Colonies, which confines the Attention of People to mere Necessaries, is now pretty well over," Franklin wrote, "and there are many in every Province in circumstances that set them at Ease, and afford Leisure to cultivate the finer Arts, and improve the common stock of knowledge." Perhaps he overestimated the level of leisure time he and his fellow colonists had. It was not until the late 1760s that the APS fully began to realize Franklin's ambitions for it.

The year 1769 was a watershed for the American Philosophical Society. The society purchased a telescope from David Rittenhouse to participate in an international project to map the transit of the planet Venus across the sun (and thus aid in the process of establishing longitude readings), and it built an observation tower on the State House lawn near the present site of Philosophical Hall to carry out its observations.

The Philosophical Society was hard hit by the American Revolution. Loyalists and Quaker

The front of the library presents a Niche, which is to be distinguished by a statue of the venerable and illustrious Franklin.

—Judith Sargent Murray, June 12, 1790

Scientist and instrument maker David Rittenhouse (1732–1796), in a portrait by Charles Willson Peale.

Philosophical Hall, the American Philosophical Society's headquarters since 1789, was under construction when the Constitutional Convention met in Independence Hall next door in 1787. At right is Old City Hall, the last of the State House Square's buildings, where the U.S. Supreme Court sat from 1791 to 1800.

pacifists who held membership left, and the society's collections of books and scientific curiosities were scattered. But the return of the Society's founder finally reinvigorated it. In 1785, Benjamin Franklin returned from Paris after serving as American minister there for almost nine years. Franklin's reputation as a natural philosopher was now paired with international recognition as a statesman, and his return to the APS led to new growth for the society. The Pennsylvania State Assembly gave the APS the plot of ground on State House Square on March 28, 1785. By the time the delegates gathered to debate the Constitution in the Pennsylvania State House in 1787, the building was under construction.

That building was Philosophical Hall, the home of the American Philosophical Society since 1789, the same year George Washington became America's first president. The APS continues to use the broad eighteenth-century definition of the term "philosophy," encompassing science, history, and several other fields. Today, the reconstructed Library Hall and the museum rooms in Philosophical Hall house a collection that is far beyond the wildest dreams of Benjamin Franklin when he proposed the Society in 1743. In addition to priceless items associated with early members, the building houses a vast collection of rare books and manuscripts that draws scholars from around the world to the Independence Hall neighborhood. The APS library includes Franklin's papers, the journals of Lewis and Clark, and vast holdings of scientific writings.

Even in its first years, Philosophical Hall became a destination for men and women seeking "useful knowledge" and a better understanding of the ways the new learning of the Enlightenment would influence their lives. In 1794, Charles Willson Peale rented the building for his famous museum, and moved into the building on the State House lawn complete with his large family, pets, and scientific equipment.

Many of the artistic treasures Charles Willson Peale and his family created are now located in Philadelphia's National Portrait Gallery in the Second Bank of the United States, the Parthenon-like structure that is the focal point of its block.

As late as the era of the American Revolution, this area was still on the city's outskirts, filled with the "rural" homes and lavish gardens of some of Philadelphia's leading families. "It was in that day considered as placed in the western extremity of the city," Deborah Norris Logan recalled of her birthplace in the 1820s. Logan was the daughter of Charles Norris, a Quaker merchant, and his wife Mary Parker. In the early 1800s, she recognized that the world around her was changing, and she became one of Philadelphia's first historians.

Deborah Norris Logan (1761–1839) witnessed the creation of the new nation from her parents' garden, located where the Second Bank stands today.

Educated in Anthony Benezet's Quaker school, she developed an interest in historical study that led her to collect the letters between William Penn and James Logan, the grandfather of her husband George. She also recorded the reminiscences of Charles Thomson, secretary to the Continental Congress, and in her own writings she preserved the look and feel of her parents' residence in the days of her youth. "I want to present to those who may come after me, some idea of the comfort, convenience, and delightsome rural beauties, that rendered conspicuous at that time, my honoured Father's home," she wrote. She described the layout of the house, built in the mid-eighteenth century, its hothouse and closets, and especially the lavish gardens that surrounded it: "a walk in the garden was considered by the more respectable citizens as a treat to their friends from a distance, and as one of the means to impress them with a favourable opinion of the beauty of their city." From her parents' garden, the fifteen-year-old Deborah heard Col. John Nixon as he read the Declaration of Independence in public for the first time on July 8, 1776. Perhaps witnessing history inspired a love of it that she maintained until her death in 1839.

Deborah Logan's world was shaped by the transformations in Philadelphia's and America's economy during her lifetime, changes that pushed the city's economic district further west after 1800 and led to the construction of the Second Bank of the United States in 1818.

By the 1790s, when the federal government sat in Philadelphia, city residents liked to boast that they lived in "the Athens of America." Like that ancient city, Philadelphia represented the

☛ Charles Willson Peale

Charles Willson Peale was born in 1741 in Queen Anne's County, Maryland, the son of a schoolmaster. Peale's father died in 1750, leaving his widow with five small children. The family resettled in Annapolis, living in colonial Maryland's capital when it was at its height of sophistication. During this period, Peale became a saddle maker. However, a business trip to Norfolk in 1762 changed his life and early American art. Peale, who at the age of twenty-one had never seen a painting before, went to purchase leather at the home of a Scottish merchant, where he recalled that he saw "several landscapes and one Portrait, with which he had decorated his rooms. They were miserably done."

Peale visited Philadelphia that year on his quest to learn to be an artist. At Christopher Marshall's shop at the corner of Front and Market streets he purchased the book *The Handmaid of the Arts*, a how-to book for painters. After studying the book for a few days, Peale purchased what supplies he could afford and returned to Annapolis. In Maryland, he observed the work of John Hesselius, a noted portrait painter. Peale's saddle business soon brought him troubles; his partner absconded with their funds, and when Peale became actively involved in politics in the Maryland elections of 1764, members of the opposing party drove him out of the colony by suing for debts. He fled to Boston for a brief time, studied art and painting, and returned to Maryland.

Peale came to the attention of John Dickinson, already well known for his *Letters from a Pennsylvania Farmer*. Peale painted Dickinson and his wife, as well as Dickinson's kinsman John Cadwalader and his family. The two men's encouragement led Peale to finally move to Philadelphia early in 1776. It was in the city that Peale's career flourished.

The revolution was a defining moment in Peale's life. He was present on the State House lawn when the Declaration of Independence was first read on July 8, 1776, and he joined the local militia and was elected one of its officers. He saw action at Princeton, was encamped at Valley Forge, and carried the memories of serving in the revolution for the remainder of his life. Peale's personal fortunes ☛

Charles Willson Peale (1741–1827), early Philadelphia's most important artist and portrait painter, spent much of his adult life celebrating and recording the history of the American Revolution. This self-portrait shows him in his military uniform.

John Dickinson (1732–1808), in a portrait by Charles Willson Peale.

Charles Willson Peale's portrait of the victorious George Washington, after the Battle of Princeton on January 3, 1777. In the distance at left is Nassau Hall, now the centerpiece of Princeton University and one of Philadelphia architect Robert Smith's masterpieces.

As a painter, his likenesses were strong but never flattered; his execution spirited and natural.

—Artist Rembrandt Peale describing his father, Charles Willson Peale, in 1855

suffered from his political convictions. The artist was a staunch revolutionary and was extremely anti-Tory at the end of the British occupation of Philadelphia. He helped confiscate the homes of Loyalists, including former Assembly speaker Joseph Galloway, who had left with the British. Peale also helped lead the political charge against Robert Morris and other aristocratic, if pro-American, leaders. Many of the wealthy who could afford the cost of Peale's artistry would not condescend to have such a strident revolutionary paint them.

In 1783, Peale wrote to a friend: "I have painted thirty or forty portraits of Principal Characters. The collection has cost me much time and labour and I mean to keep adding as many of those who are distinguished by their

Actions or Office as opportunity will serve." Peale, living in an era long before the camera was invented, saw the importance of recording the appearance of the faces of those who had led the American Revolution. His portraits are simple, showing only carefully recorded faces and enough of the sitter's clothing to designate military rank or social station.

In 1784, Peale's brother-in-law, Colonel Nathaniel Ramsay, stopped in Philadelphia to see his family. Upon entering Charles Willson Peale's "picture room," he remarked most on the mastodon bones that a local physician had loaned to the artist. He said he would have "walked twenty miles to behold" the bones. "Doubtless, there are many men like myself who would prefer seeing such articles of curiosity than any painting whatever." It was this conversation that led Peale to found one of America's first museums, growing out of his own diverse interests. He threw himself into his Philadelphia museum with gusto. First located at the Peale family residence at Third and Lombard streets, the museum moved to Philosophical Hall in 1794 and finally to the upper floors of Independence Hall in 1802. Basing his ideas on the neatly ordered universe of natural philosopher Carl Linneus, with its hierarchical view of the natural world, Peale's museum showed everything from mastodon bones and taxidermied animals to portraits of America's founding fathers, who symbolized the pinnacle of the natural world for Peale and his contemporaries. The museum continued, in various forms, until after Peale's death in 1827. Among his sixteen children were the painters Rembrandt and Raphael and naturalists Titian, Rubens, Franklin, and Titian Ramsay Peale. ✐

James Peale, Jr., and Augustus Runyon Peale pose at the entrance to Independence Square with a boy worker sometime in the 1840s. Note the snow on the ground and on the roofs.

Nineteenth-century water-color of the Second Bank of the United States.

new nation's cultural, artistic, economic, and political center. The Second Bank, the elegant Greek Revival building once the center of the United States's economy, became one of the most hated institutions in the country for some Americans, the center of a major political battle, and perhaps the cause of one of the worst economic depressions the United States ever faced. Its marble columns and stately interior rooms belie the intensity of the political struggle that was associated with it.

Congress incorporated the Second Bank in 1816. The bank was the successor of Alexander Hamilton's Bank of the United States, which had been at the center of a political battle between Hamilton, Jefferson, and their supporters a generation earlier. The First Bank's charter had expired in 1811, and many blamed the loss of the bank for the economic strife that came with the War of 1812. President James Madison, though a strident Jeffersonian, created the

Second Bank, located in Philadelphia and, eventually, headed by the aristocratic, brilliant Nicholas Biddle. Biddle, one of the city's most prominent men of business as well as letters, brought new architectural style to his native city with the building of the Second Bank.

Born in 1786, Biddle followed in the footsteps of many wealthy young men and went on a grand tour of Europe after his graduation from college. But Biddle broke with tradition, and changed Philadelphia in the process. He traveled extensively in Greece in 1806, considered by some Anglo-Americans to be too ancient and barbaric to visit. There, as one of his kinsmen later wrote, "he was seized with the lasting conviction that there were only two perfect truths in the world—the Bible and Greek architecture." Biddle would spend the decades that followed championing that second truth as a leader of the Greek Revival movement, and would create perhaps the most important architectural revolutions in early American history in the process.

President James Monroe had not yet appointed Biddle to be a director of the bank when its board called for a "chas[t]e imitation of Grecian Architecture in its simplest and least expensive forms," but Biddle's taste-making influence was obvious. Biddle's friend William Strickland won the contest, copying the design for the bank's north and south facades from an engraving of the Parthenon in James Stuart and Nicholas Revett's *Antiquities of Athens*. As a member of its board, Biddle saw to it that branches of the national bank throughout the country were modeled on Greek temples. In the years to follow, Strickland would design the Merchants' Exchange, the United States Naval Asylum

The portico of this glorious edifice, the sight of which always repays me for coming to Philadelphia, appeared more beautiful to me this evening than usual. . . . How strange it is that in all the inventions of modern times architecture alone seems to admit of no improvement— every departure from the classical models of antiquity in this science is a departure from grace and beauty.

—Philip Hone, February 14, 1838

Greece was free; in Greece every citizen felt himself an important part of his republic.

—Architect Benjamin Henry Latrobe

William Strickland
(1787–1854) painted by
John Neagle in 1829.

He found us living in a
city of brick, and he
will leave us in a city
of marble.

—Joseph R. Chandler,
toasting architect
William Strickland,
1833

along Grays Ferry Avenue near the Schuylkill River, and a host of public buildings that would lead early nineteenth-century Americans to call Greek Revival architecture "the national style," with its center in Philadelphia.

A New Jersey native, William Strickland was born in 1788. In 1790, his family moved to Philadelphia. From 1803 to 1805, Strickland was apprenticed to Benjamin Henry Latrobe, best known for his work on the United States Capitol and the White House, among other structures, in the new nation's capital in Washington, D.C. For the next few years, Strickland carried out several trades, including painter, surveyor, and engraver as well as architect, but he had designed only four buildings before winning the competition to design the Second Bank of the United States in 1818. The design catapulted Strickland to fame. He designed at least eighteen buildings in the next six years.

While Strickland is most famous for his Greek Revival buildings, he designed in at least nine architectural styles. Another famous example of his work is the re-created wooden steeple on Independence Hall. Badly damaged by weather and rot, the original was removed in 1781. Strickland's Georgian design was an early example of American historic restoration architecture.

Ironically, a series of events in one of Strickland's creations also brought his career in Philadelphia to an end. A battle between President Andrew Jackson and bank president Nicholas Biddle led to the Panic of 1837. Strickland's business in Philadelphia suffered, and he accepted the job of designing and con-

ᴅ Architecture: Greek Revival

Americans were intrigued by Grecian culture by the 1820s. They identified classical Greece with democracy but they also sympathized with the freedom struggle that modern Greeks were waging against the Ottoman Turks at the time. Copying Greek decorative styles allowed Americans to break with the Italian-inspired architecture that defined the homes of their British adversaries.

In addition to its use for public buildings including banks and churches, Greek Revival architecture was also wildly popular for private homes. Nicholas Biddle set the fashion when he hired Thomas U. Walter, Strickland's protégé, to transform Andalusia, his rural Georgian-style home, into a Grecian temple overlooking the Delaware River north of Philadelphia. In the city, the style was widely adopted in building early nineteenth-century row houses. The popular press spread the fashion, and Greek Revival buildings with their street-facing pediments and covered front porches became the vogue throughout the United States in the years before the Civil War.

Old Pine Presbyterian Church.

GREEK REVIVAL BUILDINGS IN HISTORIC PHILADELPHIA
Old Pine Presbyterian Church, Fourth and Pine streets; Atwater Kent Museum (built as the Franklin Institute, 1825), 15 S. Seventh Street; Dorrance Hamilton Hall, University of the Arts, 320 S. Broad Street (built as the Pennsylvania Institution for the Deaf and Dumb, 1824–26); Founder's Hall, Girard College, Girard and Corinthian avenues (1833–47). Examples of Greek Revival row houses include the private homes built by the estate of Stephen Girard from 1831 to 1833 (326–334 Spruce Street) and Portico Row (900–930 Spruce Street).ᴄ

326–334 Spruce Street.

Atwater Kent Museum.

Founder's Hall, Girard College.

Nicholas Biddle (1786–1844), whose personal taste helped shape Americans' love of Greek Revival architecture in the nineteenth century.

structing the new State Capitol in Jackson's home state, Tennessee, in 1845. He died in Nashville in April 1854, and was buried under the still-incomplete building's north portico.

The Second Bank of the United States was soon at the center of its own controversies. The bank drew strong support from Philadelphia-based business leaders who still followed Alexander Hamilton's theory of a strong connection between mercantile and manufacturing economy and the government. Biddle's bank created a strong, centralized American currency and economy. But many Americans hated the Second Bank and its branches that Biddle established around the young nation. Opponents in Maryland attempted to restrict the bank by taxing its notes in 1819, leading to the U.S. Supreme Court decision *McCullough v. Maryland,* in which Chief Justice John Marshall ruled that a national bank was allowed under the Constitution's necessary and proper clause, and that states could not tax federal entities—a landmark in American federalism. The controversy did not end there. Some believed that the bank's "questionable practices" (which limited the amount of money in circulation and acted as a regulator of the paper money being issued by state banks) led to the major economic panic in 1819. New York's Wall Street financiers, newly powerful from the trade generated by the creation of the Erie Canal, felt jealous of the Philadelphia-based institution. And southern and western farmers particularly distrusted the bank, seeing it as an "aristocratic" institution. None seemed to see the irony that their hatred of "aristocracy" was financed by the labor of enslaved people.

Andrew Jackson, a Tennessee plantation owner and military hero of the War of 1812, became the leader of the Second Bank's opponents. Jackson had an almost manic hatred of banks and bankers. Early in his career, he had lost money in land speculation and blamed banks for the rest of his life. When he was elected president in 1828, Jackson brought these feelings with him to the executive branch. Jackson thought that both the national bank and paper money were unconstitutional. He saw the power vested in the national bank as a threat to the republic.

The Second Bank became a political football during Jackson's administration. Senator Henry Clay of Kentucky was running for president in 1832 against Jackson. A staunch supporter of the bank and friend of Nicholas Biddle, Clay thought that bringing its charter to a vote before Congress in an election year would embarrass Jackson. If the president were to veto the charter, mercantile interests throughout the country might rally against his reelection. If he did sign a new charter, it might infuriate Jackson's rural supporters.

Nicholas Biddle applied to recharter the bank in January 1832. Both houses of congress passed the bill, throwing the decision of the bank's continuation to Jackson. When Martin Van Buren, a staunch Jacksonian Democrat (and soon to be Jackson's vice president) visited the White House on July 4, he found the president sick in bed. Jackson took Van Buren by the hand and said, "The bank, Mr. Van Buren, is trying to kill me, but I will kill it!"

President Andrew Jackson's veto of the 1832 bill that would have renewed the charter of the Second Bank cemented his reputation as a hero to some. Others, however, saw him as a despot who was trying to impose his will over the entire nation, and they lambasted him as "King Andrew I." Anti-Jackson politicians formed the Whig Party, a term that connected them to Britons and American revolutionaries who had sought to curtail the power of monarchs.

We reached the city, late that night. Looking out of my chamber-window, before going to bed, I saw, on the opposite side of the way, a handsome building of white marble, which had a mournful ghost-like aspect, dreary to behold. . . . I hastened to inquire its name and purpose, and then my surprise vanished. It was the Tomb of many fortunes; the Great Catacomb of investment; the memorable United States bank.

—Charles Dickens, 1841

Jackson's veto of the bank bill was a declaration of the ideals of Jacksonian Democrats. In it, he said that the bank was "unauthorized by the Constitution, subversive of the rights of the states, and dangerous to the liberties of the people." Jackson railed against the bank's stockholders, northeastern businessmen whom he called pro-British and who drew the money of southern and western planters out of those regions, he said. Positioning himself as the protector of the republic and its common citizens, Andrew Jackson was reelected by a landslide in 1832.

Jackson saw his reelection as a mandate to kill the bank as quickly as possible. Jackson's cabinet doubted the logic or legality of the move, and he removed two secretaries of the treasury before he finally appointed Roger B. Taney of Maryland, who agreed to carry out Jackson's plan. Taney withdrew all governmental deposits and placed them in state banks. Nicholas Biddle responded to the "killing" of his bank by announcing that he must clean up all banking affairs before closing the institution, and called in all outstanding loans. A financial panic followed, leading to a nationwide depression.

Opponents to Jackson's heavy-handed practices responded by forming the Whig Party, taking their name from the British political party that attempted to curtail the power of the monarch there. This elegant building thus played a key role in creating the Second American Party System and the rough-and-tumble world of antebellum politics.

The Second Bank building was acquired by the National Park Service in 1935, after spending almost a century as Philadelphia's customs house. Preserved because of its artistic and historic importance, the Second Bank's banking room and offices now hold one of America's great collections of early American portraits.

Entering William Strickland's Roman-style, barrel-vaulted main banking room, visitors can encounter the faces—famous and less famous—whose lives were connected with Philadelphia's story in the early national period. Large panels reproduced from William Birch's *Views of Philadelphia* set the scene to walk the early city's streets and observe "conversations" between the men and women of Philadelphia, meeting the people who experienced Philadelphia's rise to being the intellectual center of the American colonies, the capital of its revolutionary government, and the cultural capital of the new nation.

Society Hill's sun-dappled streets are lined with surviving Georgian, Federal, and Greek Revival residences, including the home of Samuel and Elizabeth Powel (left), as well as outstanding examples of modern architecture that date from the area's renewal in the 1960s.

SIX

Society Hill

B Y THE MID-1700S, Philadelphia's economy was booming as the city became a major hub for commerce and trade in the Atlantic World. Just as the city's elite residents now had access to the latest trends in Enlightenment thought, they also had the means to buy the best goods and homes to display their wealth, refinement, and taste as members of the genteel class. By the time the Continental Congress arrived in Philadelphia, Society Hill—the city's first "suburb," located just south of Walnut Street between Second Street and Washington Square—already had a reputation as one of the grandest neighborhoods in any American city. The large brick houses, sumptuously appointed with the finest goods that the British Empire could provide and surrounded by lavish gardens,

In addition to welcoming settlers seeking religious freedom, William Penn hoped to draw merchants, craftsmen, and traders to his colony, and he extolled the land's virtues and opportunities in his published letter to the Free Society of Traders. The company did not last long, but its name continues, in Philadelphia's Society Hill.

outbuildings, and coach houses, all revealed America's most impressive high society.

But that is not why Society Hill acquired its name. The Free Society of Traders bought this land from William Penn in 1681, and the name stuck. Penn knew that if his "holy experiment" were to succeed, it would need artisans and merchants who could create the colony's economy, bringing people, trade, and crafts to Pennsylvania and exporting goods throughout the Atlantic World. He knew that any colonial endeavor that did not deal with practical matters was doomed to fail.

The Free Society addressed those needs: they planned to bring two hundred indentured servants to the colony; to rent land to new settlers; to trade whale oil, lumber, grain, hemp, and fish; and to establish a fur trade with Native Americans. By late 1682, they raised £12,500 in subscriptions, many from Penn's relatives and friends or members of the Quaker mercantile elite in England. In return, Penn gave the society his public support and privileges for office holding.

The Free Society never developed as Penn had hoped. From the beginning, both the traders who were already in the colony prior to its arrival (many of whom had been there before Penn received his colonial charter) and other merchants resented their monopoly, and the colonial assembly restricted their political privileges. By 1686, the Free Society had begun to collapse. The business continued for a time, selling off their large tract of land.

Society Hill emerged as a place of high society in the mid-eighteenth century. By then, the center of Philadelphia at Second and High streets near the court house and market had become a crowded, polluted place, with a mix of commercial, governmental, and residential buildings. The families who moved to Society Hill were seeking more pleasant surroundings as well as new styles of architecture and domestic space.

The outstanding surviving example of these homes is the one that Samuel Powel III bought in 1769. Powel's grandfather had come to Pennsylvania as an apprentice in 1685, and he learned his trade well. By the time he died, "the rich carpenter" left his grandson a large fortune and much land. Both Powel's father and grandfather had followed the building trades, but he received a formal education as one of the first students at the College and Academy of Philadelphia that Benjamin Franklin had founded, graduating in the college's second class. He then spent seven years on a grand tour of Britain and the European continent, attending concerts and balls, meeting dignitaries ranging from the pope to Voltaire, and studying art and architecture. He visited the archaeological sites at Pompeii, which was just then being excavated, and shipped home furniture and artwork from Europe.

Powel purchased his Third Street town house just before he married Elizabeth Willing at Christ Church in 1769. His wife's parents were among the first fashionable Philadelphians to move to Society Hill, where they planned a mansion with carvings, portraits, and furnishings that placed them at the pinnacle of Anglo-American power and prestige. Charles Willing died before building the entire compound of buildings he envisioned just south of Walnut

Dined at Mr. Powells, with Mr. Duché, Dr. Morgan, Dr. Steptoe, Mr. Goldborough, Mr. Johnson, and many others.—A most sinfull Feast again! Every Thing which could delight the Eye, or allure the Taste, Curds and Creams, Jellies, Sweet meats of various sorts, 20 sorts of Tarts, fools, Trifles, floating Islands, whippd Sillabubs &c. &c.— Parmesan Cheese, Punch, Wine, Porter, Beer, &c. &c.

—John Adams, September 8, 1774

Samuel and Elizabeth Powel's Georgian townhouse was at the height of elegance in late colonial Philadelphia, with its marble steps, bricks laid in a Flemish bond pattern, and neoclassical door frame.

Street, at Third. By the end of the century, Mrs. Powel's brother Thomas Willing lived in the inherited house their father had completed, her sister lived next-door, and her niece Anne lived down the block with husband Senator William Bingham. The street became the residential compound of one of the city's wealthiest and most powerful families.

The Powels' "splendid seat," as John Adams called it—an observation that points out that the area was still very rural in 1774—was a fine example of Georgian design with a large entrance hall leading to a splendid Santo Domingo mahogany staircase ascending to the upper floors. Two large parlors opened off the entrance hall, and Powel designated one as "my dining room," making him perhaps the first man in the city to have a room just for eating.

The second floor was even more lavish than the first. The large room at the front was one of Philadelphia's most beautiful spaces. Hercules Courtenay—one of the best carvers then working in Philadelphia—created elaborate cornices, paneling, and baseboards. The fireplace became the focal point. On the mantle, Courtenay carved a classical fable: Aesop's story of the greedy dog who lost his bone by attacking his own reflection in a pool. At the top, Samuel Powel's recently created family crest disclosed his identity as a wealthy Briton living in the colonies' largest city.

Anne Shippen Willing (1710–1791) and her husband Charles were one of the first prominent merchant families to move into Society Hill in the 1750s. This portrait, by Matthew Pratt, shows her in the 1780s.

Yet by the time Powel put the finishing touches on his house, the British Empire had begun to crumble. In 1774, Samuel Powel pledged money to the "relief of the poor at Boston" after Parliament closed that city's port to punish the colony for the Boston Tea Party. Powel's apparently noncommittal stance during the revolution is a reminder of the old adage that one-third of the colonists supported the revolution, one-third opposed it, and one-third didn't get involved. Elected mayor of Philadelphia in 1773—a position that his grandfather, father, father-in-law, and brother-in-law all held— Powel was at the State House on July 8, 1776, to hear the first reading of the Declaration of Independence. He left no record of his feelings about the Declaration, and he took no part in the war that followed.

In the autumn of 1777, British troops under General Howe captured the city, and Samuel and Elizabeth Powel found themselves hosts to an uninvited guest during the occupation. The

The Powels' elegant second-floor drawing room, or ballroom, disclosed the couple's high status with its richly carved walls and fashionable furnishings. During and after the revolution, the room would host leaders of the new nation as well as international visitors.

Earl of Carlisle confiscated the main portion of their mansion. He came to negotiate a peace plan, but the rebellious colonists were furious at the king for sending German mercenaries and for destroying American towns, and they rejected it. The *Pennsylvania Packet* reported that "Lord Carlisle, with his three mistresses, is quartered at Mr. Powel's the late mayor, the family having retreated to the back building."

Neither Powel left a record of their feelings at having the British invade their home. But both befriended the American cause and its leaders. Samuel Powel eventually swore a loyalty oath to the new American government; Elizabeth Powel became one of the leading hostesses in the city once the Americans recaptured Philadelphia.

As Society Hill developed into Philadelphia's fashionable residential area in the 1750s and

ᛞ Elizabeth Willing Powel

"Contrary to American custom, she plays the leading role in the family—la prima figura, as the Italians say," the Marquis de Chastellux wrote of Elizabeth Powel in 1780. The French diplomat was visiting the new nation's capital and was impressed by what this woman of the republic had to say: "She received me in a handsome house furnished in the English manner and, what pleased me most, adorned with fine prints and some very good copies of the best Italian paintings," he wrote, "but what chiefly distinguishes her is her taste for conversation and the truly European manner in which she uses her wit and knowledge."

Born in Philadelphia in 1743, Elizabeth Willing was part of the large, wealthy family of Charles Willing, a prosperous merchant and civic leader and Anne Shippen Willing. Her father's untimely death in 1754 left Eliza in an unenviable position, moving into a smaller rented house so her brother could claim his inheritance. Later, gossips quipped that she was too outspoken to win a husband, and she had already reached the advanced age of twenty-five when she wed Samuel Powel in 1769. Together, they became one of Philadelphia's most prominent couples. "It would be difficult to separate two persons who have for twenty years lived together in happiest union, I shall not say as man and wife, which would not in America convey the idea of perfect equality, but as two friends, unusually well matched in understanding, taste, and knowledge," Chastellux wrote.

Elizabeth Powel was a leader in the emerging culture of women entering into the political sphere. These women, long denied a public political role under the old standards of the colonial system, now saw the benefit of participating in the debates. Denied the vote and membership in the elected government, women asserted themselves in the public viewing balconies in the House and Senate chambers, and especially in the salon culture in the city's parlors. Abigail Adams, who met Elizabeth Powel when she arrived in Philadelphia as wife of the vice president, said, "Of all the ladies I have seen and conversed with here, Mrs. Powell is the best informed. She is a friendly, affable, good woman, sprightly, full of conversation." ᛞ

Elizabeth Willing Powel (1743–1830), portrayed by an unknown artist at the time of her marriage in 1769. Her wit and intelligence would make her one of the preeminent women of the new nation at the time Philadelphia served as its capital.

William Birch's view of Third Street, when Society Hill was the social center of the United States capital. At left is the grand Federal-style home of Senator William Bingham and his wife, Anne Willing Bingham. The Binghams' mansion and gardens were based on neoclassical designs imported from London. In the distance is the Powel House. The Powels had added a three-story bow room a few years earlier, a fashionable addition similar to those seen on Congress Hall and the President's House. The room was removed by a later owner in the 1820s.

☞ While wealth and intelligence shaped Powel's life, she also experienced tragedy. Each of her three or four children died in infancy, a fact she commemorated when she had Matthew Pratt paint her portrait as a mourning mother, just before her fiftieth birthday in 1793. That year would bring another tragedy: Samuel Powel died in the yellow fever epidemic that ravaged the city that autumn. Her interest in the American cause never waned, though. She was a friend and frequent correspondent of George and Martha Washington, proffered advice to civic leaders and family members, and, when she died in 1831, left a large part of her sizable fortune to a charity striving to abolish slavery in the United States. ☜

1760s, its new residents were concerned with having convenient access to the same institutions that they would have had in the central part of colonial Philadelphia. New Market's construction gave them access to fresh foods, and

members of various religious congregations founded houses of worship in the neighborhood in the years prior to the American Revolution.

By mid-century, Quakers had become a numerical minority in Philadelphia, but they still had power and influence. In 1753, Friends founded the Pine Street Meeting, building their meetinghouse on land donated by Samuel Powel's father. Like the Friends' Great Meetinghouse at Second and High, the building was brick, plain in style, and without a steeple.

Samuel Powel left his parents' Quaker faith by the time he returned from his European grand tour and he, his neighbor John Cadwalader, and his future in-laws were all among the "Gentlemen of the South End" noted in the parish records who became supporters of St. Peter's, established in 1758 as a "chapel of ease" for members of the Church of England in Society Hill. The United Church of Christ Church and St. Peter's (as the single congregation with two church buildings called itself) shared clergy, administrative structure, finances, and theology—all carefully crafted by

Two views of New Market. The first, showing the view from the south in 1788, with Christ Church's steeple in the distance, reveals the commercial side of life in Society Hill in the late eighteenth century. The Federal Style headhouse (below) was added in 1804 to provide space for fire companies.

their rector, Richard Jenney, to ensure that Anglicans maintained their ties to the mother country and its official church in the face of the theological debates in this era and the religious diversity in Pennsylvania. Reverend Jenney was alarmed at many factors that he saw challenging the church's role in Pennsylvania, including the 1760 creation of St. Paul's, an evangelical Anglican church on Third Street north of the Powel House, where the congregation embraced George Whitefield's more emotional brand of Christianity.

Just across Fourth Street from St. Peter's is the Third Presbyterian Church of Philadelphia, affectionately known as Old Pine. The two churches followed different theologies and had different congregational compositions, but they shared two important factors: both responded to the needs of large numbers of Philadelphians moving to Society Hill, and both turned to one of early America's greatest architects to design their buildings.

Robert Smith immigrated from Dalkeith, Scotland, around 1748 when he was in his mid-twenties. Smith mastered the art of Georgian architecture and created many of the outstanding American buildings of the time, including Nassau Hall at Princeton, New Jersey, Carpenters' Hall in Philadelphia, and the tower on Christ Church. St. Peter's appears almost as it did when Smith completed the building in 1761, with the exception of the bell tower added in the 1840s. Smith's design included an elegant Palladian window facing east and a three-aisle layout inside the church. The original wineglass pulpit and sounding board remain in place; historic paint analysis in 1997 discovered that the

Robert Smith's architectural mastery shone in the construction of St. Peter's Church, completed in 1761. Thomas and Richard Penn granted the land for the "chapel of ease" for the Anglican people of Society Hill, and the Penn family crest is carved into the original woodwork above the pulpit's sounding board.

gold leaf on the carved sounding board above the minister's pulpit is the original applied in Smith's day. The box pews are also original and have the very rare feature that allows the congregation to stand, turn, and sit facing the other direction when the service moves from sermon to the Lord's Supper. The magnificent rococo organ case was carved by William Rush in 1831.

All of this original detail is in sharp contrast to Old Pine. Like St. Peter's, Smith designed that church following outstanding architectural and building techniques of his day, but he also observed the religious customs of the two churches. The Presbyterian Church followed American Calvinist customs by placing the main entrance in the center of the longer east wall, facing the burial ground. Inside the church, the congregation faced the pastor's desk and pulpit along the western wall.

Why, then, does the church appear so different today? The building was extensively renovated after the revolution, and appears today in the Greek Revival style that was fashionable at the time John Fraser oversaw its redecoration in

[The revolution is] nothing more or less than a Irish-Scotch Presbyterian Rebellion.

—a Hessian officer, 1778

1857. But the need for those extensive changes dates back to independence. When the revolution began, George Duffield was Old Pine's pastor. An avid revolutionary, Duffield supported the cause for independence, led many of his congregants to join the military, and served throughout the war as chaplain to Pennsylvania's militia.

When the British invaded Philadelphia in 1777, they took their revenge on the rebels' church building. At various points it became a hospital and a horse stable, its pews and woodwork stripped and burned for fuel when farmers refused to bring firewood into the city. Hessian mercenaries from the Battle of Brandywine were buried in an unmarked mass grave in the churchyard.

In contrast, St. Peter's Church lost only its fence during the war. The current brick fence dates to the years immediately after independence. But the United Church suffered other losses, including its pastor. The Rev. Jacob Duché was a lifelong Anglican, born in Philadelphia in 1724. Following his ordination in England, Duché moved into one of the loveliest homes in Society Hill, just diagonally across Third Street from St. Peter's. In September 1774, Duché became chaplain to the Continental Congress. Samuel Adams called him "a gentleman of piety and virtue, who was at the same time a friend of his country." John Adams, often a tough critic, was impressed by the minister's style: "Heard Mr. Duche read Prayers. . . . A Prayer, which he gave us of his own Composition, was as pertinent, as affectionate, as sublime, as devout, as I ever heard offered up to heaven. He filled every Bosom present."

The Reverend Jacob Duché's elegant town-house, painted by an unknown artist, sat on Third Street, across Pine Street from St. Peter's. Duché's decision to change his support to the British during their occupation of the city led to the house's confiscation after the British returned to New York City and Duché had fled to England. Duché estimated that the house, grounds, and furnishings were worth £2000 when he filed his 1784 claim as a Loyalist. The house was razed in the early nineteenth century.

When the Congress fled Philadelphia as the British invaded, Duché stayed at his post, and General Howe had him arrested in September 1777. The minister then vacillated, and the following month wrote an infamous letter to George Washington, asking the general either to convince the Congress to rescind the Declaration of Independence or to go around them and work with the British himself. Local Tories were delighted, but Duché's patriot friends and neighbors were furious. "Words cannot express the grief & Consternation that wounded my Soul at sight of this fatal performance," wrote Francis Hopkinson, the Declaration signer who was married to Duché's sister. In December 1777, Duché sailed for England, promising to return as soon as he safely could. His former congregants never forgave him. Years later, he wrote to Elizabeth Willing Powel that he planned to return, but she responded coolly that the town had not forgotten his actions. By that time, his mansion had been confiscated by the state of Pennsylvania. Despite much advice to the contrary, Duché did return to Philadelphia in 1792, where he died five years later. He is buried near the Palladian window in St. Peter's churchyard.

Just across Pine Street from the churchyard, near the site of Duché's house, stands a modest dwelling, but one also closely associated with the history of Philadelphia when it was the nation's capital. There, in a boardinghouse owned by Ann Relf, Tadeusz Kosciuszko lived from November 1797 to May 1798. Kosciuszko had first arrived in Philadelphia in August 1776, the son of a lesser Polish nobleman who—like many other European gentry—was drawn to the cause of the American war for independence by the wealth and glory it might bring. Born in 1746, Kosciuszko had studied in Poland and in Paris, had gained both military prowess and a fascination with the Enlightenment's promises of human equality, and came to America with impressive engineering skills. The Pennsylvania Committee of Defense charged him with fortifying the Delaware River in 1776, and he was given the commission of colonel in the Continental Army in October of that year.

Kosciuszko's engineering abilities quickly proved beneficial to the American cause. He was instrumental in the key American victory at

General Tadeusz Kosciuszko rented rooms in the house at the corner of Third and Pine when he returned to Philadelphia, an injured revolutionary. Here, he met with Thomas Jefferson and other leaders of the new federal government.

Saratoga, then oversaw the fortification of West Point on the Hudson River from 1778 to 1780. Kosciuszko accompanied General Nathanael Greene south in 1780 as chief of engineers and contributed to further military success when the American army retook Charleston, South Carolina, in 1782. In 1783, he joined American officers in founding the Society of the Cincinnati, the patriotic society begun by George Washington's officer corps that continues as a hereditary society today.

Kosciuszko returned to Europe after the revolution in 1784. He remained in retirement for four years, then in October 1789 became major-general of the Polish army, entering into the longstanding struggle with Russia for control of his native land. In March 1794, Kosciuszko led an uprising and became dictator of Poland. During his brief rule, he attempted to push through a series of liberal reforms, but that

Polish revolutionary and Patriot Tadeusz Kosciuszko (1746–1817), in a late nineteenth-century portrait by Julian Rys, based on an earlier engraving.

October, Russia invaded and defeated the Polish army. Kosciuszko received serious head and leg wounds, and he was captured and imprisoned by the Russian army of Empress Catherine the Great.

After Catherine's death, Kosciuszko was permitted to return to Philadelphia in August 1797. Severely wounded, the Polish hero spent his time in this house recovering and seeing old friends from the American Revolution. One frequent visitor was Vice President Thomas Jefferson, who came to sit in his friend's rooms. The friendship would lead to a tragic incident.

Kosciuszko had grown convinced that the Enlightenment must lead to expanded freedoms. The revolutions in America, France, and Haiti showed that the world could change. During the years he fought to free Poland, Kosciuszko emphasized that aristocratic Poles must also be willing to free their serfs—servants bound to land—if they were to demand their own national liberty. His fellow Polish leaders were not convinced. When he returned to America to secure the years of back pay and interest that the U.S. Congress had promised him, Kosciuszko's belief in freedom expanded to include the end of slavery in the United States. He was well acquainted with American blacks. Agrippe Hull, a free African man from Massachusetts, had served as his aide for seven years during the war. In Europe, Kosciuszko was likewise aided by a man known as Negro John, who stayed with him for years and helped him after his wartime injuries in Poland.

On April 20, 1798, Kosciuszko wrote in the first draft of his will: "I beg Mr. Jefferson this in the case I should die without will or testament he should bye of out my money So many Negroes and free them, that the restante sums should be Sufficient to give them aducation and provide for ther maintenance, this is to say each should know before, the duty of a Cytyzen in the free Government." In the final version of the will, Kosciuszko amended that section to say: "I hereby authorize my friend Thomas Jefferson to employ the whole thereof in purchasing Negroes from among his own or any others." The $18,912 in back pay that Congress had granted Kosciuszko was a small fortune in 1798; it would have allowed Jefferson to free numerous enslaved people at no financial loss to himself, and to make a strong abolitionist statement at a moment when slavery was becoming a sectional issue and dividing the young nation.

The tragedy was that Jefferson never carried out the promise he had given his friend. Kosciuszko returned to Europe in 1798 and never came back to the United States, but he stayed in close contact with Jefferson, and just before his death in 1817 wrote the former president, "You know the fixed destination" of his American funds. Kosciuszko died on October 15, 1817, one month later. When Jefferson died in 1826, however, the money remained in trust, and the enslaved people he could have freed with his friend's bequest were sold at auction to pay his massive debts.

One of the grandest houses in Kosciuszko's neighborhood was the mansion built by wine merchant Henry Hill on Fourth Street, now known as the Physick House, honoring Philip Syng Physick, a later owner famous for being

Henry Hill built his city house in 1786, using the wealth he had acquired as one of the country's leading Madeira wine merchants. The elegant Federal-style dwelling included a more flat, classical appearance and larger windows, including the elaborate fan light above the front door, setting it apart from its Georgian neighbors. The house was later owned by Dr. Philip Syng Physick, the father of American surgery.

"the father of American surgery." After the revolution, Society Hill became even more fashionable, and more and more wealthy merchants built town houses there, including Hill. Architecturally distinct from the Powel House and its colonial neighbors, the house Hill began to build in 1786 reveals the neoclassical tastes that came to dominate Great Britain and the United States in the last decades of the eighteenth century. The elegant simplicity of the house, with its less-ornate façade and impressive windows and size, all spoke to the builder's wealth, ambitions, and desires in the years immediately after the American Revolution.

Henry Hill was born near Annapolis, Maryland, on September 18, 1732. His father, a physician and merchant, ran into debt and moved part of his family to the island of Madeira, located off the northwestern coast of Africa. That island was the home to a particu-

☞ Architecture: Federal Houses of Philadelphia

Federal or "late Georgian" architecture reached Philadelphia just after the American Revolution. Citizens of the new nation believed that their republic restored ancient Roman traditions and values of liberty, civic virtue, and the sovereignty of the people to shape their own government and lives, and this style gave a physical presence to those ideas. Several public buildings, including Old City Hall and Congress Hall, as well as the center wing of the Pennsylvania Hospital and the headhouse at New Market, are outstanding examples. The Federal style was also extremely popular in domestic architecture.

William Bingham, the English-born merchant who married Elizabeth Powel's niece Anne Willing and later served as one of Pennsylvania's first senators, built the grandest Federal house in the city on south Third Street near Spruce, a building that was razed in the mid-nineteenth century. But many others survive, including the houses constructed for Henry Hill and Bishop William White, both of which reveal the Federal style in their large front windows and the "republican simplicity" of the houses' architectural details.

The Federal style was strongly influenced by British architect Robert Adam, who used the classical patterns of Georgian architecture but brought his own interpretations of Roman elements to them. Simplicity replaced the richness of the Georgian style. Pilasters, pillars, and moldings are more flat or narrow; use of ovals, including oval ☞

The Bingham mansion, at the corner of Third and Spruce streets was one of the grandest Federal houses in the new nation. Its elaborate entrance, second floor Palladian window, and third floor fan light, as well as its carvings, furnishings, and lavish walled garden, set it apart as a beautiful, if controversial, city house. Other Philadelphians used some of these same Federal architectural elements, if on a more restrained scale.

☞ rooms like those in Philadelphia's Lemon Hill in Fairmont Park and the White House in Washington, D.C., became fashionable. Windows narrowed and grew taller, and more delicate wooden mullions separated the large glass panes in them.

FEDERAL STYLE BUILDINGS IN PHILADELPHIA

Congress Hall, Old City Hall, the Physick House, Bishop White House, Fairmount Waterworks (along Schuylkill River, near the Philadelphia Museum of Art), Girard Warehouses (18–30 N. Front Street), Lemon Hill (Fairmount Park), New Market Headhouse (Second and Pine streets), Pennsylvania Hospital (center wing, Eighth and Pine streets), and numerous row houses in Society Hill. ☜

Lemon Hill, located in Fairmount Park, is one of Philadelphia's most splendid surviving country houses. Its Federal architecture, including three stories of oval parlors similar to those built in the White House during the same decade, have made it one of America's most notable houses since its construction in 1799–1800.

larly desirable commodity for Anglo-Americans: wine. Since North American colonization had begun, entrepreneurs had sought a way to grow wine-producing grapes in the colonies, but with no luck. Spirits were an important part of the diet in the eighteenth century. Although people did not know exactly why water could be unhealthy—and placed wells and outhouse pits in close proximity to each other, as archaeolo-

gists have found—they did know that possibly
fatal cases of dysentery and other diseases might
follow drinking it. Colonists drank beer and
hard cider at breakfast, rum throughout the day,
and a variety of other spirits. But wine remained
hard to come by in the new world. Wine
imported from Europe didn't travel well; bottles
broke and casks became so warm in the hulls of
ships sailing through the Caribbean that their
contents turned into swill.

Madeira wine proved to be the answer.
Importers found that travel through warm
waters actually improved its warm, rich taste.
Like china, glassware, houses, and clothing,
Madeira became a highly desirable commodity
as well as an indicator of superior tastes and elevated station, and the Hill family developed a
lucrative trade network that traversed the
Atlantic World. George Washington was their
customer as early as the 1750s, perhaps acquiring a taste for the beverage at about the same
time that his marriage to the wealthy widow
Martha Dandridge Custis provided him with
the means to purchase it. Benjamin Franklin—
himself a lover of Madeira—chose his friend
Hill to be one of the executors of his will. Hill's
familiarity with the nation's founders was
revealed by a task Benjamin Franklin left for
him to carry out after his death: he was charged
with delivering Franklin's legacy to President
Washington: a "crab-tree walking stick, with a
gold hat curiously wrought in the form of the cap
of liberty." Franklin's will included the codicil
that the walking stick went "to my friend, and
the friend of mankind, General Washington. If
it were a Sceptre, he has merited it, and would
become it."

Archaeologists digging at
Monticello discovered the
remnants of Thomas
Jefferson's Madeira wine
decanter, a beverage that
eighteenth-century
colonists enjoyed so much
that merchants sometimes
referred to it as "American
wine." Merchant Henry
Hill's family network sold
Madeira throughout the
Atlantic World.

Henry Hill's life and career show the complexity of Anglo-American trade and relations during the revolutionary period. His kinship ties in Philadelphia connected Hill to Patriots Samuel Meredith and George Clymer, a signer of the Declaration of Independence and Constitution. In his correspondence, Hill referred to "our British oppressors" and he hosted members of the Continental Congress at his country home outside Philadelphia in 1775, including an ill-fated dinner where Peyton Randolph, delegate from Virginia and president of the Congress, collapsed during the meal and died of a "parylitick fit."

Yet as this house reveals, Philadelphia's elite did not sever ties to the mother country when they declared independence. When Hill began to plan this house, he turned to London to outfit his residence. Hill's sister Mary Lamar became not just his personal shopper in London, but the arbiter of taste for early national Philadelphia. For Hill's house, she selected wallpapers, furniture, and fabrics; worked with carvers to design the marble mantelpieces for its parlors; and selected the style and number of tables and sofas. She also worked with James Keir to create the magnificent fanlight and windows that adorn the front of the house.

While the Hills' house was splendid, their domestic life was filled with sadness. His wife Ann Meredith Hill died in 1787 following "a tedious and painful illness," the *Pennsylvania Gazette* reported. Henry Hill completed the house and moved in, but he lived there just over a decade. In 1798, he contracted yellow fever and died on September 15.

In addition to being a place of gracious living, Society Hill had a diverse population unknown almost anywhere else in the English-speaking world. At the corner of Willings Alley and Fourth Street stood Old St. Joseph's Church, one of the few places in the American colonies where Roman Catholics could worship freely. British people on both sides of the Atlantic were prejudiced against Catholics in the eighteenth century. Henry VIII's break with the Church of Rome in the 1520s and his Roman Catholic daughter Mary's persecution of Protestants was a common theme in their collective memory. Colonists also identified Catholicism with the wars that had pitted French Canadian and English colonists against one another for decades. But Roman Catholic missionaries had reportedly come to Philadelphia as early as 1708, and Father Joseph Greaton, an English priest, had arrived in 1720 or 1721. Construction on the church began in 1733.

"A House lately built in Walnut Street . . . sett apart for the Exercise of the Roman Catholick Religion and . . . commonly called the Romish Chappell" was Lieutenant Governor Patrick Gordon's description of the residence of Father Joseph Greaton in 1734. The house was located on Fourth Street between Willing's Alley and Walnut Street, an area still on the distant outskirts of Philadelphia at the time.

Not everyone was thrilled with the news that a Roman Catholic parish was to be located in Philadelphia. On July 25, 1734, Lieutenant Governor Patrick Gordon told the Provincial Council:

> he was under no small Concern to hear that a House lately built in Walnut Street, in this City, had been set apart for the Exercise of the Roman Catholick Religion, and is commonly called the Romish Chappell, where several Persons, he understands, resort on Sundays, to hear Mass openly celebrated by a Popish Priest; that he conceives the tolerating the Publick Exercise of that Religion to be contrary to the Laws of England . . . but

> those of that Perswasion imagining they have
> a right to it, from some general Expressions
> in the Charter of Privileges granted to the
> Inhabitants of this Government by our late
> Honourable Proprietor.

William Penn's religious toleration won out, and the "Romish Chappell"—St. Joseph's Church—became a part of the religious fabric of Philadelphia.

At the time the original church was constructed, St. Joseph's was on the outskirts of the colonial settlement. By 1754, when the church acquired a plot of land between Fourth and Fifth streets for a burial ground, the area had begun to acquire more residences, and when the trustees of the ground conveyed a portion of the land to Father Robert Harding in May 1763 to begin construction on St. Mary's Church, some of Society Hill's noteworthy houses were already being planned. Construction of the second Catholic chapel in Philadelphia reflects the increasingly diverse population in the city by the second half of the eighteenth century. Two hundred and twenty-two people subscribed to the construction of the new church. The majority were Irish, along with thirty Germans and fifteen French.

Harding, an English Catholic, came to Pennsylvania in 1750. He took an active interest both in his parish and in the growing city, contributing funds to Pennsylvania Hospital, joining the American Philosophical Society, and becoming the only Catholic to join the Sons of St. George, a charity that aided English immigrants. Jacob Duché called him "a decent, well-bred Gentleman . . . much esteemed by all denominations of Christians in this city, for his

Early parishioners at St. Mary's Roman Catholic Church entered the building from Fifth Street, rather than the nineteenth-century addition facing Fourth. The church, set far back from the street, was reacting to anti-Catholic prejudices held by many English colonists in the eighteenth century.

prudence, his moderation, his known attachment to British liberty, and his unaffected pious labors among the people to whom he officiates." When Harding died on September 1, 1772, the city's lay and clerical leaders attended his funeral mass at St. Mary's Church.

Both St. Joseph's and St. Mary's churches bowed to the reality that many colonists were prejudiced against Catholics, and both structures kept a low profile. The small building that housed St. Joseph's, which was razed in the 1830s and replaced by the current church, had "more the appearance of a stable than of a church," Father Adam Marshall mused. Fearing attacks by anti-Catholic mobs, St. Mary's early parishioners built their church entrance facing Fifth Street, with the burial ground separating it from the street.

The members of the Continental Congress were astonished by the religious pluralism in Philadelphia. On October 9, 1774, George Washington and John Adams attended mass at St. Mary's. The adamantly Protestant Adams gave rich details about the impressive experience, writing to his wife Abigail, "I wonder how Luther ever broke the spell?"

National Park Service historical architects re-created colonial America's "most genteel tavern," where America's founders socialized and celebrated, using original art, archaeological findings, and documentary evidence.

SEVEN

City Tavern Block

F OR VISITORS TO LATE eighteenth-century Philadelphia and the merchants and civic leaders who welcomed them, City Tavern was one of the clearest signs that the city was a place of refinement and gentility. The tavern, built in an elegant style and fitted up in the most genteel manner, was located just two blocks from the bustling Delaware River waterfront on one of the city's busiest streets, and it proclaimed that Philadelphia was a leading port of the Atlantic World. During the last quarter of the eighteenth century, the tavern would host business leaders, revolutionaries, British officers, and the delegates who wrote the Constitution of the United States.

John Adams visited City Tavern immediately after arriving as a delegate to the First Continental Congress on the evening of August 29,

1774. The Massachusetts lawyer and his fellow delegates from New England arrived in Philadelphia to seek redress for grievances against the king and Parliament. Adams recalled the last leg of his weeklong trip in detail:

A Number of Carriages and Gentlemen came out of Phyladelphia to meet us. Mr. Thomas Mifflin, Mr. McKean of the Lower Counties [Delaware], one of their Delegates, Mr. Rutledge of Carolina, and a Number of Gentlemen from Philadelphia. . . . We were introduced to all these Gentlemen and most cordially wellcomed to Philadelphia.

"We then rode into Town," Adams wrote,

and dirty, dusty, and fatigued as we were, we could not resist the Importunity, to go to the Tavern, the most genteel one in America. There we were introduced to a Number of other Gentlemen of the City—Dr. Shippen, Dr. Knox, Mr. Smith, and a Multitude of others, and to Mr. Linch and Mr. Gadsden of S. Carolina. Here we had a fresh Welcome to the City of Philadelphia, and after some Time spent in Conversation a curtain was drawn, and in the other Half of the Chamber a Supper appeared as elegant as ever was laid upon a Table.

John Adams was participating in a carefully orchestrated pageant that evening, as Philadelphia's elite welcomed leaders from the Massachusetts Bay Colony, which had been shocked by the Boston Tea Party the previous December, as well as the killing of five colonists during the Boston Massacre in 1770.

The Philadelphians who had constructed City Tavern just a few years earlier could not have anticipated the causes that brought the Congressional delegates to their city, nor could they have imagined the changes that the tavern and city would witness in the years ahead. But the role that it played that August evening was exactly what they had expected. Leaders from throughout the colonies were welcomed by Philadelphia's grandees and by Daniel Smith, the tavern master they had hired for his skill and affability. They gathered in an elegant room, discussed their affairs, and then enjoyed a splendid repast. Little wonder that John Adams called the tavern America's "most genteel."

"There is nothing which has yet been contrived by man, by which so much happiness is produced as by a good tavern or inn," the British wit and man of letters Dr. Samuel Johnson wrote in 1776. What was true for Johnson and London's taverns was also true for the patrons of City Tavern in British America's largest city. Taverns were social centers, locations for clubs to meet and communities to gather. Benjamin Franklin, whose autobiography gives us one of the best glimpses into life in eighteenth-century Philadelphia, recalled that one of his first stops upon arriving in the city was in a tavern near the market at Second and High streets. "Walking again down towards the River, and looking in the Faces of People, I met a young Quaker Man whose Countenance I lik'd, and accosting him requested he would tell me where a Stranger could get Lodging. We were then near the Sign of the Three Mariners. Here, says he, is one Place that entertains Strangers, but it is not a reputable House; if thee wilt walk with me, I'll show thee a better. He brought me to the Crooked Billet in Water-Street. Here I got a

Dinner. And while I was eating it, several sly Questions were ask'd me, as it seem'd to be suspected from my youth and Appearance, that I might be some Runaway. After Dinner my Sleepiness return'd: and being shown to a Bed, I lay down without undressing, and slept till Six in the Evening; was call'd to Supper; went to Bed again very early and slept soundly till the next Morning." Later tavern visits allowed Franklin to befriend his fellow artisans, get to know the colonial governor, and launch a host of civic improvements. Taverns were integral to community life in the eighteenth century.

City Tavern's origins dated to 1772, when a group of Philadelphia gentlemen that included Edward Shippen, Jr., George Clymer, Henry Hill, Joseph Shippen, Jr., John Cadwalader, John Wilcocks, and Samuel Meredith leased a plot of ground on Second Street near Walnut from Samuel Powel to build a tavern for refined entertainment. The men collected fifty-two subscriptions of £25 to build the building, and later in 1776 they created a formal trust, much like the joint-stock companies that financed early colonies. As the city had grown, men of wealth and sophistication wished to establish separate public spaces for themselves, away from the noise and bad behavior of the "lower sort"; the tavern and other institutions including Philadelphia's Dancing Assembly and the Schuylkill River Fishing Club allowed the well-off merchant class to indulge themselves in a developing sense of privacy, as well as ideals of refinement and gentility.

City Tavern was not just an entrepreneurial venture for these men, but a way that they could promote their city and at the same time provide

a fine business venue for their friends and colleagues. An account in the *Pennsylvania Journal* explained "the Proprietors have built this tavern without any view of profit, but merely for the convenience and credit of the city." To manage their property, they advertised to hire a tavern keeper who would oversee an inn as great as any in the English Atlantic World. Their advertisement assured applicants that "the terms will, of convenience, be made easy to the tenant: the extensiveness of the undertaking, in superintending so capital a tavern as this is proposed to be, requires some stock beforehand, as well as an active obliging disposition."

The proprietors chose Daniel Smith to fit that description. As City Tavern prepared to open, Smith took the unusual action of carrying out what later business leaders would call an advertising campaign. In colonial newspapers from New England to the South, Smith ran

Birch's 1799 view of City Tavern showed the building when it was part of Philadelphia's prospering postrevolutionary economy. At right is the Bank of Pennsylvania, the first Greek Revival building in America, designed by Benjamin Henry Latrobe in 1798 and demolished in 1870.

notices that City Tavern was now furnished "perfectly in the style of a London tavern."

City Tavern's clientele must have been struck by how different it looked than other taverns in Philadelphia. In the eighteenth century, liquor licenses were often distributed as a form of social welfare, given to support one of the few careers that a widowed woman could pursue. Tavern rooms were most often located in the first floor front of small dwelling houses, much like those on Elfreth's Alley or Betsy Ross's house. At times, clubs would make special arrangements with the innkeeper to use another room for their meetings, as Benjamin Franklin's Junto club had done decades earlier.

City Tavern, however, was built and decorated on a far grander scale. Its tall, Georgian facade presented a picture of prosperity and gentility that reflected the status of the men who were its intended customers. Visitors entered the first floor of the tavern via a wide set of steps set twenty feet back from Second Street, a distance that allowed observers to appreciate its fifty-foot-wide front and lodgers to avoid some of the noise and dust of the street. The entrance hall was flanked by two rooms where merchants and other gentlemen met, drank coffee, and discussed the latest news available in Daniel Smith's stock of publications. On the second floor was the tavern's most elegant feature: a long gallery ideal for large banquets and dancing. No longer were Philadelphia's gentry content to hold their dances in a warehouse. Instead, the ladies and gentlemen of Philadelphia's wealthy merchant class displayed their carefully studied dance steps and manners in their stylish English clothing here. Also on the second floor were two smaller

rooms, where, Francisco de Miranda, a visitor from Venezuela, reported, "those who do not like to dance play cards on tables prepared for that purpose."

Man Full of Troubles Tavern, located near the Delaware River port at Second and Spruce streets, was typical of the size and style of colonial pubs.

But the empire in which City Tavern was built was about to change. Soon, the tavern became a gathering spot of the revolutionary movement. On October 26, 1774, the *Pennsylvania Gazette* reported: "On Thursday last an elegant entertainment was given at the *City Tavern*, by the Assembly of this province, to the Gentlemen of the Congress." John Adams reveals his Yankee prejudice against Quakers in his anecdote about the Assembly members in City Tavern that night, but he also noted that diverse groups were coming together in the

Dined with the whole Congress at the City Tavern, at the Invitation of the House of Representatives of the Province of Pensylvania, the whole House dined with Us, making near 100 Guests in the whole—a most elegant Entertainment. A Sentiment was given, "May the Sword of the Parent never be Stain'd with the Blood of her Children." Two or 3 broadbrims [Quakers], over against me at Table—one of em said this is not a Toast but a Prayer, come let us join in it—and they took their Glasses accordingly.

—John Adams's Diary, October 20, 1774

growing protest against Britain. The following June, the Congress bade farewell to George Washington with a formal banquet in the tavern, just before he left to lead the new Continental Army at Boston. Washington's fellow Virginian Thomas Jefferson recorded purchasing frequent bowls of punch "at Smith's" to share with his fellow delegates in 1776.

The next year, the political climate of the tavern changed profoundly. When the British captured Philadelphia in 1777, officers claimed City Tavern as their own, and the Tory *Pennsylvania Ledger* announced balls where those soldiers would dance with the daughters of prominent Tory families. Indeed, the revolution's challenge to old loyalties would become very personal for Daniel Smith.

After Daniel Smith left with other Loyalists at the end of the occupation in 1778, City Tavern's subscribers hired a new manager and continued to run the tavern until 1785, when they sold the building to Samuel Powel. Powel, owner of many properties throughout Philadelphia, hired Edward Moyston to run the tavern. Under his management, the adjacent Three Crowns Tavern building was purchased so ladies as well as gentlemen could find accommodations there in a respectable and sophisticated manner.

The tavern offered privacy, but it also continued to be a location of major public events and celebrations for the city and nation's wealthy and powerful in the years to follow. On September 15, 1787, George Washington and the delegates to the Constitutional Convention gathered to celebrate their just-completed work. The party the delegates threw appears to have been a memorable one. The fifty-six guests consumed fifty-

four bottles of Madeira wine, sixty bottles of claret, eight bottles of old stock, twenty-two bottles of porter, eight bottles of cider, twelve bottles of beer, and seven large bowls of punch.

In addition to being a center of entertainment, City Tavern's role as a center of the new nation's business world grew after the revolution. In 1789, Moyston arranged for the Merchant's Coffee House and Place of Exchange to use the front rooms on the tavern's first floor. Meeting every afternoon and evening, the exchange brought together ship captains, merchants, and other businessmen. By the early nineteenth century, it would grow enough to move into the elegant Philadelphia Merchants' Exchange building just west of City Tavern, across Dock Street.

The Coffee House and Exchange was just one example of the rising power and influence of Philadelphia's merchant class during the years

Tobacconist Isaac Jones's advertisement for his shop—"in front street, between race and vine streets, Philadª."—showed a scene that regulars at any of Philadelphia's colonial taverns would have recognized: men gathered around a table sharing a friendly glass, clay pipes at hand, and sociable conversation.

The business being thus closed, the members adjourned to the City Tavern, dined together and took a cordial leave of each other; after which I returned to my lodgings, did some business with and received the papers from the Secretary of the Convention, and retired to meditate on the momentous work which had been executed.

—Diary of George Washington, September 15, 1787

☞ Daniel Smith, City Tavern's Tory Tavern Keeper

When Daniel Smith opened the doors of City Tavern in 1773, he probably looked at the changes of his life as a collection of positive advances. He was Irish-born and had immigrated to the colonies six years earlier, shortly after peace was finally secured following years of warfare between the French and British empires. Smith left no record of what he had done in his first years in America or where he had lived, but as City Tavern's owners were careful to advertise for a person of skill and experience, it seems likely that he managed a tavern during that time, and perhaps in Ireland as well.

Smith's first years running City Tavern were prosperous ones. He started a family, and his business success allowed him to purchase land outside Philadelphia as an investment. Later, Smith would value his personal property at £700 at the start of the revolution.

We know that amount because Daniel Smith filed a claim with the British government to recoup some of his considerable financial losses during the war. The documents that he filed included letters from some of Britain's leaders, including a statement by Lord Cornwallis that Smith "bore an exceeding good character in America" and noting that the tavern keeper "suffered much on Account of his Loyalty" to King George III and his government.

Like many colonists, Daniel Smith did not take an immediate stand on the movement toward independence. He played host to revolutionary leaders, but drew the ire of their supporters, as well. When Patriot troops engaged the British at Quebec, they captured Colonel Robert Prescott and brought him to Philadelphia as a prisoner of war. Like officers on both sides of eighteenth-century conflict, the captured Briton was released on parole, and he was allowed to rent quarters in City Tavern rather than be imprisoned in a cell. Obviously, revolutionaries in Philadelphia did not like that situation. Smith "made himself obnoxious" to the crowd who attempted to attack Prescott while he was lodged at City Tavern, and he "exerted himself in protecting him and shewed him in other respects all the kindness in his power." Smith's business prospered during the British occupation of Philadelphia, but when the British withdrew in 1778, Smith and his young family accompanied them and returned to

> CITY TAVERN, PHILADELPHIA.
>
> DANIEL SMITH begs leave to inform the PUBLIC, that the Gentlemen Proprietors of the CITY TAVERN have been pleaſed to approve of him, as a proper perſon to keep ſaid tavern; in conſequence of which he has compleatly furniſhed it, and, at a *very great expence*, has laid in every article of the firſt quality, perfectly in the ſtile of a London tavern: And in order the better to accommodate ſtrangers, he has fitted up ſeveral elegant bed rooms, detached from noiſe, and as private as in a lodging houſe. The beſt livery ſtables are quite convenient to the houſe.
>
> He has alſo fitted up a genteel Coffee Room, well attended, and properly ſupplied with Engliſh and American papers and magazines.
>
> He hopes his attention and willingneſs to oblige, together with the goodneſs of his wines and larder, will give the public entire ſatisfaction, and prove him not unworthy of the encouragement he has already experienced.
>
> The *City Tavern* in Philadelphia was erected at a great expence, by a voluntary ſubſcription of the principal gentlemen of the city, for the convenience of the public, and is by much the largeſt and moſt elegant houſe occupied in that way in America.

Daniel Smith's advertisements for City Tavern appeared in numerous newspapers throughout the colonies, including this one, which appeared in the *Pennsylvania Gazette* of February 16, 1774

Great Britain. The new state of Pennsylvania confiscated Smith's real estate and other property as punishment for his Loyalist actions.

In England, Smith resumed his career as a tavern keeper. On September 19, 1784, Loyalist Samuel Shoemaker, a prominent Philadelphia Quaker, saw "little Smith who formerly kept the City Tavern in Philada. He now keeps a Tavern on the road to South Hampton somewhere near Bagshot." Shoemaker saw Smith again the following year while journeying from Southampton to London. His coach stopped at Smith's "very genteel house," and Smith invited his fellow former Philadelphian to stay at the tavern "and said it should not cost me a farthing." Shoemaker had to decline, but as the coach left Smith sent him "a quantity of very fine Gooseberrys and currants which were very acceptable to refresh us on the road."

Smith's business in England failed, and in 1787 he presented a claim to the government, signed by Lieutenant General Prescott and a number of prominent Loyalists from Pennsylvania. Smith noted that he "is not at present worth more than One hundred Pounds." The crown granted Smith a £30 annual pension.

A teacup and saucer bearing the initials "JB" for John Barry, the celebrated Irish-American naval hero. Barry ordered the set in Canton, China, when he captained the second American merchant trip from Philadelphia to the Far East in 1788.

following independence. A thriving economy based in both international trade and domestic transportation and manufacturing paid for the cultural advances of the city. In 1784, Robert Morris's *Empress of China* had opened the profitable trade with Asia. By 1800, over forty ships would be engaged exclusively in commerce with China. In the first quarter of the century, Philadelphians made vast fortunes in overseas trade. By the 1830s, the city was a major mercantile port and other economic opportunities, including coal and iron production, mills along the Schuylkill River at Manayunk and Kensington, and new roads and canals, all brought further prosperity to the city.

The Merchants' Exchange Building was the embodiment of the maritime economy of this era. Commodity brokers awaited news of incoming ships and the fine goods they would bring from Asia and Europe. Real estate sales, auctions, and numerous other types of business transactions were carried out in the grand exchange room on the second floor of the building.

The founding of the Philadelphia Exchange Company in 1831 marked the formal establishment of business practices that had been going

on for years in nearby City Tavern. The merchants who formed the organization now needed an official space in which to conduct their business. An advertisement in the *Philadelphia Inquirer* of October 28, 1831, announced a $100 prize "for *the plan which shall be adopted* of an Exchange Building, contemplated to be erected upon the scite bounded by Walnut, Dock, and Third streets in the city of Philadelphia."

A committee of Philadelphia merchants chose William Strickland to create the monumental building. The Merchants' Exchange, constructed between 1832 and 1834, was one of his masterpieces. Strickland's foremost challenge was building on a triangular lot, created when city leaders had finally capped over the polluted, stinking Dock Creek from Walnut Street to Front in the 1780s, altering William Penn's urban grid plan. Strickland met the challenge by placing a curved Corinthian portico in the east end of the structure. This element tied in well

The Merchants' Exchange Building, designed by William Strickland, was the commercial center of early nineteenth-century Philadelphia. At right is the First Bank of the United States.

The Lanthorn, or
Choragic Monument of
Lysicrates, illustrated in
volume one of *The
Antiquities of Athens* by
James Stuart and Nicholas
Revett, served as William
Strickland's inspiration for
the cupola atop the
Merchant's Exchange
Building

with the Corinthian front of the First Bank
across Third Street. As in his design for a Second
Bank building a few years earlier (see Chapter
5), Strickland copied details from Stuart and
Revett's *Antiquities of Athens* to produce details,
including the elegant cupola, or "lantern," atop
the building. Three stories of windows surrounded the building's main section.

The finished building was sumptuous.
Merchants arriving to trade commodities could
climb the marble steps on the east front to the
building's trade floor, passing marble lions,
carved by Henry and Battin Fiorelli, the first of
which was installed in 1838. Inside, mosaic tiles
covered the trading floor, and a domed ceiling
painted with frescos was supported by marble
pillars. These elements were destroyed during a
remodeling in 1900.

The Merchants' Exchange went out of business during the Civil War, and the building was
used for many purposes. By the early twentieth
century, the area had become the city's wholesale
food district, and awnings of corrugated metal
encircled Strickland's once elegant portico. A gas
station, marking the beginnings of the age of the
auto, stood on the building's north side by the
1920s. When the National Park Service began to
create Independence National Park in the 1950s,
the federal government acquired the building,
restoring its exterior to Strickland's masterful
design. In the early twenty-first century, the
National Park Service renovated the building's
interior, and it reopened in 2005. The one-time
center of Philadelphia commerce, successor of
the area's revolutionary-era business life, is now
the park's administrative headquarters.

By the early twentieth century (above), Philadelphia's leading merchants and central post office had long since moved west, and the once-elegant Merchants' Exchange was surrounded by Philadelphia's wholesale food distribution center, with tin-roofed stalls surrounding Strickland's magnificent portico. The National Park Service restored the building's exterior to its Greek Revival splendor (below), and it now serves as the headquarters for Independence National Historical Park.

Carpenters' Hall, an outstanding example of Georgian architecture designed by Robert Smith, sits nestled at the center of its block, bounded by Walnut and Chestnut streets, between Third and Fourth.

EIGHT

Carpenters' Hall Block

O F ALL THE BLOCKS IN Independence National Historical Park, the one surrounding Carpenters' Hall provides the best glimpse of what life was like in eighteenth-century Philadelphia. Before the days of mass transportation, personal automobiles, or even the bicycle, most people lived in a world that was defined by how far they could walk. Certainly, horses were a means of transportation, but they were expensive to keep and convenient only for long trips. City blocks like this one contained a variety of public and private places. This pattern continued until the nineteenth century, when mass transportation became available and businesses moved away from residential neighborhoods. The historic sites and spaces of this block show how eighteenth-century Americans' dom-

The members of the Carpenters' Company had completed work on their hall just a year before the First Continental Congress made use of the meeting room to the left of the front door in the fall of 1774, overcoming sectional prejudices to form a united resistance to British colonial policy. The Carpenters' Company of the City and County of Philadelphia has owned the building since its construction.

estic, economic, educational, and manufacturing lives all existed within a few steps of each other.

The centerpiece of this block is Carpenters' Hall, still owned by the Carpenters' Company of Philadelphia. Founded in the 1720s, the Carpenters' Company's objective was to maintain the quality of building in the Philadelphia area, setting high standards for craftsmen and providing charitable relief to members' widows and orphans. In many ways, the company was similar to European craft guilds and organizations of artisans and craftsmen which were springing up in villages in the American colonies at that time. Barbers, tailors, glaziers, printers, ropemakers, shoe cobblers, and others created groups where members could be entertained, carry out philanthropic work, learn from their fellow craftsmen, and protect their interests.

Within decades of its founding the company had become a leader in improving the quality and aesthetic appearance of structures throughout the region. The middle decades of the eighteenth century saw a transformation in building styles in Philadelphia. Prior to that time, lack of materials, workmen, knowledge, or funds kept most residences in simple, vernacular styles much like the structures which today line Elfreth's Alley or the Letitia Street House, now located in Fairmount Park, though a few buildings, like James Logan's home Stenton, broke from that mold. But a combination of new information and new wealth brought about changes, and the Carpenters' Company was to play an important role.

In part, the change in building followed changes in reading. Printed materials were becoming more available in Philadelphia after 1730. The Library Company of Philadelphia increased the number and type of published works available to city residents after its first shipment of books arrived from London. Among the most popular of these works were architectural plan and design books, which imported the classical symmetry inspired by sixteenth-century Italian architect Andrea Palladio to American colonists who had never been to Europe. That, along with the wealth that Philadelphia's merchant class was acquiring, allowed Americans to create buildings which mimicked those of their wealthy counterparts in the Old World.

One of the chief aims of the Carpenters' Company became the education of its members in mastering modern architectural techniques. The company began a library by 1734, and in

The *Articles of the Carpenters Company of Philadelphia* guided members in the style, and pricing of their craft, after its 1786 publication. The book, considered so secret that members refused to provide a copy for Thomas Jefferson, included a floor plan for Carpenters' Hall (upper right).

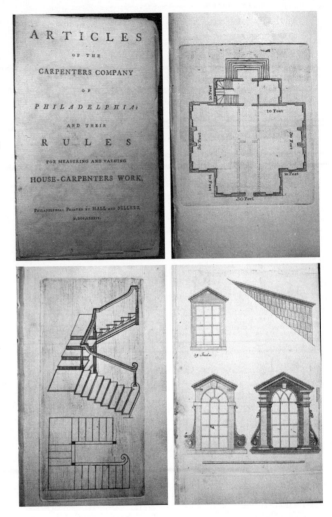

the years that followed collected and shared some of the outstanding works on architecture and style then available.

Another goal of the Carpenters' Company was restricting access to the "art and mystery" of members' craft skills. Several times in the early decades of the eighteenth century, builders petitioned the leadership of the colony to ban any more artisans in the construction trades from entering the colony. Each time, the assembly or council flatly denied the request, deciding that a plentiful supply of artisans was vital to the growth of the colony. The debate was one of supply and demand: keeping builders scarce and their wages high, or expanding the trades and lowering those wages. When they failed to restrict immigration, the builders instead turned their attention to other ways of gaining prominence for their members. Members determined prices to be charged for building and wages to be paid to employees. In 1786, the company published a guide to building for members, with styles and prices. The book was kept strictly secret; members actually visited the widows of deceased craftsmen to secure their copies.

By the 1760s, the Carpenters' Company was an organization of elite master builders. The company's annual dues of £4, compared to the rival Friendship Carpenter's Company's charges of five shillings, shows the exclusivity expected of the group. The Carpenters' Company never achieved the power or authority of European guilds, but of the city's artisan organizations, the company was both the longest-lived and most successful in promoting and improving its craft.

In 1770, the Carpenters began constructing their hall, which would be both a showcase for the skills of local artisans and a meeting place for the members. When it was completed in 1773, Carpenters' Hall was one of the largest, grandest buildings in the city, a fitting exemplar for the master builders who were members of the company. Robert Smith (1722–1777), America's first great architect, designed the structure. Scots-born and well trained as both architect and builder, Smith designed a plan calling for a building that was both functional and beautiful, and which could draw rental income to support

At Ten, The Delegates all met at the City Tavern, and walked to the Carpenters Hall, where they took a View of the Room, and of the Chamber where is an excellent Library. There is also a long Entry, where Gentlemen may walk, and a convenient Chamber opposite to the Library. The General Cry was, that this was a good Room, and the Question was put, whether We were satisfyed with this Room, and it passed in the Affirmative. A very few were for the negative and they were chiefly from Pennsylvania and New York.

—John Adams, September 5, 1774

the Carpenters' Company's plans for education of young artisans and charity.

For his plan, Smith combined his experience in Scotland and his study of Palladian architecture for the Carpenters' Company's use. The Flemish-bond brick structure was built on a Greek-cross plan, a building type often used for town houses or market houses in Scotland. Smith had used a very similar plan when he designed the courthouse for Northampton County, Pennsylvania, in 1765.

The first floor of the structure was divided into two large meeting rooms, with a hallway separating them. The Library Company of Philadelphia moved into rented rooms on the second floor in 1773. When the delegates to the First Continental Congress arrived in Philadelphia in September 1774, they found one of the American colonies' largest collections of books, where the Rev. Manasseh Cutler reported, "every modern author of any note, I am told, is to be met with here, and large additions are annually made. The books appeared to be well arranged and in good order." The library's second room held its Cabinet of Curiosities, a collection of natural history specimens, Native American artifacts, and scientific equipment that constituted Philadelphia's first museum.

Carpenters' Hall's most famous moment in history came in the autumn of 1774. Britain's Parliament was furious that colonists in Massachusetts Bay had carried out the Boston Tea Party the previous December, and it closed Boston's port in retaliation. Even conservatives saw the brutality of that action, which would soon lead to poverty and starvation for innocent people in the Bay Colony. Leaders from throughout the colonies voted to meet in Philadelphia in September to plan a mutual reaction to London's actions. When the Congress arrived, they were immediately faced with a controversy over where they should meet.

The Pennsylvania State House was one obvious choice. Delegate James Duane wrote, "I observed that if the State house was equally convenient it ought to be preferred being a provincial and the Carpenter's Hall a private House. And Besides, as it was tendered by the Speaker it seemed to be a piece of respect which was due to him, at least to enquire whether the State House was not equally convenient. The Question was however called for; and a great Majority fixed upon Carpenter hall."

Congress chose Carpenters' Hall because Assembly Speaker Joseph Galloway objected to strident opposition to Britain. Galloway had been Benjamin Franklin's political protégé in the 1750s and 1760s, countering the Penn family and their policies. Like Franklin, he had been defeated in the nasty election of 1764, when personal attacks flew between the supporters of the Penn family and members of the "Quaker Party"—Galloway and Franklin's side—who demanded that the Penns should pay their share of taxes to protect the colony. But by 1774 Galloway had regained his seat and risen to lead the Assembly, and he saw independence as unthinkable. John Adams and other congressmen preferred to keep Galloway and his state house at a distance.

The Congress that met from September 5 through October 26, 1774, in Carpenters' Hall was a turning point in the history of the American colonies. Up to that time, intercolo-

The First Continental Congress met in the east room of Carpenters' Hall on the first floor from September to October 1774, formulating plans to protest Great Britain's taxation policies and the closing of the Port of Boston after the Boston Tea Party.

Government is dissolved; we are in a state of nature. The distinctions between Virginians, Pennsylvanians, New Yorkers, and New Englanders are no more. I am not a Virginian, but an American!

—Virginia Delegate Patrick Henry, October 1774

nial meetings were rare (only two had ever occurred, the Albany Congress in 1754 and Stamp Act Congress in 1765), as colonists identified primarily with their local areas or their colonies. While each colony felt a level of grievance against the king and Parliament, those feelings differed significantly from region to region. The main goal of the Congress was to break down sectional differences and find compromises and common ground.

Congress ignored Galloway's plan for an "olive branch" petition to the king and instead created the Continental Association. Figuring that the best way to get Britain's attention was through its pocketbook, it called for a boycott of all British goods to start the following spring. The delegates hoped to unite all Americans behind the cause by advocating self-sacrifice.

When the Congress finished its work in Carpenters' Hall that fall, it voted "that another Congress should be held on the tenth day of May next, unless the redress of grievances, which we have desired, be obtained before that time." By the time that meeting took place, Massachusetts' militia had defended their military stores and political leaders at the Battle of Lexington and Concord. The American Revolution had begun.

As the walls of Carpenters' Hall rang with the pronouncements of the First Continental Congressmen, the space just west of their meeting was likely filled with the equally boisterous sounds of a busy schoolhouse. On Fourth Street, near Carpenters' Hall, the National Park Service has erected two brick rectangles which might seem to be little more than flower beds. In fact, these spaces outline the locations of two impor-

tant buildings in eighteenth-century Philadelphia: the schoolhouse and meetinghouse of the Society of Friends, or Quakers. The meetinghouse was torn down in 1859, followed by the razing of the schoolhouse in 1867, but this space reveals the continuing importance of William Penn's fellow Quakers in eighteenth-century Pennsylvania.

The Fourth Street Meeting House was built in 1763–1764, mostly to accommodate the religious meetings of Quaker youths who were members of the other meetings in town. The building's first schoolmaster was Anthony Benezet, a French-born Quaker who was one of the most significant citizens of eighteenth-century Philadelphia. Benezet removed corporal punishment from the school, substituting Quaker gentleness for beatings. He transformed the curriculum, teaching an impressive list of subjects including French, and stressed Quaker literature and manners.

The two-story brick Quaker meetinghouse stretched seventy-six feet along Fourth Street, and was forty-two feet deep. Nearby, the Quaker schoolhouse was a two-story brick building, thirty-four by sixty feet, which the Society of Friends built in 1744–1745 at a cost of £149. William Breton's image of the buildings included easily recognizable members of the Friends' meeting in the street scene, as well as two African American boys rousting a pig, a common sight in the colonial city, where pigs foraged for food in the streets.

After teaching the youth of this city near forty years, I have solicited & obtained the office of teacher of the Black children & others of that people, an imployment which tho' not attended with so great pecuniary advantages as other might be, yet affords me much satisfaction. I know no station in life I would prefer before it. Indeed my kind friend the object of slavery is still an object worthy the deepest consideration of a philosophic mind.

—Anthony Benezet to his neighbor Benjamin Franklin, 1783

☞ Anthony Benezet and his "African School"

When the Philadelphia Friends Meeting hired Anthony Benezet in 1742, Quaker education in the city was limited. Quakers believed in a very personal religious experience, one that did not require a college-educated clergy. Many of the first Quakers in seventeenth-century England were members of the poorest classes, and a limited emphasis on literacy and education persisted. But Anthony Benezet changed that. In his letter outlining his teaching abilities, he wrote that he was prepared to teach reading and writing, various forms of arithmetic, bookkeeping, French, German ("as that the learner might read and perfectly understand the bible, and talk it as to be unable to buy, sell, and talk of common things"), and skills relating to measuring timber, brickwork, and land.

But beyond what he could teach, it was the students he taught that was most significant. In 1754, Benezet began teaching what is believed to be the first girls' school in the American colonies. Young women were given an education far beyond anything offered anywhere else, with reading, writing, arithmetic, and grammar among the subjects. His pupils included women who became some of the leading citizens in late eighteenth-century Philadelphia.

The educational revolution that Anthony Benezet began in the 1740s was part of a cultural transformation in Philadelphia. In the decades to follow, he and his contemporaries changed the Quaker City from being a backwater to the leading city for early American arts, education, and culture.

The members of the Carpenters' Company were brilliant builders and architects, but they were also savvy businessmen. They knew that the land they owned along Chestnut Street would be valuable, so they placed their own building at

This new school was his second educational initiative. In 1750, Benezet began night classes for African American students. He taught these lessons in his home on the north side of Chestnut Street between Fourth and Fifth. Benezet devoted much of the remaining decades of his life to educating African American children. French traveler Jacques Pierre Brissot de Warville visited the school in the 1780s and reported that Benezet's black students "read well, repeat from memory, and calculate with rapidity. I have seen a picture painted by a young negro, who never had a master: it is surprisingly well done. . . . The Black girls, besides reading, writing, and the principles of religion, are taught spinning, needle-work, & c. . . . They have the appearance of decency, attention, and submission."

Benezet's interest in African American education led him to become one of Pennsylvania's first abolitionists. Through correspondence, petition, and writing, he strove for the rest of his life to eradicate slavery.

Anthony Benezet died May 3, 1784, leaving a legacy as an educator, philanthropist, and civil rights pioneer that was felt throughout Philadelphia and the world. ◄

"Residence of the late Anthony Benezet No 115 Chestnut Street" as drawn by William Strickland in 1818, was located between Third and Fourth.

the center of the block in a court, a common practice in eighteenth-century Philadelphia.

In the 1950s, the National Park Service opted to re-create the buildings that had surrounded the hall at the end of the eighteenth century, rather than preserve the Victorian buildings that had taken their place in the following century— an action that many preservationists have come to regret. After painstaking research, the NPS rebuilt New Hall, the rental property and meeting hall that the Carpenters' Company had built in 1791 for its own use at the time they rented Carpenters' Hall to the newly established Bank of the United States. New Hall ran sixty-one feet

By the mid-nineteenth century, the residences that had once faced Chestnut Street were long gone, replaced by commercial architecture, but Carpenters' Hall remained at the center of its court in a busy urban center.

along Carpenters' Court and was nineteen feet, eight inches deep. On its first floor were three separate offices, each complete with a fireplace: additional rental spaces for the company's income. On the second floor was a large meeting room, suitable for meetings of the company. In the early years of the republic, the carpenters rented New Hall to the United States War Department, and as such, this diminutive building served as America's first Pentagon. Here General Henry Knox, secretary of war under President George Washington, worked with his staff of five men.

Just across the lane leading from Chestnut Street to Carpenters' Hall is the reconstructed Pemberton House, now used as a National Park gift shop. Merchant Joseph Pemberton leased

New Hall, constructed by the Carpenters for rental and meeting space, housed the United States War Department during Philadelphia's decade as the nation's capital from 1790 to 1800. Much altered and damaged over the 150 years that followed, the building was reconstructed by the National Park Service and is now a museum of military history.

the spot from the Carpenters' Company for an annual ground rent of 69 1/3 Spanish milled pieces of eight in January 1775. Pemberton was the son of Israel Pemberton, called "King of the Quakers" due to his positions in the Pennsylvania Assembly and leadership in the Society of Friends' Annual Meeting. The younger Pemberton and his wife, Ann Galloway, lived for only a short time in the elaborate town house he built. His business suffered both from his overextending his finances and Americans' decision to enter into a nonimportation agreement to protest British taxation. Thus, the agreement reached by the Congress in nearby Carpenters' Hall a few months before Pemberton began to build his house led to his loss of that house a few years later. Pemberton's "large, elegant and commodious new brick house" went to his creditors, and was sold to merchant William Savery in 1777. Likewise, Savery was a victim of uncertain financial times, and in 1790 he also went bankrupt, the same year that the new nation's first secretary of the treasury issued a call for the

Alexander Hamilton
(1755-1804), by Charles
Willson Peale.

creation of a national bank, to be headquartered in Philadelphia.

Stabilizing the American economy was one of the central purposes of the new federal Constitution, and when George Washington appointed his friend and former aide Alexander Hamilton as the first secretary of the treasury in September 1789, Hamilton laid out a series of bold plans to do just that. A man of ability, ego, and ambition, Hamilton was born in poverty on the island of Nevis, educated at King's College (Columbia University), rose to success in the military and as a lawyer, and married into a prominent New York family. Hamilton crafted a series of reports that advocated an economy closely allied with northern merchants. A national bank, modeled somewhat on the Bank of England, was integral to his plan. His programs revealed that Hamilton feared "the mob" as much as he respected the wealthy.

Hamilton first tackled the massive national debt that Americans had run up during the revolution, developing a plan that allied northern mercantile interests which had speculated in government debt with the new national government. James Madison and Thomas Jefferson opposed the scheme, and the compromise the three men worked out included the relocation of the capital from Hamilton's home in New York City to Philadelphia in 1790.

Next, in December 1790 Hamilton issued a plan for a national bank into which the government could deposit tax revenues while drawing in the support of merchants who would buy shares in it. The bank would issue paper money backed by government gold and silver, finally creating a stable, single American currency.

Hamilton's plan was a major extension of the powers of the federal government. Nowhere in the Constitution were banking powers outlined, but Hamilton posited that Article One of the document allowed the government to make any laws "which shall be necessary and proper for carrying into Execution the foregoing Powers, and all other Powers vested by this Constitution in the Government of the United States, or in any Department or Officer thereof," and thus allowed for his bank. Thomas Jefferson disagreed. In a report to President Washington, Jefferson stated: "The incorporation of a bank, and the powers assumed by this bill, have not, in my opinion, been delegated to the United States, by the Constitution."

After much consideration, and over much opposition, Washington signed the legislation, and the bank was created in February 1791. Alexander Hamilton's plans for the American economy had both good and bad effects. To be sure, Hamilton's programs stabilized the national economy. The bank convinced northeastern merchants to support the new federal government, and brought their considerable financial resources to the support of the young nation. His call for a tax on the manufacture of whiskey by western farmers kept grain prices lower, but also asserted the right of the federal government to manipulate the economy. Hamilton's plans helped develop American manufacturers and wean the United States off its dependence on European-produced goods.

But Hamilton's programs were increasingly viewed as heavy-handed or unfair by those outside his circle. "Congress may go home. Mr. Hamilton is all-powerful, and fails in nothing he

attempts," complained Pennsylvania senator
William Maclay. Many of Hamilton's economic
plans ignored or attacked the economic well-
being of western and southern agrarian interests,
a large and important part of the American population. Indeed, the combined power of Washington's support and northeastern interests
passed many of Hamilton's ideas, but led to levels of opposition that would have long-lasting
implications for the American political scene. By
1793, the tone of the American political debates
became intensely bitter, with congressmen and
other opponents attacking Hamilton's character
as much as his programs. In 1794, Washington
had to lead federal troops into western
Pennsylvania to put down the Whiskey
Rebellion, a potential uprising of farmers who
protested Hamilton's tax on the whiskey they
manufactured.

Hamilton's early constitutional debates with
Jefferson continued to echo in the wrangling
over the role of government throughout the
nineteenth century, long after President James
Madison allowed the bank's charter to expire in
1811. The constitutional power of the federal
government was one of the issues that led to the
Civil War, and still plays a role today in the discussion of the balance between the federal government and the rights of individuals.

Within a short walk of these important public
buildings stood the homes of people who lived
near each other, but whose lives were divided by
levels of wealth, power, and culture. The three
historic residences of this block—the homes of
the White and Todd families, as well as the space

☞ Architecture: The First Bank and Neoclassical Architecture

The construction of the First Bank of the United States was one of the earliest opportunities the government of the United States had to send a message to the American people through architecture. Built within the first decade of the new Constitution's rule, the bank uses the language of neoclassical architecture to announce the longevity, stability, and strength that bank leaders and government officials wanted to see in both institutions.

The First Bank was designed by amateur architect Samuel Blodget, Jr., a New Englander who moved to Philadelphia in 1789. Blodget's plan was inspired by the work of Andrea Palladio, whose neoclassical style was then the rage in England and the United States.

Above the Corinthian columns which faced Third Street, the plan called for a carving of an American bald eagle, one of the first times an image of the national bird was used to ornament a public structure. Artist Charles Willson Peale provided a live example of an American bird as a model, as the carvers working on the mahogany facing only knew Roman eagles. Blodget originally planned for the entire building to be faced in marble, but costs made that impossible, and the sides and back of the architect's masterpiece were made of red brick.

The bank's charter expired in 1811 and merchant Stephen Girard bought the bank building. ☞

> On viewing this building, the first impression is, one plain and beautifully proportioned whole. . . . an elegant exhibition of simple grandeur and chaste magnificence.
>
> *—Gazette of the United States,* December 27, 1797

The First Bank of the United States, built in 1795, is an outstanding example of neoclassical architecture. The bank façade's carved wooden eagle, on the pediment, was one of the first times the national bird adorned a public building.

Billy White was born a Bishop. I never could persuade him to play anything but Church. He would tie his own or my apron round his neck, for a gown, and stand behind a low chair, which he called his pulpit; I seated before him on a little bench, was the congregation; and he always preached about being good.

—A childhood friend of the Rt. Rev. William White

preserved as the site of an artisan-class home—reveal that people of varying social classes lived in close proximity to one another in early America. That fact is even more striking when we consider what *did not* survive from the period. The two small lanes that meet just behind the Bishop White House, Harmony Lane and Whale Bone Alley, were the locations of tanneries in the eighteenth century. Tanners dumped the carcasses and chemicals used to create leather into nearby Dock Creek, the body of water that intersected the block; the creek had been deep enough to sail a schooner inland in the time of William Penn, but it had filled with silt and pungent waste by the mid-eighteenth century. The smell was so bad that Benjamin Franklin and others sought ways to clean up the water supply by moving the tanners out of the city in the late 1730s. Their plan failed, and eventually Dock Creek was capped over to reduce the stench.

William White, the longtime rector of the combined parish of Christ Church and St. Peter's, was one of Philadelphia's best-loved clergymen in the revolutionary and early national periods. That White was "born a Bishop" was even more remarkable, due to the animosity most colonists felt toward that church office. Many early American Protestants, remembering the ways their forebears had been abused by the Roman Catholic English Queen Mary I, squirmed at the idea of any bishop, even an Anglican one, setting foot on American soil. Yet throughout the colonial period, as the number of colonists who were members of the Church of England grew, the lack of a bishop caused hardship. Anglican men had to travel to London for an extended stay to receive ordination. The result was a lack of clergy in many colonies that persisted until the late eighteenth century. But White's kind and generous personality won out, to the point that numerous Philadelphians—including members of the Quaker meeting—came to call him "our bishop."

William White was born in Philadelphia in 1747, the son of a wealthy Anglican family. He received bachelor's and master's degrees from the College of Philadelphia, and was ordained in London in 1772. He returned to Philadelphia and was appointed assistant pastor of the combined parish where he would spend his career. Thus, he became a clergyman of the Church of England in one of the most critical eras in the church's history.

Bishop William White (1748–1836), in a portrait by Charles Willson Peale.

Since King Henry VIII's break with the Roman Catholic Church in 1531, the monarch had been the head of the national church. Every clergyman undergoing ordination swore allegiance to the king or queen. By the time William White stepped to the pulpit, his congregation included leaders of both political factions in the growing breach with England. White decided that, despite the worsening situation, his first duties would be to his congregation. "I never beat the ecclesiastical drum," White recalled. "Being invited to preach before a battalion, I declined; and mentioned to the Colonel (who was one of the warmest spirits of the day, Timothy Matlack), my objections to the making of the ministry instrumental to the war." But White eventually did side with the American cause, unlike many of his fellow American Anglican clergymen. "I know my dan-

The Bishop White House, on Walnut Street near Third, a Federal-style brick townhouse, reflects Americans' postrevolutionary tastes as well as the continuing attachment to British building patterns.

ger," White told another Philadelphian at the time he took his loyalty oath to the new United States, "and that it is the greater on account of my being a clergyman of the Church of England; but I trust in Providence. The cause is a just one, and I am persuaded, will be protected."

William White and his family began construction on their Walnut Street home after the revolution, and work continued on it while White, the newly elected bishop of Pennsylvania, traveled to England to be consecrated by the archbishops of Canterbury and York and the bishop of Bath and Wells on May 4, 1787. The

Bishop White House offers an outstanding glimpse into the lives of elite Philadelphians in that era. White was not the wealthiest man in town, but his social status was certainly near the top. His neighbors included Supreme Court Justice James Wilson across the street and the eminent physician Dr. Benjamin Rush next door, and just down Third Street lived Thomas Willing, merchant and president of the Bank of the United States. From his home, White presided over an active congregation and a large family in the first half century of the new republic.

When Bishop White returned from London, the family took up residence in their town house. Built in the late Georgian, or Federal, architectural style, the house's front is of Flemish bond brick, with three bays of windows and a front door with a neoclassical frame. Inside, the layout of the house was quite typical of those built in Philadelphia in the era. Visitors entered through a "passage," which served as a waiting area to ensure the family's privacy and led to the staircase to the upper floors. On the first floor are two large parlors, one used as a formal sitting room and one an elegantly appointed dining room. The second floor was White's realm, with his spacious bedroom connected to his library. The bishop never lived in this house alone. The upper floors of the house were filled with the Whites' children and numerous grandchildren, along with frequent guests. At that time, the family consisted of the bishop and his wife, and their children Elizabeth, Mary, Thomas, William, and Henry, ranging in ages from eleven to two. Also moving into the house were three domestic servants. Young Henry White died in

Mr. [Samuel] Powell is indefatigable in hurrying the Workmen about the House; he told me this day he was afraid that there would not be as much of the plaistering done this season as you expected and he wished for; it is his opinion I should have some of the Chimneys measured and the dimensions sent you for marble, which I shall inclose, you can do what you think best; he tells me you will save near one-half by bringing it with you.

—Mary White writing to her husband in London, November 27, 1786

Bishop William White's book-lined study and adjacent bedroom (with mosquito netting draped around the bed) provided the busy clergyman with a modicum of privacy in a household filled with servants, children, grandchildren, and frequent guests.

1788, followed by his brother William in 1797. Mrs. White also died that year. Bishop White would continue to live in his Walnut Street home for the next thirty-nine years as a widower.

By the early nineteenth century Bishop White lived in a multigenerational household that rarely left him lonely or alone. Both of White's daughters moved from the house when they married, but Thomas White and his wife resided with the bishop, along with their five children. When she was widowed in 1813, Elizabeth White Macpherson and her two daughters moved in, and Mary White Bronson's five children moved in with their grandfather when she died. By 1826, the bishop and his two surviving offspring lived there with his eleven grandchildren. The White family was expansive in other ways, as the bishop took in others in need of a place to stay. When Justice James Wilson fled Philadelphia due to financial troubles and eventually died in North Carolina, his daughter Mary moved in with the Whites. Visiting clergy, children of friends sent to Philadelphia for an education, and numerous others joined Bishop White's family in this home for short or long stays.

The Whites' neighbor John Todd lived in a far smaller house, representative of the rising number of professionals who were members of Philadelphia's "middling sort" and the diversity of the neighborhood in the 1790s. Jonathan Dilworth had built the house as a rental property in 1775, and subsequently rented to several tenants. Todd purchased this house from Dilworth's widow on November 23, 1791, for £1,350 and moved in on the same day. At the time, Todd was a prosperous attorney with a young family who appeared to have a bright future ahead of him.

When John Todd hung out his shingle at Fourth and Walnut, he was following a common practice, joining his next-door neighbor, Dr. Samuel Powel Griffiths, and other professionals

Attorney John Todd and his wife, Dolley, resided at Fourth and Walnut streets from 1791 to 1793. The house's Georgian architecture reflected Todd's place as a prospering middling-sort professional, a career cut short by the yellow fever epidemic that hit Philadelphia in 1793.

and master craft workers in row houses throughout the city in running his business out of his home. The Todds' house had a simple floor plan: main rooms in the front, with a "dependency" at the rear of the building that held the kitchen and service spaces, with sleeping rooms for children and servants above. The front section of the house had two rooms, and Todd, like many other middling men, used the front one, facing Walnut Street, for his work space. Artisans, craftsmen, lawyers, and doctors all plied their trades within their homes, almost always in the first floor room with easiest access to passersby. French immigrant Peter Du Ponceau wrote of Philadelphia row houses, "The front room was devoted to business. If the master of the house was a lawyer, it was his office."

John Todd had been practicing law in Philadelphia since 1783, and had built up a thriving practice. On February 8, 1791, Todd was admitted to practice law before the Supreme Court of the United States, which was holding its first session in Philadelphia since the government relocated the previous fall. The Todds' new home was within walking distance of the business, social, and political centers of the nation's capital.

John Todd, Jr., married Dorthea "Dolley" Payne on January 7, 1790. The bride was born in North Carolina in May 1768 and lived in Virginia until her father decided that the cultural climate was not conducive to the way he wanted to raise his Quaker family. After freeing his slaves in 1783, John Payne moved his family to Philadelphia. Dolley's father loved the new role he played as a leading Quaker in the largest Quaker community in the United States. But while Payne's spiritual life prospered, his role as a capitalist did not. His starch manufactory failed, leading his fellow members of the Pine Street Friends Meeting to "read him out" in 1789. Probably depressed, he took to his bed and remained incapacitated for the next three years. Dolley's mother became the sole provider for her family, running a successful boarding-house on Chestnut Street, a space that would influence Dolley's later happiness.

Dorothea Payne Todd, in a 1797 portrait by James Sharples, Sr. Left a widow in 1793, "Dolley" married Congressman James Madison and became one of the most famous women in the United States.

She came upon our comparatively cold hearts in Philadelphia, suddenly and unexpectedly with all the delightful influences of a summer sun.

—Anthony Morris, recalling the arrival of Dolley Payne, in 1783

Oh my dear Brother, what a dread prospect has thy last letter presented to me! A revered Father in the jaws of Death, & a Love'd Husband in perpetual danger. . . . I am almost destracted with distress & apprihension, is it two late for their removal? Or can no interfearance of their Earthly friends rescue them from the two general fate? I have repeatedly Entreated John to leave home from which we are now unavoidably Banished, but alas he cannot leave his Father. . . . I wish much to see you, but my Child is sick & I have no way of getting to you.

—Dolley Payne Todd to her brother, 1793

Perhaps seeking a stable domestic life in the face of her family's financial problems, twenty-one-year-old Dolley accepted the marriage proposal of John Todd, a successful twenty-seven-year-old attorney who was also a member of the Quaker meeting. After their marriage, the Todds set up housekeeping with Dolley's younger sister, Anna, living with them and two young sons joining the family in the three years that followed. But the family's contentment in this residence was short lived. In the autumn of 1793, a yellow fever epidemic broke out in Philadelphia. Like other men with the means to do so, John Todd sent his wife and two sons out of Philadelphia to escape the disease. While Dolley Todd nursed her sick children near Grays Ferry on the Schuylkill River, John stayed in Philadelphia, where lawyers were much in demand writing wills and taking care of other legal matters. John Todd caught the disease and died on October 24.

The widow Dolley Todd and her sole surviving son returned to Philadelphia late that fall. Dolley's widowhood led her to a much different life than she could have expected as a young Quaker wife. Through friends and the people who lived in her mother's boardinghouse, she became acquainted with numerous people who returned to the capital that fall. By the following spring Congressman James Madison of Virginia persuaded Senator Aaron Burr of New York to introduce him to the pretty, vivacious widow.

"The great little Madison"—as Dolley Todd referred to her future husband—was then one of the most powerful men in the new nation's capital, belying the diminutive five-foot-four frame.

Married on September 15, 1794, James and Dolley Madison had an extremely close, loving relationship that lasted until James Madison's death in 1836. Few letters between them survive, largely because they insisted on not being separated for extended periods of time. The Madisons moved to his family plantation when he retired from politics in 1797, but when Thomas Jefferson defeated John Adams in the election of 1800, Madison became secretary of state and the new president's chief advisor. The widowed Jefferson selected his friend's wife to act as his official hostess. Dolley Todd Madison began a career as a popular Washington, D.C., hostess that would continue for the next sixteen years, through Jefferson's two terms and her husband's that followed. Dolley's vivacity was often contrasted with her husband's shyness, her beauty with his less-than-attractive looks that led Washington Irving to describe him as "a withered little apple-John."

> Thou must come to me, Aaron Burr says that the great little Madison has asked to be brought to see me this evening.
>
> —Dolley Todd to her friend Eliza Lee, 1794

Just behind the Todd House, the National Park Service has marked a small rectangle on the site of a small frame building that housed working Philadelphians in the late eighteenth century. Unlike today's residential areas where different social classes rarely live in close proximity to each other, eighteenth-century Philadelphians shared tightly packed housing areas. Families of high social status like the Whites or of rising professional ambitions like the Todds lived within a few steps of the craftsmen and workers whose small houses lined Harmony Lane and Whalebone Alley, or in the small artisans' house that this site commemorates.

William Birch captured the ways different social classes mixed together in his 1799 print of Library Hall (detail). Like their neighbors one block away, the residents who lived on the Carpenters' Hall block in the eighteenth century included rich, middling, and poor families, with residential, public, and commercial buildings a short walk from one another.

Early city directories reveal that the people who lived here worked as coachmen, a cordwainer, a turner, a tavern keeper, and a coppersmith. Their inclusion in these published directories and their listing by careers shows that these families were of middling ranks—below the professional groups like John Todd but slightly above the "lower sort," poor people who earned daily wages for manual labor, and who often only entered the historical record when they sought charity at the almshouses or at the Pennsylvania Hospital.

Life in this small house along Fourth Street must have been transitory for late eighteenth-century Philadelphians. The city directories, published in six different years during the 1790s, show six different families living in the small, wood-frame building. Historical archaeology has allowed us to more fully understand the lives of early Philadelphia craftspeople, revealing the diets, material possessions, and other aspects of the lives of people who left little written record.

Each of the people who lived and worked on the Carpenters' Hall block in the last quarter of the eighteenth century witnessed a variety of revolutions that shaped their lives. Politics, the economy, education, family patterns, and medical experiences all changed during these decades, and each of these changes made its presence felt on the lives of Philadelphia's residents, whether they were famous theologians, young professionals, struggling craft workers, or the host of others who called the Quaker City home during that era. But at the center of those changes was the revolutionary break from Great Britain, first discussed in whispers as the First Continental Congress met in Carpenters' Hall in 1774, and then shouted about when Congress returned the following year.

The Declaration House, reconstructed by Independence National Historical Park in time for America's 1976 bicentennial, re-creates the home where Thomas Jefferson rented rooms in the summer two centuries earlier. While living there, Thomas Jefferson wrote the Declaration of Independence.

NINE

The Declaration House

LIKE OTHER VISITORS IN THE 1770S, Thomas Jefferson enjoyed Philadelphia's numerous sources of entertainment. He spent hours browsing in the city's shops; he enjoyed conversations, drinks, and meals at City Tavern; and he found amusement in the city's streets, parlors, and meeting rooms. But throughout his life, Jefferson preferred a country setting. In the summer of 1776, he moved out the heart of noisy, smelly, dusty Philadelphia to the corner of Seventh and High streets. Here, Jefferson wrote the Declaration of Independence.

Jefferson was on his third visit to Philadelphia in 1776. In 1769, he had come to be inoculated for smallpox, a process that was almost as debilitating as the disease itself. Then in 1775 he arrived for the Second Continental Congress,

When Thomas Jefferson rented rooms at the corner of High (Market) and Seventh streets in 1776, the area was on the city's outskirts, as revealed in this detail of Benjamin Easburn's map dated the same year.

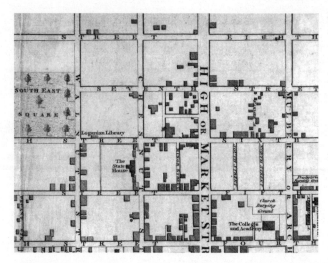

joining Virginia's delegation that included George Washington, Richard Henry Lee, and Benjamin Harrison. During that stay, Jefferson lodged in the home of cabinetmaker Benjamin Randolph. But disliking the noise and heat of city living, Jefferson made plans only a few days after returning to Randolph's house in 1776 to seek a more "rural" climate.

While Jefferson's mission in Philadelphia would prove to be historic, his mind was often filled with the same everyday concerns that travelers have today. His family was one of those concerns. His mother, Jane Randolph Jefferson, had died that spring, and he purchased a mourning ring—a traditional symbol of grief— during his stay in Philadelphia. His beloved wife Martha Jefferson was often in fragile health, and he thought of her often, buying household goods and luxury items to take to her and toys and clothing for their daughters in Virginia.

Jefferson tried to get over his worries about home by finding a residence that reminded him of his preferred surroundings. He wrote to a friend that summer: "I am at present in our old lodgings, tho' I think, as the excessive heats of the city are coming fast, to endeavor to get lodgings in the skirts of the town where I may have the benefit of a freely circulating air."

The move he made, from his rooms in Randolph's house on Chestnut Street near Carpenters' Hall to the house of Jacob Graff on Seventh Street, may seem minor to us today. But the city was very different then. Philadelphians considered Sixth Street to be the edge of town as late as the end of the 1700s. When Jefferson moved into Graff's house, he was trading a cramped block for a more open location. His daily walk to the Pennsylvania State House had a rural feel; "if not then the only house on that part of the street, I am sure there were few others yet built near it," Jefferson recalled decades later.

Jefferson found the rural environment he sought in the rooms he rented from Jacob Graff for thirty-five shillings a week. Graff, a prosperous German American mason, had just moved into his home at Seventh and High streets. The house was in the modern Georgian style, an excellent example of a city house. Philadelphians who passed as they headed east to the busy market just up High Street saw a façade laid out in the Flemish bond pattern of alternating "stretcher" and "header" bricks, a style that was both elegant and durable. Each window was crowned with a stone lintel that included a keystone design on both the two windows that faced High Street and the five "bays" (neatly symmetrical windows and doors) that faced Seventh. Graff chose to have his home face the side street rather than High, which even at the outskirts of

Thomas Jefferson (1743–1826), as painted by Charles Willson Peale.

I lodged in the house of a mr Graaf, a new brick house 3. stories high of which I rented the 2d floor consisting of a parlour and bed room already furnished. . . . in that parlour I wrote habitually and in it wrote this paper particularly.

—Thomas Jefferson, on writing the Declaration of Independence, 1825

☞ Architecture: Reconstructed Buildings

What we now call the Declaration House, the family home of Jacob Graff in 1776, is one of the few buildings in Independence National Historical Park that is a re-creation. While some early preservationists venerated the site, businessmen razed it in 1883 to build a bank. By the time Congress created the national park in 1948, a hamburger stand sat on the site of Jefferson's Philadelphia residence. The house was rebuilt in the 1970s as part of the celebration of America's bicentennial.

National Park Service policy on reconstructing buildings has changed over the years. While it was once common practice to rebuild lost structures—the original plans for Independence National Historical Park considered rebuilding the homes of William Penn and Benjamin Franklin, among others—the practice often led to mistakes. Reconstructions were placed on the wrong spot, built in the wrong style, or made of inaccurate materials. Indeed, a group of well-meaning preservationists had Thomas Jefferson's long-lost birthplace outside Charlottesville, Virginia, "rebuilt" in the 1960s. Subsequent archaeological

By the time Americans began to attach importance to the buildings associated with their nation's founding in the nineteenth century, the Graff house had been much altered. This 1854 photograph shows the building had acquired an additional floor and a large addition to the west, more than doubling the house that Thomas Jefferson had known in 1776.

research showed that the new structure was in the wrong place and looked nothing like the original home. The re-created "birthplace" was later moved and sold to a restaurant.

The NPS chose to reconstruct the historically noteworthy Declaration House for several reasons. Intensive research uncovered significant information on the original building. Park historians discovered essential documentation, including an 1802 fire insurance survey that recorded the building's measurements, style of paneling, and woodwork. An 1854 photograph, as well as a floor plan of Jefferson's rented rooms that a later owner sketched in 1855, provided visual proof that backed up the documentation. These discoveries allowed the NPS to construct a historically accurate building at the corner of Seventh and Market streets.

Today, the National Park Service focuses on preservation, rather than re-creation. The few structures in Independence Park that were reconstructed, including the Declaration House, City Tavern, the Pemberton House, and the façade of Library Hall, are based on painstaking research by historians, architects, curators, and archaeologists and accurately re-create significant spaces integral to the story of independence. ◁

Visitors to the site of Thomas Jefferson's 1776 residence in 1947—the year before Congress created Independence National Historical Park—saw the location filled with a Tom Thumb hamburger stand.

July 4.
Pd. Sparhawk for a
thermometer £3-15.
Pd. For 7 pr. Women's
gloves 27/.
Gave in charity 1/6.

—Thomas Jefferson's
Memorandum Book,
July 4, 1776

town must have been a busy road on market days. Graff was a member of the large German community that had first settled in Pennsylvania in the 1680s. His grandfather immigrated to Philadelphia in 1741, during an era when political upheaval in Europe pushed many to emigrate. Jacob Graff and his wife, Maria, had married in 1774 and had one son by the time Thomas Jefferson moved into his rented rooms.

It was common for "middling sort" families to take in boarders to supplement their incomes. Philadelphians had long hosted scores of visitors, as the political and mercantile capital of Pennsylvania drew members of the Assembly, merchants, and ship captains who needed housing in the town on a regular basis.

One of the frequent duties that Thomas Jefferson assigned to Robert Hemings, his enslaved servant who accompanied him throughout his time in Philadelphia, was picking up packages that he had purchased. Jefferson loved to shop, a fact that is clearly in evidence in the re-created parlor at the Graff house. Stacks of crates and parcels were filled with the treasures he found in Philadelphia shops, all awaiting his return to Monticello, the home he was building near Charlottesville, Virginia. His papers tell us a story of a man marveling at the goods that were available. Books, clothing, scientific equipment, artwork, and household items were among his purchases in the summer of 1776. Jefferson, a man whose love of spending would leave him bankrupt at the end of his life fifty years later, found time nearly every day to browse in local shops.

☞ Robert Hemings and the Hemings Family

Thomas Jefferson did not come to Philadelphia alone in the summer of 1776. He brought his young slave Robert Hemings as his personal servant. Robert, his sister Sally, and other members of their family had come into Jefferson's possession at the time of his marriage a few years earlier. The Hemingses were half siblings of Martha Wayles Jefferson, the children of her father and Betty Hemings, an enslaved woman whom Wayles owned.

We have no record of fourteen-year-old Bob Hemings's reaction to Philadelphia, no clues if he wondered why his owner's famous statement that "all men are created equal" did not apply to him. What we do know of Bob was that his labor was a valuable asset to Jefferson that summer, as he took care of laundry and ran countless errands. We can tell from Jefferson's meticulous account book that he rewarded his slave's special duties with the purchase of items of clothing, including shoes and stockings, which were not provided to field hands. Bob Hemings also probably had the opportunity to meet members of Philadelphia's large free and enslaved African American community, an experience that was far different than that of living in slave quarters on plantations or in the comparatively small towns of Williamsburg and Charlottesville in Virginia.

The work Bob Hemings did that summer, while living in the Graff house, allowed his owner to maintain a comfortable life and enjoy the city. Like many of the men who proclaimed American freedom that summer, Thomas Jefferson was cared for by an enslaved American. ☞

Robert Hemings saw to Thomas Jefferson's daily needs in his rented bedroom in the Graff house, a room re-created by National Park Service curators and architects, based on Jefferson's meticulous accounts of his expenditures during the summer of 1776.

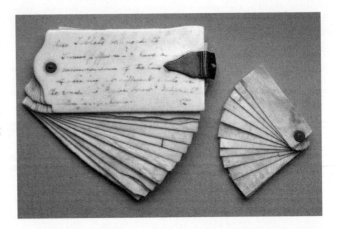

Thomas Jefferson left no diary and few letters from the summer during which he wrote America's founding document. But Jefferson was a methodical bookkeeper, and his memorandum books, recording his daily expenditures, allow us to glimpse his day-to-day activities during those critical months. Jefferson wrote each expenditure on thin, polished sheets of ivory, held together by a hinge and clamp, and then transferred the information to his ledger book.

These debts had become hereditary from father to son for many generations, so that the planters were a species of property annexed to certain mercantile houses in London.

—Thomas Jefferson, 1786

But entertainment and shopping were not why Jefferson and other Continental Congressmen were in Philadelphia that summer. They gathered after a decade when the affection that bound the British Empire together began to weaken. British culture dominated the American colonies in the second half of the eighteenth century, and as Thomas Jefferson grew up in colonial Virginia, the fashion, language, literature, architecture, and political thought of his fellow colonists all celebrated a close connection between the mother country and its prospering American colonies.

By the time Jefferson reached his maturity, however, the world of Virginia's planter aristocrats had begun to disintegrate. To be a member of the colonial elite meant one assumed a genteel air and expensive taste in clothing, food, beverages, housing, furnishings, entertainment, and scores of other ways. That elite culture led wealthy Virginians to run up massive debts to British merchant houses. At the same time, tobacco prices began to fall, and planters required more land to cultivate larger crops and they borrowed more money to keep their per-

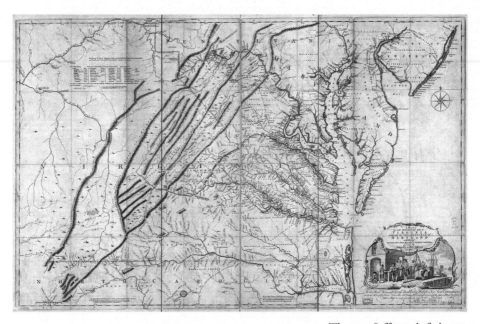

sonal economy afloat. Unlike New Englanders, Virginians were not as angered by the first import taxes Britain levied—they had always paid taxes when exporting tobacco and importing fine goods from England. But by the 1760s, at the end of the Seven Years' War, Virginia's leaders began to see that their economy and culture rested on a crumbling foundation.

George III ascended to the British throne in 1760, and he immediately sought ways to improve the financial state of his empire. He and his ministers pushed for tax reform that would relieve the disastrous financial burden on his subjects at home. In late 1763, the young king attempted to avoid further warfare on the frontier by establishing the Proclamation Line, limiting how far west American colonists could settle. Virginia's elite saw an end to their lucrative speculations in western lands as a serious threat to their financial stability.

Thomas Jefferson's father, Peter Jefferson (1708–1757), collaborated with Colonel Joshua Fry on this 1751 map of Virginia, the first accurate depiction of the Appalachian Mountains. The Jefferson family's wealth and status depended on continuing to expand their colony to the west, a practice that came into conflict with British imperial policy in 1763, which continued a chain of events that ultimately led to the colonies' decision to break with England.

Jefferson proposed to me to make the draft, I said, "I will not do it. You shall do it." "Oh no!" "Why will you not?" "You ought to do it." "I will not." "Why?" "Reasons enough." "What can be your reasons?" "Reason first: you are a Virginian and a Virginian ought to appear at the head of this business. Reason second: I am obnoxious, suspected and unpopular. You are very much otherwise. Reason third: You can write ten times better than I can."

—John Adams to Timothy Pickering, 1822

These economic realities and a keen interest in political theory and history led Thomas Jefferson to be an early advocate for colonists' liberties. In 1765, George III's government passed the Stamp Act, a law that taxed colonial newspapers, public documents, and even playing cards. Colonists from northern New England to the Caribbean rioted in protest of the act, and as a law student in Williamsburg Jefferson stood in the doorway of the Virginia House of Burgesses to hear Patrick Henry deliver his famous speech that compared King George to the tyrants of history. In the decade that followed, Virginians and their fellow colonists became convinced that Parliament was determined to pursue policies that would destroy the plantation culture they had created in the New World. Taxes rose, incomes fell, and the London-based government ignored the colonists' opposition.

A sense of paranoia spread up and down the coast of British North America, and royal officials seemed determined to make matters worse. At first, Virginia's gentry saw little logic in opposing the British government. That began to change by April 1775, when John Murray, Lord Dunmore, Virginia's last colonial governor, had British marines seize barrels of gunpowder stored in Williamsburg's powder magazine and move them to a British ship anchored nearby. Why would their governor take away their means of defense, if he did not mean to attack, they asked? The question might have seemed ridiculous to some, but a few days later, word reached Williamsburg that a similar attempt had been repelled by force in Massachusetts Bay,

where colonists had taken up arms and fought the British Regulars at Lexington and Concord.

Outrage over the removal of the gunpowder grew, and on June 8 the Burgesses learned that the governor had fled the capital with his family and taken up residence on a nearby warship. Anger turned to hysteria when Dunmore issued a proclamation on November 15, 1775, that declared that any enslaved men who agreed to fight as a part of the king's forces would be freed. Wealthy Virginians saw these actions as attacking the very foundation of the slavery-dependent society they had established in America. It was these beliefs that brought Virginians to the Continental Congress in Philadelphia, and Jefferson to the house at the corner of Seventh and High streets.

Jefferson wrote the Declaration of Independence on a small writing desk in Jacob Graff's second floor parlor during the busy weeks leading up to July 1776. Surrounding his work space are crates of the books, scientific equipment, and household materials that he bought to take back to Monticello. The original desk is now in the Smithsonian.

The work Jefferson did at the Graff house was to be the most important of his life. In his parlor, Jefferson explained the logic of American inde-

How is it that we hear the loudest yelps for liberty among the drivers of negroes?

—Dr. Samuel Johnson, British essayist and Tory, August 1775

pendence. Over the course of three weeks in June 1776, he detailed the rights that he believed human beings had at birth, calling on history and Enlightenment political theory to lay out "an expression of the American mind." That expression included some of the most important statements on human liberty that have ever been put on paper.

Jefferson also detailed the charges of the American colonists against the king, explaining the ways in which George III had usurped the lawful rights of his subjects in America. The Declaration cited dozens of instances in which the king had attacked these rights. The right to trade, to be secure in one's person, to assemble, and numerous other infringements on colonists' liberties combined to damn the king as a tyrant "unfit to be the ruler of a free people."

It was one issue—slavery—that led to the most heated arguments in the Continental Congress in July 1776. As Jefferson assessed the actions of King George, he laid the most striking inequities of the British Empire squarely at the feet of the monarch: "He has waged cruel War against human Nature itself, violating its most sacred Rights of Life and Liberty in the Persons of a distant People who never offended him, captivating and carrying them into Slavery in another Hemisphere, or to incur miserable Death, in their Transportation thither. This piratical Warfare, the opprobrium of infidel Powers, is the Warfare of the Christian King of Great Britain."

Opposite: Thomas Jefferson wrote out this copy of the Declaration for his colleague Richard Henry Lee, who had returned to Virginia, and added changes in the left margin as Congress amended the document. The Lee family later gave this copy to the American Philosophical Society, where it has remained since the 1820s.

The statement is odd. George III did not own a single slave; Thomas Jefferson owned more than 200. Slavery had always been a part of Jefferson's life. One of his earliest memories was

a Declaration by the Representatives of the UNITED STATES OF
AMERICA in General Congress assembled.

When in the course of human events it becomes necessary for one people to dissolve the political bands which have connected them with another, and to assume among the powers of the earth the separate and equal station to which the laws of nature and of nature's god entitle them, a decent respect to the opinions of mankind requires that they should declare the causes which impel them to the separation.

We hold these truths to be self-evident, that all men are created equal; that *certain in-* *alienable rights* they are endowed by their Creator with inherent and inalienable rights; that among these are life, liberty, and the pursuit of happiness; that to secure these rights, governments are instituted among men, deriving their just powers from the consent of the governed; that whenever any form of government becomes destructive of these ends, it is the right of the people to alter or to abolish it, and to institute new government, laying it's foundation on such principles and organising it's powers in such form as to them shall seem most likely to effect their safety and happiness. prudence indeed will dictate that governments long established should not be changed for light & transient causes; and accordingly all experience hath shewn that mankind are more disposed to suffer, while evils are sufferable, than to right themselves by abolishing the forms to which *& alter* they are accustomed. but when a long train of abuses and usurpations, begun at a distinguished period & pursuing invariably the same object, evinces a design to reduce them under *left out* absolute despotism, it is their right, it is their duty, to throw off such government, & to provide new guards for their future security. such has been the patient sufferance of these colonies; & such is now the necessity which constrains them to expunge their former systems *alter* of government. the history of the present king of Great Britain is a history of unremitting *repeated* injuries and usurpations, among which appears no solitary fact to contradict the *left out* uniform tenor of the rest, but all have in direct object the establishment of an absolute *having* tyranny over these states. to prove this let facts be submitted to a candid world, for *left out* the truth of which we pledge a faith yet unsullied by falsehood.

He has refused his assent to laws the most wholesome and necessary for the public good.
he has forbidden his governors to pass laws of immediate & pressing importance, unless suspended in their operation till his assent should be obtained; and when so suspended, he has neglected utterly to attend to them. *utterly ne-* *glected* he has refused to pass other laws for the accommodation of large districts of people, unless those people would relinquish the right of representation in the legislature; a right inestimable to them, & formidable to tyrants only.

All eyes are opened, or opening, to the rights of man. the general spread of the light of science has already laid open to every view. the palpable truth, that the mass of mankind has not been born with saddles on their backs, nor a favored few booted and spurred, ready to ride them legitimately, by the grace of god. These are grounds of hope for others. for ourselves, let the annual return of this day forever refresh our recollections of these rights, and an undiminished devotion to them.

—Thomas Jefferson's last letter, remembering the Declaration of Independence fifty years later, June 24, 1826

riding on horseback, seated on the lap of a slave, as his family traveled across Virginia. Jefferson inherited about fifty slaves from the estate of his father, who died in 1757, and 135 more came as part of his wife Martha's dowry and inheritance. Slavery made every aspect of Jefferson's life possible: the laborers who worked his extensive farms and had begun construction on Monticello created the wealth that supported his luxurious lifestyle and allowed him the leisure hours to read the Enlightenment thinkers who influenced the Declaration. Had Jefferson been required to work his own lands to feed himself and his family, he might not have traveled to Philadelphia to participate in the Congress. The labor of enslaved people made the lives of Thomas Jefferson and many other signers of the Declaration of Independence easier, wealthier, and more cultured.

Slavery was not just a southern phenomenon. There were an estimated 1,100 slaves in Philadelphia by the 1760s, with a total of 4,000 in the colony of Pennsylvania, and slavery existed in each of the northern colonies. One account noted that, while the Congress met during the summer of 1776, enslaved persons sat along the walls of the hallway in Independence Hall, awaiting orders to run errands for their masters.

When the Congress debated Jefferson's anti-slavery clause, it became evident that the delegates from the Deep South were unwilling to include slavery among their charges against the king. Congress cut the passage before approving the final draft of the Declaration of Independence on July 4, 1776.

Thomas Jefferson lived at the Graff house from May 23 to September 3, 1776, when he went back to Virginia. He never returned to the house. But Jefferson's residence there for a few months made this Philadelphia corner famous. Today, we can easily imagine Jefferson stepping out of the house's front door onto Seventh Street, turning right, and walking two blocks to the Pennsylvania State House, where the Continental Congress was meeting.

Independence Hall, as seen from Chestnut Street, constructed by the colony of
Pennsylvania as its State House beginning in 1732.

TEN

Independence Square

T HE SCENE AT THE STATE HOUSE on the morning of Monday, July 8, 1776, was remarkable. Thousands had gathered, knowing that a major announcement was coming from the Continental Congress whose members had been meeting there for over a year. The previous January, these same Philadelphians had seen the first copies of *Common Sense* come off the presses at Robert Bell's printing house on Third Street. The small pamphlet made a huge impression, spreading from colony to colony, arguing, as its author Thomas Paine stated, that the king of England had no legitimate hold on the people of America.

Congress had reconvened the following May, just weeks after news had arrived that Massachusetts' Minute Men had gone to battle on

"Congress Voting Independence," by Robert Edge Pine and/or Edward Savage. Although historians have debated which of the two artists completed which part of this image, architectural research has found that the engraving accurately captures the look of the Pennsylvania Assembly Room at the time Congress declared independence. Benjamin Franklin is seated in a Windsor chair in the foreground, with John Adams at his left. Behind them, Thomas Jefferson lays the declaration on John Hancock's desk.

April 19 at Lexington and Concord with the British troops who had occupied their colony for seven years. In the months since, delegates had discussed and debated, trying to unify thirteen of His Majesty's colonies into a common course of action to protest the king's taxes as well as to respond to some Britons' belief that the colonists had somehow lost their natural British rights because they lived in colonies rather than in the mother country. American colonists disagreed with that idea, and they had protested, boycotted, and now fought in response. What would happen next?

The answer came at noon on that Monday. The crowd gathered in the square directly south of the State House, an unlandscaped space surrounded by a seven-foot-high brick wall with a large gate facing Walnut Street. The square was used as a storage lot for the colony's canon and a field for the militia to practice. As patriot Christopher Marshall recorded it in his diary, the rebel leaders who formed Philadelphia's Committee of Inspection and Committee of Safety gathered at the meeting room of the American Philosophical Society near Christ Church and then "went in a body to the State House Yard." With the colony's militia standing at formation, Marshall and his colleagues watched as Sheriff William Dewees and Colonel John Nixon of the Pennsylvania militia walked out of the south door of the State House. They were greeted by Mayor Samuel Powel and members of Philadelphia's common council, and then walked to a stage on the square, near the current site of Philosophical Hall. Dewees walked to the platform's railing and announced to the large crowd below: "Under the authority of the Continental Congress and by order of the Committee of Safety, I proclaim a declaration of independence." Nixon then stepped forward and began reading from the broadside that John Dunlap had just printed at his shop at High and Second streets:

The first printing of the Declaration of Independence, by John Dunlap. This copy descended in the family of Colonel John Nixon, and is believed to be the one Nixon read on the State House Square on July 8, 1776, the first public reading of the document.

> When in the course of human events it becomes necessary for one people to dissolve the political bonds which have connected them with another, and to assume among the powers of the earth the separate and equal station to which the laws of nature and of nature's God entitle them, a decent respect to the opinions of mankind requires that they should declare the causes which impel them to the separation.

Yesterday, at twelve o'clock, independency was declared at the State-House in this city, in the presence of many thousand spectators, who testified their approbation of it by repeated acclamations of joy.

—*Pennsylvania Evening Post,* July 9, 1776

As Nixon read the conclusion, "And for the support of this declaration, with a firm reliance on the protection of divine providence, we mutually pledge to each other our lives, our fortunes, and our sacred honor," Marshall recorded, "The company declared their approbation by three repeated huzzas."

The cheers echoed off the walls of the yard as citizens entered the State House, crossed the brick-floored entrance hall to the room that filled the building's western half, and approached the carved wooden symbol that proclaimed that this was a court of justice under the auspices of King George III. What they did next was not a spontaneous reaction. Earlier that morning, Elbridge Gerry of Massachusetts wrote to a colleague that "A formal Declaration is to be made of Independence at ye State House this Day & the burning of the Kings Arms is to succeed it." Burn they did, but not before jubilant revolutionaries dragged the carved wooden lion and unicorn through the streets of Philadelphia, ending their long parade at Center Square, where City Hall now stands. The symbol of royal authority went up in flames that night, an evening Marshall described: "Fine starlight, pleasant evening. There were bonfires, ringing bells, with other great demonstrations of joy upon the unanimity and agreement of the declaration."

The monumental events of July 1776 were a far cry from the inauspicious beginnings of Pennsylvania's State House. The colony was already fifty years old when its leaders began to plan for a permanent home for its legislature in 1732,

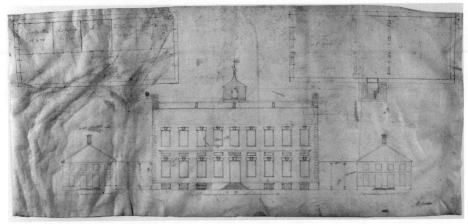

amid outrage that sailors and laborers were disrupting the meetings that took place on the second floor of the Court House, at High Street and Second. To placate cries that the Assembly should move the capital to a more rural area away from boisterous crowds, Pennsylvania politicians chose a plot of land on the edge of town, so far from the business of the city that bureaucrats complained bitterly at having to work there. The assemblymen took sixteen years to get their new home completed. In 1750, the Assembly voted to expand the project by adding a tower to the building's south side, complete with a bell chamber at the building's top.

The State House displayed the wealth, artistic sophistication, and ideals of eighteenth-century Pennsylvania's leadership. On the first floor the entrance passage and the stair tower to the south featured beautifully paneled walls and elaborate carvings. The Assembly room on the east side of the entrance hall showed both the Georgian style but also the colony's Quaker heritage: the room was paneled, but not elegantly carved, painted, or furnished.

Andrew Hamilton's drawing of the proposed State House, 1732. In the upper right, the second floor's plan called for the creation of the largest room in the colony for public meetings and receptions, as well as offices and committee rooms. In the upper left, the first floor showed the plan for the assembly room on the left, with the courtroom at right and a staircase filling the southern end of the building's central hallway. The floor plan was altered in 1750, with the addition of the tower and new staircase.

The Pennsylvania colony's legislative and judicial branches were both located on the State House's first floor, with the assembly room (top) on the east end of the building, and the supreme court—whose open entrances reflected William Penn's demand for public trials—on the west.

A Handsome State House, a Well finished Steeple, A Healthful Country but, a Perverse People.

—Provincial Secretary Richard Hockley to Proprietor Thomas Penn, November 6, 1753

Opposite: While the still Quaker-dominated assembly room remained relatively plain in its decorations, the entrance hall and stair tower featured intricate carvings by some of Philadelphia's most skilled craftsmen.

In contrast, the colony's courtroom across the hall was far more elaborate in highlighting the artistic skills of the town's workmen—perhaps indicating the tastes of the increasingly prosperous Philadelphia lawyer. The room reveals a quirk particular to Georgian architecture: the era was obsessed with balance and control, and to establish it in their design, the architects included a blind, or false, door, to keep the west wall's panels symmetrical. Similar blinds can be found in other nearby Georgian buildings, like the Powel House in Society Hill and Mount Pleasant in Fairmount Park.

The State House's second floor illustrated the sophistication that Philadelphia's artisans had achieved by the mid-eighteenth century. Elite gentlemen could aspire to a seat on the proprietary governor's council and a chair in the elegant chamber above, which they reached by climbing the splendid stairway in the tower's base. The elaborate carving that surrounded ascending council members and visitors, the rich Prussian blue paneling, and the light streaming through the elaborate Palladian window all embodied their power and the new ideas of the Enlightenment. Next to the council's chamber, those same elite gentlemen might hope to dance with their wives in the long gallery, one of the largest rooms in the colonies.

The State House was completed just as a rift was widening between the governors of the colony and the leaders of the popularly elected Assembly, a situation that would eventually help provoke Pennsylvania's movement to independence. A member of the Penn family always held the position as governor and chief proprietor, and the family often appointed a lieutenant governor to manage the colony in Philadelphia. As warfare broke out on the Pennsylvania frontier—prompted in part by the 1737 "Walking Purchase" land grab that made the Penn family and their supporters in the Proprietary Party richer—strife increased in the colony and in the State House. Many Quakers, once the leaders of the Assembly, left office because they could not participate in conducting war due to their pacifist beliefs. A new group of political leaders, including Benjamin Franklin, rose to power in

The governor's council room on the second floor of Independence Hall reflected the elevated status of the men whom the Penn family chose to advise them. A copy of a portrait of founder William Penn, painted prior to Penn's conversion to Quakerism and showing him in armor, hangs above the fireplace.

the 1750s and 1760s. By the 1770s, the State House was no stranger to controversy.

From 1775 to 1776, the first two years that it met in Independence Hall, the Continental Congress orchestrated a tremendous change in American politics and society. Since 1763, King George and his ministers had looked for ways to increase tax revenues from the American colonies to relieve the empire's staggering debts. Britain's leaders had understood that the colonists didn't want to pay these new taxes. Protests, riots, printed rebukes, and a host of other means all shouted that fact across the three thousand miles of ocean that separated the two lands. But what those leaders didn't understand was that this anti-tax sentiment was backed up by some very British ideals: no one should be taxed or ruled by anyone who didn't represent them, and the American colonists were not represented in the British Parliament. In their history books, political pamphlets, newspapers, sermons, letters, and discussions, that fact was stated again and again. Thousands of Americans now saw representation as an inalienable right,

☞ Architecture: Georgian Architecture

A modern architectural drawing of the north elevation of Independence Hall commissioned by the Historic Architecture and Building Survey and completed in 1987.

Georgian architecture embodied changing ideas about human ability that we call the Enlightenment. This style expressed people's desire to control the environment and to organize life along neat, symmetrical lines.

Like many American ideas and fashions of the era, Georgian architecture was an import from England. In 1666, London experienced a devastating fire that destroyed much of the city. In place of the medieval timber and stucco buildings which had burned, architects influenced by Sir Christopher Wren and others set about a rebuilding campaign that closely followed classical building styles. The style and design of these new buildings, reflecting new science and new philosophy, was transferred across the Atlantic by merchants who adopted the architectural style that represented the power and status of old world leaders. The four kings, members of the House of Hanover, who ruled Britain for most of the eighteenth century, gave their name to the widely popular architecture style.

The Pennsylvania State House is an excellent example of this transfer of knowledge and patterns. Designed, historians believe, by attorney and politician Andrew Hamilton—who, like many early American architects, was an amateur—the Chestnut Street facade closely resembled that of the house of the Earl of Buckingham in London. Edmond Wooley, a master builder and member of the Carpenters' Company, drew the plans for the building and supervised the actual construction. The building is a two-story, nine-bay symmetrical layout, with the door at the center. The brick facade is framed by cornerstones, ☞

Cliveden, the country estate built by Chief Justice Benjamin Chew in 1767, one of Philadelphia's preeminent Georgian residences. Above, a dormer with console bracket, pedimented frontispiece above the door, keystones above the windows, and cornerstone quoins.

➣ or quoins, with soapstone panels between the first- and second-story windows, and marble keystones on top of each window. The square tower, reproducing styles common in the English capital and other towns, continued the Georgian pattern.

The ways Philadelphians learned of new building styles changed by the early eighteenth century. For centuries, architectural techniques and styles had passed from craftsmen to apprentices, generation after generation. Georgian architecture spread through the printed word and the expert. As early as November 1732, Benjamin Franklin and members of the newly formed Library Company of Philadelphia ordered a copy of Andrea Palladio's *Architecture*, one of the preeminent texts of the neoclassical Georgian movement, for their shelves. Texts and prints taught builders about the style. Decades later, Thomas Jefferson would call Palladio "my bible." He and other members of the Continental Congress would see a common language of architecture that was immediately familiar when they arrived at the Pennsylvania State House.

SIGNIFICANT GEORGIAN STRUCTURES IN PHILADELPHIA

Carpenters' Hall, Christ Church, St. Peter's Church, Germantown White House, Todd House, Cliveden (6401 Germantown Avenue), Mount Pleasant (Fairmount Park), Powel House (244 S. Third Street), Shippen-Wistar House (238 S. Fourth Street). ◁

A View of the State-House in Philadelphia.

something they were born with. Sadly, few in Parliament or in the king's palace understood the American commitment to this right until war was declared.

On July 2, 1776, in Pennsylvania's Assembly Room, Congress approved the Virginia Resolution, which Richard Henry Lee had proposed weeks earlier, a simple statement but one that held monumental consequences: "These united colonies are, and of right ought to be, free and independent states."

John Adams wrote home to his "dear partner" Abigail Smith Adams: "The Second Day of July 1776, will be the most memorable Epocha, in the History of America.—I am apt to believe that it will be celebrated, by succeeding Generations, as the great anniversary Festival. It ought to be commemorated, as the Day of Deliverance by solemn Acts of Devotion to God Almighty. It ought to be solemnized with Pomp and Parade, with Shews, Games, Sports, Guns, Bells, Bonfires and Illuminations from one End of this

London's *Gentlemen's Magazine* published this "View of the State House in Philadelphia" in its September 1752 issue, celebrating the high-style English Georgian building in Pennsylvania's capital more than two decades before it played a central role in bringing down Britain's American empire.

In the State House's second floor long gallery, colonial Pennsylvania's elite held celebratory banquets, danced, and practiced politics. Benjamin West's portrait of Governor James Hamilton hangs at left. The room was used as a hospital during the revolution.

Continent to the other from this Time forward forever more."

Adams compared the thirteen colonies' simultaneous decision to declare independence as being like "Thirteen clocks [that] were made to strike together: a perfection of mechanism which no artist had ever before effected." Adams was accurate in that assessment. Despite ideas to the contrary, the decision to declare independence was not unanimous: George III had colonies in Canada and the Caribbean that did not attend the Congress and did not leave the empire in 1776. That thirteen colonies did speak in one voice was amazing, indeed.

The words with which the Congress spoke were Thomas Jefferson's, of course. Just thirty-three when he penned the declaration, Jefferson crafted eloquent phrases to explain not just why each region of the colonies believed that their rights had been attacked, but also a brilliant expression of Enlightenment ideals about what rights humans possessed. After much editing and days of debate, the Second Continental Congress approved Jefferson's Declaration of Independence on July 4, 1776. Jefferson himself

John Adams

History owes a great deal to each of the delegates who signed the Declaration of Independence in 1776, but perhaps historians owe the most to John Adams. Scholarly, hot-headed, cantankerous, John Adams understood the significance of what was happening during his days as a Congressman from Massachusetts, and his diary and letters home to his wife, Abigail, are some of our best sources for understanding the events that surrounded American Independence.

John Adams was born in Braintree, Massachusetts, in 1735, a fifth-generation New Englander whose ancestors had settled in the first decade of the Puritan colony. Adams graduated from Harvard College in 1755, taught in Worcester, Massachusetts, for a brief time, and then began studying law.

In 1764, Adams married Abigail Smith, the daughter of a prosperous parson. The marriage was a love match, but also one that brought two keen intellects together. While developing his new law practice, John Adams often had to ride the court circuit alone, and the couple became frequent and skilled correspondents—a practice that would benefit later historians.

John Adams gained fame when he defended the British soldiers who, on March 5, 1770, had fired into an angry crowd in what we have come to call the Boston Massacre. Adams saved the men from the gallows based on points of law, but his intense feelings that the king's policies were wrong continued to grow. His skill as an orator and writer led to a prominent position within the resistance movement, and in 1774 he was elected one of the delegates to the First Continental Congress, meeting in Philadelphia to seek common ground to protest the king's policies, particularly the closing of the Port of Boston following the Boston Tea Party in 1773.

Adams's descriptions of Philadelphia in 1774 and the years to follow give us an outstanding glimpse into the ideas and actions of the city, and his diary and letters reveal the often contentious movement toward American independence. Adams could ruffle feathers. He acknowledged that his fellow delegates often found him obnoxious and disliked him. But his persistence in the cause paid off. Adams signed the Declaration, helped negotiate the ☞

John Adams, in a 1782 German publication identifying him as "minister plenipotentiary," while Adams was carrying the new nation's diplomatic message to the old world. This engraving is one of the first public portraits of Adams.

About 3 o Clock last Friday morning the members of Congress were warned by an express from one of Genl. Washington aids, Coll. [Alexander] Hamilton, to leave this city immediately as the enemy could throw a body of troops into it. . . . Upon so strong an alarm . . . your Colleagues with their brethren of Congress took to the Saddle without loss of time governed by different fancies of the road.

—James Lovell to Robert Treat Paine, September 24, 1777

☞ peace treaty that ended the Revolutionary War in 1783, and served as the country's first vice president and second president. He retired to Massachusetts in 1801 after he lost his bid for reelection, and he continued to farm and practice law. One of the last surviving signers, he was asked for a public statement to be read on the golden anniversary of American Independence, and he said simply and succinctly "Independence forever." When he died on July 4, 1826—the fiftieth anniversary of the Declaration of Independence—his last words were "Jefferson still lives." His colleague, friend, and onetime adversary Thomas Jefferson had died just a few hours earlier, at his home in Virginia. ☜

oversaw the document's preparation at Dunlap's printing house in the days that followed. On July 8, congressmen and thousands of Philadelphians listened together as John Nixon read from one of those copies to the assembled crowd, and public readings followed in each of the new states in the days that followed.

After the public reading of the Declaration, Congress set about forming and running a new country that was at war with the most powerful empire on earth. One of the first needs of the new government was, as the Declaration stated, to lay the causes of the country before that "candid world." To that end, Congress dispatched Benjamin Franklin to Paris, to attempt to gain diplomatic recognition for the new nation from the king of France and, it hoped, financial and military support. Franklin's scientific discoveries and writings made him undeniably the most famous living American, and he used that fame to further his country's cause.

The Pennsylvania State House served as the nation's first Capitol in the year following inde-

The second floor committee room in Independence Hall, where American prisoners of war were held during the British occupation of 1777–1778.

pendence, but as the war reached Pennsylvania, the building would suffer many indignities. By September 1777, the British army seemed almost unstoppable, and after victories at Brandywine and Germantown, General William Howe set his sights on the capital. Congress fled to Lancaster, Pennsylvania, and Howe and his men settled into Philadelphia for a winter's encampment while George Washington and the American army suffered—and trained—at Valley Forge. British officers delighted in the entertainments Philadelphia Tories offered them; the British army likewise seemed to enjoy wreaking havoc on the place where Independence was declared. The State House became a hospital and prison for the Americans wounded in battle. Years later, restoration crews would

We remain'd in this manner 'till the 7th Octor when the Commisy of Prisoners inform'd Us he had order to take us to the State House where we were to be kept in close confinement, . . . Many of us were here for six days without having any provision serv'd to us—and for many Weeks after, Our allowance did not exceed from 4 to 6 ounces of salt Pork & abt half a pound very ordinary Biscuit p. day—and had it not been for the supply we had from the Citizens We must have all inevitably Perished. . .

▷ The Declaration of Independence

Despite familiar myths, the members of the Second Continental Congress did not solemnly line up in Independence Hall on July 4, 1776, to sign the Declaration of Independence. Only the congress' president, John Hancock of Massachusetts, and secretary, Charles Thomson—a man so committed to the cause that John Adams called him "the Samuel Adams of Philadelphia"—signed it that day, as was customary for acts Congress passed. Congress immediately made plans to have the document published. A draft appeared in one Philadelphia newspaper on July 6, while Dunlap was setting the type for the published broadside. Colonel Nixon and his descendants kept his copy of the Declaration, and today it resides in the Great Essentials display in Independence Hall's west wing.

On July 19, after the thirteenth colony, New York, formally adopted the Declaration, Congress voted to have it "fairly engrossed on parchment, with the title and stile of 'The unanimous declaration of the thirteen United States of America' and that the same, when engrossed, be signed by every member of Congress." Congressmen began to add their signatures to this hand-lettered copy on August 2, 1776.

find bloodstained beams below the long gallery on the second floor, where injured Americans had been placed on straw pallets in 1777.

When Congress returned from exile after the British evacuation in 1778, members found the city, and especially its meeting place, in a sorry state. Congressional President Henry Laurens wrote "from various impediments I could not collect a sufficient number of States to form a Congress earlier than . . . [July] 7th . . . one was the offensiveness of the air in and around the State House, which the Enemy had made an Hospital and left it in a condition disgraceful to

Visitors to that document, now on display in the National Archives in Washington, D.C., often ask the question: "But if Congress sent this copy to England, how did we get it back?" The answer is that it never left. Congress didn't plan to send the original, or indeed any copy, directly to the king. The Declaration was a public, formal statement, not a personal letter. It was meant to show "a candid world" why independence was justified and essential, but was not a personal gripe at the monarch. The parchment copy stayed with the Continental Congress as it moved from capital to capital in the first years of the American republic, and then Secretary Thomson deposited it in the newly created State Department once the Constitution was ratified.

So King George III never got the "original" document, because Congress never sent it. But eventually the king did get the message. ✄

Charles Thomson (1729-1824), by Charles Willson Peale, 1784.

... We were often refused the liberty of going from one Room to the other, the Windows also, nail'd down, though the smoke occasion'd by a stove below stairs in the guard Room & badness of the Chimnies had been for many Days together, almost intolerable[.] [T]here were forty of Us in the two upper chambers in the State House which serv'd for every purpose of Kitchens & Bed Chambers.

　—Colonel Persifor Frazer, describing his imprisonment in the Pennsylvania State House during the British occupation

the Character of civility. Particularly they had opened a large pit near the House, a receptacle for filth, into which they had also cast dead horses and the bodies of men who by the mercy of death had escaped from their further cruelties."

After having the building cleaned, whitewashed, and repaired, the Continental Congress resumed its meetings in the Pennsylvania State House. Soon, it would host some of the grandest occasions in the life of the new nation. On August 6, 1778, French Minister Gérard presented his credentials as ambassador to Congress

Congress meets in a large room on the ground floor. The chamber is large and without any other ornament than a bad engraving of Montgomery, one of Washington and a copy of the Declaration of Independence. It is furnished with thirteen tables each covered with green cloth. One of the principal representatives of each of the thirteen states sits during the session at one of these tables. The president of Congress had his place in the middle of the hall, upon a sort of throne. The clerk is seated just below him.

—Prince Charles Louis Victor de Broglie, 1782

in the Assembly Room. Three years later, in 1781, Congress received twenty-four stands of colors captured from the British at Yorktown, where Washington had gained the decisive battle ending the fighting of the American Revolution.

One of the central challenges to the newborn United States was finding a system of government that all thirteen states could agree to. Each state was jealous of its autonomy and fearful that a powerful national government might be as bad as the king and his henchmen from whom they had just freed themselves. The result was the Articles of Confederation. Franklin proposed the first plan for the articles in 1775, but the idea was tabled. It was not until 1781, and many revisions later, that states finally adopted the Articles. The Articles solved many problems, including giving citizens of one state full citizenship in all, deciding what to do with western land claims, and managing the war. But weaknesses abounded, too.

These weaknesses of the government were made dramatically clear by events that took place at the Pennsylvania State House. While British troops had not been successful in permanently driving the Continental Congress from Philadelphia, the American army was able to do just that. The Articles of Confederation created a decidedly weak form of government and gave Congress no power to levy taxes, and financial crises plagued the United States from the beginning. By the summer of 1783, the Continental Army had been disbanded, but Congress had no way to provide back pay to soldiers. A group of angry veterans surrounded the State House on June 21 and demanded their money. No member of Congress was harmed, but most were frightened by the urban mobs that had once been an ally in their cause but now seemed to pose a continual threat to their safety. The Confederation Congress adjourned and reconvened in Princeton, New Jersey. It never returned to Philadelphia.

Over the course of the American Revolution, Pennsylvania's State House—eventually known as Independence Hall, so named by the Marquis de Lafayette a half century after the Continental Congress first met—was transformed from a simple government building to the birthplace of a new nation, a prison, and an armed encampment. But these changes were representative of what the hall's neighbors would go through in this same era. In the neighborhoods surrounding the State House Yard, Philadelphians of differing backgrounds, and beliefs, experienced the tumult that accompanied the creation of the United States.

On Sunday the 9th instant, at night, a fit time for the sons of Lucifer to perpetuate the deeds of darkness, one or more volunteers in the service of hell, broke into the State House in this city, and totally defaced the picture of his excellency general Washington and a curious engraving of the monument to the patriotic general Montgomery, done in France in the most elegant manner.

—*Freeman's Journal*,
Wednesday,
September 12, 1781

The tomb of the unknown Revolutionary War soldier in Washington Square features a copy of the Jean-Antoine Houdon statue of George Washington in the Virginia State Capitol in Richmond and an eternal flame marking the final resting place of an unidentified member of Washington's army. The phrase "Freedom is a Light for Which Many Men Have Died in Darkness," often misattributed to Washington, was actually written by a copywriter at a Philadelphia advertising firm in the 1950s.

ELEVEN

Washington Square

O N APRIL 13, 1777, John Adams wrote to his wife, Abigail, recounting how the cost of independence from Britain was close at hand: "I have spent an Hour, this Morning, in the Congregation of the dead. I took a Walk into the Potters Field, a burying ground between the new stone prison and the hospital, and I never in my whole Life was affected with so much Melancholly. The Graves of the soldiers who have been buryed, in this Ground, from the Hospital and bettering House, during the Course of the last Summer, Fall, and Winter, dead of the small Pox, and Camp Diseases, are enough to make the Heart of stone to melt away."

Adams's walk that morning allows us to see the consequences of the Declaration of Indepen-

Southeast Square (later, Washington Square) was still an unlandscaped, fenced pasture on the edge of Philadelphia when this engraving was created around 1767. At left (*D*) stands Pennsylvania Hospital's east wing, with the Pennsylvania State House, or Independence Hall (*e*), right of center. Christ Church is at far right (*f*). Detail of "A View of the House of Employment, Alms-house, Pennsylvania Hospital, and part of the City of Philadelphia," by Nicholas Garrison, engraving by James Hulett.

dence. Whether he started at his rented rooms "in a pleasant Part of Town, in Walnutt Street, in the south side of it, between second and third Streets, at the House of Mr. Duncan" or from Independence Hall, perhaps crossing the State House Square, we cannot know. But certainly, Adams realized that as he took his walk that day he was leaving the "settled" part of Philadelphia, and traveling to its outskirts. The "stone prison" he described was the Walnut Street Jail, a Georgian-style edifice designed by master builder Robert Smith. That building, completed just a few years before, was at the very edge of town. The nearest landmark that Adams noted, Pennsylvania Hospital, was four blocks away, and considered "in the country." The "Potters Field" (or Strangers' Burying Ground, as Philadelphians knew it, now known as Washington Square) that Adams visited was literally and figuratively on Philadelphia's margins.

In the distance as he walked among the graves of the dead from Washington's army, John Adams could see Pennsylvania Hospital, the oldest public medical facility in the American colonies, founded by Dr. Thomas Bond and Benjamin Franklin. Bond was born in Calvert County, Maryland, in 1712. He studied medicine with Dr. Alexander Hamilton of Annapolis, and later continued his studies in Paris. By 1734, he was practicing medicine in Philadelphia in partnership with his half-brother, Dr. Samuel Chew, and advertising the sale of the most modern pharmaceuticals in their shop in High (Market) Street. By the 1760s, Bond and his brother, Phineas, had a thriving practice headquartered in his house on Second Street, where he both treated patients and provided medical training to a series of apprentices, the common educational method of the time.

Dr. Thomas Bond (1712–1784), founder of the Pennsylvania Hospital.

Bond developed a medical reputation that spread throughout the colonies. Caesar Rodney traveled from Delaware to seek Bond's surgical skill in the removal of a cancerous growth in 1768; Robert Treat Paine came from Boston in 1751 to have himself inoculated against the dreaded smallpox, still a very controversial procedure. By the end of his life Bond described himself as a "surgeon" rather than a "physician."

Bond's plan for Pennsylvania Hospital was unique in the era. He conceived an institution that would receive public support to care for poor sick people "whether Inhabitants of the Province or Strangers," Franklin recorded. The hospital was a charity, but one that did not depend upon church support or distinguish who would receive care there based on religious persuasion. Bond's plan grew from the realities of

William Penn's diverse colony. Since no single church dominated Pennsylvania, none could or would bear the burden of caring for all of the city's poor. Bond's unique proposal met with little initial success, however. It was when he turned to Franklin, his "particular Friend," that the plan took shape. Franklin wrote:

> Dr. Thomas Bond . . . conceived the Idea of establishing a Hospital in Philadelphia, for the Reception and Cure of poor sick Persons. . . . A very beneficent Design, which has been ascribed to me, but was originally his. He was zealous and active in endeavouring to procure subscriptions for it; but the Proposal being a Novelty in America, and at first not well understood, he met with small Success. At length he came to me, with the Compliment that he found there was no such thing as carrying a public Spirited Project through, without my being concern'd in it; for, says he, I am often ask'd by those to whom I propose Subscribing, Have you consulted Franklin upon this Business? And what does he think of it? And when I tell them that I have not . . . they do not subscribe.

Franklin was at the height of his powers as the organizing genius in Philadelphia at that time. In the previous five years, he had led the effort to meet the long-neglected educational needs of the colony by establishing the Academy and Charity School of Philadelphia, now the University of Pennsylvania, and he had seen to the security of the colony by establishing Philadelphia's first militia, known as the Associators. Franklin had retired in 1748 from

active control of his printing office, but used his skills as a persuasive writer in the *Pennsylvania Gazette* to arouse public support for the hospital endeavor. By subscribing his own money and persuading others to do so, Franklin added the organizational and financial stability that the hospital required, and Bond's dream became a reality. In 1755, Franklin provided the text for the cornerstone of the new hospital:

In the Year of Christ
1755
George the second Happily Reigning
(For he sought the Happiness of his People.)
Philadelphia Flourishing
(For its inhabitants were public spirited)
This Building,
By the Bounty of the Government,
And of many private Persons,
Was piously founded,
For the Relief of the Sick and Miserable.
May the God of Mercies
Bless the Undertaking!

Pennsylvania Hospital, built at the town's outskirts in the mid-eighteenth century, is America's oldest hospital. The east wing, at right, still bears the original cornerstone inscription noting that the building was begun in 1755, "George the second Happily Reigning." The center wing, with its skylit surgical amphitheater, was not completed until 1804. In the center of the hospital's garden stands a statue of William Penn, discovered by Penn's grandson John in an English antique shop and donated to the hospital in 1804.

Philadelphia became a center of medical treatment and knowledge in British North America. Colonists sent their sons to the city for training, first as apprentices to established physicians, then later as medical students at the College of Philadelphia. Medical treatment was, in fact, one of the public spectacles that entertained Philadelphians and their visitors throughout the century. Public lectures on medical topics were a popular entertainment. Once the Pennsylvania Hospital was opened in the 1750s, its wards provided an intriguing show for numerous visitors, including members of the Continental Congress and later the national government. While attending the First Continental Congress in 1774, John Adams recorded in his diary:

> Towards the Evening, Mr. Thomas Smith . . . and Dr. Shippen and his Brother and Mr. Reed, went with Us to the Hospital. We saw, in the lower Rooms under Ground, the Cells of the Lunaticks, a Number of them, some furious, some merry, some Melancholly. . . . We went into the Sick Rooms which are very long, large Walks with rows of Beds on each side, and the lame and sick upon them—a dreadfull Scene of human Wrechedness. The Weakness and Langour, the Distress and Misery, of these Objects is truely a Woefull Sight.

More than sixty years old when the revolution began, Dr. Bond took no active part in the politics of the day. But when his professional skills were needed, he answered the call. "When I see so many friends and valuable citizens exposing themselves to the horror of war, I think it is my duty to make them a tender of the best services in my power," he wrote to Philadelphia's Committee of Safety in late 1776. Bond treated both Patriots and Loyalists during the war, but saw his practice curtailed. He wrote to Franklin that his clinical lectures in Pennsylvania Hospital would require "hiring the Sick to go into it" when so many Philadelphians fled during the revolution. Bond continued his practice and philanthropic work after the war, and died March 26, 1784.

Like contemporary British hospitals of the era, Pennsylvania Hospital was located in a rural setting, where clean air could aid patients, and where their diseases might be less likely to spread. Between the hospital and the center of town was Southeast Square, one of five original town commons laid out by William Penn's surveyor Thomas Holme. (Philadelphia's five squares would be renamed in 1825 in honor of founding fathers, and Southeast Square would become Washington Square.) Penn had envisioned Philadelphia would be a country village, and provided five commons on which the owners of nearby houses could graze their farm animals. But Penn's plan never came to be, and the English settlers who flocked to Philadelphia clustered close to the Delaware River. By the 1770s, the city's population of 32,000 still crowded into the areas east of Fifth Street. Southeast Square was at the city's edge.

What Adams saw when he reached the corner of Sixth and Walnut streets was very different from what we encounter today. Benjamin Easburn, Pennsylvania's surveyor general, did not record any houses or buildings lining the square on the map he had published the year

Those of the English church, the New-lights, the Quakers, and the Germans of the Reformed religion have their burying places out of town and not near their church-es, though the first of these sometimes makes an exception. All the others bury their dead in their church-yards, and the Moravian Brethren bury where they can. The negroes are buried in a separate place out of town.

—Peter Kalm, 1750

before. In 1777, a creek still ran diagonally across the square, with a deep gully separating its two halves. Indeed, the square would not appear as a single piece of flat land until town leaders began to fill in the ravine with the soil laborers from Walnut Street Jail removed while digging the basement for Congress Hall on State House Square in 1787. The city of Philadelphia leased the square's acreage for pasturing animals. And while a fenced-in plot of ground stood at the square's center, marking the spot where the Carpenter family had buried a family member who had been denied burial in the local church-yards after she committed suicide, the other bodies relegated to the Strangers' Burying Ground—men and women who were, by reason of poverty, religion, or race, on the margins of society—lay in unmarked graves.

In the late 1760s, the square added another role to its resume: the military center of Philadelphia. In October 1767, Jacob Hiltz-heimer recorded in his diary that "General Gage reviewed the troops on the Commons." That rare event would become a regular occurrence in the next decade. Christopher Marshall recorded several instances in his diary of going there on militia business as the revolution broke out. Early in the war, soldiers would train on the square's fields, and as the years passed, some of those soldiers would return to be buried there.

Philadelphians had relatively little military experience before the Battles of Lexington and Concord. The Massachusetts men who fought there had a longstanding tradition of militia service which they used when they engaged the

☞ Colonial Burial Grounds

The ways a society treats its dead reveals a great deal about its culture and beliefs, and that holds true for eighteenth-century Philadelphians. Philadelphia's colonial burial grounds provide many clues about the personal and spiritual lives of the city's earliest residents.

Colonists followed Old World burial traditions, preferring to spend their afterlife with members of the same congregation with whom they had prayed in life. Some congregations owned cemeteries separate from their church buildings, and these burial grounds were within Phildelphia's municipal boundaries. By the 1770s there was little settlement as far west as the Friends Burial Ground at the southeast corner of Fourth and Arch streets (where Arch Street Friends Meeting now stands), land that William Penn had given to the Quaker Meeting for a burial ground in the 1680s, or the Anglican Burial Ground at the southeast corner of Fifth and Arch. Congregation Mikveh Israel followed Jewish law by locating its burial ground away from the village, near the present-day ☞

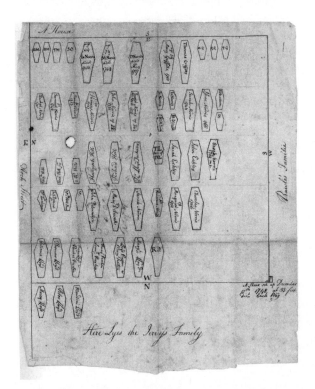

A diagram of plots for the Norris and other families in the Friends Burial Ground at Arch Street (indicated along the left side). A stone marker shown at the lower right is noted on the document to have been placed there on December 11, 1748.

NOTICE is hereby given that the City Square, commonly known by the Name of the POTTERS FIELD, containing about five Acres and three Quarters. Part of which is made use of as a Burying place for Strangers, is to be lett: Those who incline to take the same, are desired to send in their proposals to the Mayor of this City within fourteen Days for the Date hereof.

—*Pennsylvania Gazette*, April 13, 1758

☞ site of Spruce and Eighth streets. Other congregations chose to follow European custom and bury their dead in the yards surrounding their churches.

The act of burial was a symbol of acceptance. When a congregation accepted a body for internment, it was symbolically stating that it accepted that person as one of its own. From a very early date, Philadelphia also maintained a burying ground for those who did not "fit in." In 1706 Philadelphia's leaders sought "some convenient piece of ground for a comon and publick burying place for all strangers or others who might not so conveniently be laid in a particular enclosures appropriated by certain religious societies for that purpose." On January 20, 1706, Penn's commissioners of property signed a patent to use the southeast square on Holme's plan as their Strangers' Burying Ground, or potter's field. Mention of the ground appears frequently in the decades to follow, often in local newspapers, when the town government sought renters to use the still-active burial ground as a pasture land.

Although the oldest surviving tally of Philadelphia's deceased and their burial places records that there was "No account kept" for the Strangers' Burying Ground in 1736–1737, by the 1740s careful records were maintained that separated the number of white dead from those buried "in the Negroes Ground." ◁

king's forces on April 19, 1775. For the previous century, New Englanders had lived with an almost constant threat of war with the French in Canada as well as neighboring tribes of Native Americans. But in Pennsylvania, the politically dominant Quakers were pacifists who opposed military action, and they established a peaceful interaction with their neighbors that continued for decades. Only after the threat of French aggression during King George's War in 1747 had Philadelphians, led by Benjamin Franklin, created the semi-legal Associators militia to

Portrait & Uniform of An AMERICAN GENERAL.

A real representation of the Dress of An AMERICAN RIFLE-MAN.

defend the colony against an attack that never came. During the Seven Years' War a decade later, colonists established other defense associations.

But the outbreak of revolutionary hostilities would involve more men, for longer periods of time, and with longer lasting ramifications than these earlier experiences. When the Continental Congress appointed George Washington to take command of the Massachusetts troops in June 1775, the war became a national effort. Soon afterward, Congress called on Pennsylvania to supply a battalion to support the general. The colony had begun its participation in the American War for Independence.

The reality of war during the revolution was significantly different than in later American wars. The mass casualties and constant activity associated with wars in the age of advanced technologies didn't exist in the revolutionary era. Common soldiers might wait long periods to see

Edward Barnarn depicted the uniforms of a Continental Army general and an American rifleman, in his 1782 book *The New, Comprehensive and Complete History of England.* It was difficult for Europeans to believe that the American army did not have a common military dress, so they created their own often fanciful versions of how they imagined the uniforms appeared.

any military action, and when it did come, it was more likely to take the form of what would later be considered minor skirmishes rather than massive battles. But the war had profound implications for the men who fought and the communities it affected.

Reactions to the soldiers were mixed. Early in the war, one enthusiastic Philadelphia woman recorded in a letter: "Last Thursday we had a grand review of all three battalions, all dressed in their regimentals. . . . It is as compleat a companey as can be, all gentlemen and most of them young fellows and very handsome."

The matching uniforms and grand colors of the infantry and cavalry soldiers on display may have impressed some observers, but from the beginning the army had a serious deficiency in uniforms and especially boots. Colonies were expected to arm their soldiers, but they had few guns, ammunition boxes, and other military necessities, and that shortage continued. As late as 1779, General Washington wrote, "We still want for uniformity of Cloathing. We are not, like the Enemy, brilliant and uniformly attired. Even soldiers of the same Regiment are turned out in various dress; but there is no excuse, as heretofore, for slovenly unsoldierly neglect. Soldiers are to shave, have clean hands, and a general air of neatness."

Lack of hygiene was just the beginning of the continual problems that plagued Washington's army. Food was a constant concern. The army did not travel with cooks, and no mess tents dotted their camps. Soldiers received raw provisions and the men cooked them individually or in groups. The law mandated that a Pennsylvania soldier would receive one and a half pounds of flour or bread, a pound of fish, beef, or three-quarters of a pound of pork, and a quarter pint of pork or back, a half pint of beans or peas, and a quarter pint of spirits daily. But the frequent mention of soldiers being caught stealing, and the men's recollections of having to forage for food or buy their own, tell us that these ration rules were an ideal if not a reality. As the man who survived the Valley Forge encampment of 1777 noted, "we had nothing to eat for two or three days previous, except what the trees of the fields and forests afforded us."

Malnutrition was probably a contributing factor in the high disease rate that plagued the army throughout the revolution. In fact, the diseases which moved through the army—smallpox, dysentery, fevers—were often far more threatening than any English gun. John Adams stated, "Disease has destroyed ten men for us where the sword of the enemy has killed one!" Washington Square became the final resting place of many of these men.

> You can scarce walk a square without seeing the shocking sight of a Cart with five or six Coffins in it. . . . Large pits are dug in the negroes burying ground–and forty or fifty [soldier's] coffins are put in the same hole.
>
> —Sally Wistar, January 27, 1777

In its role as the Strangers' Burying Ground, Washington Square allows us to glimpse the public lives of Philadelphia's early African American community. From the beginning, Philadelphia had a community of enslaved African Americans. The first major importation of enslaved people arrived in 1684, when 150 slaves arrived in Philadelphia. Over the decades that followed, many more shiploads would arrive. By the first years of the eighteenth century, the still-small town had one of colonial America's largest African American populations per capita. Philadelphia would also be home to a

An aerial photograph of Washington Square during winter. Independence Hall can be seen at the top left and the Athenaeum, designed in 1845, is further to the right beside a multistory building.

significant population of free blacks. Historians estimate that by the outbreak of the American Revolution, Philadelphia's population of 25,000 included 1,400 slaves and 100 free African Americans.

During this era, Washington Square played a central role in the public life of this community. As the final resting place of their loved ones, the square also became one of the rare spaces where blacks could gather together. We know that the institution of slavery was not strong enough to wipe away the cultural memories of those who were held in bondage. By the burial customs, folk dances, and music that Washington Square witnessed, we see a vibrant continuation of diverse African heritages continued in Philadelphia well into the eighteenth century.

The experience of living in an urban setting influenced African Americans' lives. As the eighteenth century wore on, Philadelphia's gentry increasingly identified the ownership of slaves as an aspect of the gentility and refinement that accompanied their wealth, lavish houses, and tastes in entertaining. A glimpse into the family papers of John Cadwalader, whose Second Street house was one of Philadelphia's grandest at the time of the revolution, shows that he purchased clothing for his household slaves of a fineness that would have been unheard of in the plantation South. Similarly, Thomas Jefferson purchased shoes and stockings for his slave Bob Hemings in 1776, while they were living in the Graff house. Slaves in the city had different material lives than those on the plantation, and the enslaved men and women who were brought to Philadelphia may have taken the opportunity to rethink their position and possessions in light of their free and enslaved contemporaries' lives.

Slaveholders in the city allowed their servants to be better dressed, more for their own viewing pleasure than for the enslaved individuals' comfort. But this somewhat better material life should not obscure a very important reality of black lives in early Philadelphia: urban slavery was a very lonely existence for the people held in bondage. Historians have studied the history of colonial plantations in depth in recent decades, and they have discovered the importance of the cultures, white and black, that existed there. Life in these rural slave communities was difficult, but the cultural ties and practices that developed in them allowed enslaved African Americans to maintain and develop their own distinct culture ways.

No such shared community spaces existed for enslaved people in the growing city of Philadelphia, nor did they live together in slave quarters, set well apart from the masters. Instead, household inventories and other accounts show that they slept on pallets in basements, under eaves, or in rooms that also served as storage spaces in the houses—grand and plain—of colonial Philadelphia's master class. Slaves had no private spaces they could consider their own. And outside of the private realm, they had no public spaces where they could join together for common interests. If allowed to attend church, they went to the master's house of worship where they would be consigned to the loft or balcony, subject to the many watchful eyes of the whites seated below. Any large gathering of slaves, or slaves and free blacks, was considered dangerous by Philadelphia's white leaders and was quickly dispersed.

It is for this reason that a place like Washington Square became so important to Philadelphia's African Americans early on. Whites denied them burial in the town's churchyards, but when the Strangers' Burying Ground became the final resting place of their friends and relatives, the space took on an important symbolic meaning in the minds of colonial Philadelphia's black community, a symbolism that continued for many, many years to come. An elderly white Philadelphian in the mid-nineteenth century told historian John Fanning Watson of the days when the square would be a gathering place for Philadelphia's black community:

> It was the custom for the slave blacks, at the time of fairs and other great holidays, to go there to the number of one thousand, of both sexes, and hold their dances, dancing after the manner of their several nations in Africa, and speaking and singing in their

native dialects, thus cheerily amusing themselves over the sleeping dust below! An aged lady, Mrs. H.S., has told me she has often seen the Guinea negroes, in the days of her youth, going to the graves of their friends early in the morning, and there leaving them victuals and rum!

Watson and the people he interviewed recorded memories shaped by the racial ideas of their times, but the records they left do provide clues about the lives of Philadelphia's black community from a period when very few documents survive. Physical evidence from other parts of the city has also supported the memories Watson recorded. While archaeologists have never attempted to disinter and study the entire burial ground in Washington Square (such digs are only carried out when it is necessary to move graves), an archaeological examination at the site of the African Baptist Church on Race Street confirmed many of Watson's anecdotes. In the 1980s, archaeologists found that traditional African burial customs were used as late as the first decades of the 1800s. Even generations of enslavement could not destroy the deep-rooted cultural and religious beliefs of African Americans.

Washington Square's role as the symbolic center of Philadelphia's African American community continued in the decades that followed. By the end of the eighteenth century, the land just south of the square held "a set of negro huts and sheds," Watson wrote. These structures were the first places where free blacks exerted their rights to property ownership and private homes to form a neighborhood.

West African cultural patterns, including burial practices, continued for generations after the first enslaved Africans were brought to British North America. This skeleton, excavated when a construction project discovered the long-forgotten First African Baptist Church burial ground on Eighth Street in 1983, demonstrated the mixture of customs and material culture spanning the Atlantic World in the early nineteenth century: the deceased was interred with a dish and food placed on her abdomen. In this case, the vessel used had a Chinese pattern.

As the era of the revolution brought freedom to Philadelphia's African Americans following the Quakers' decision to discontinue slaveholding in 1776 and the Pennsylvania Gradual Abolition Act of 1780, it also fostered a desire among the members of the black community to establish free institutions to serve their growing needs. Religious congregations were among the first they created. Philadelphia's free African Americans created Mother Bethel African Methodist Episcopal Church, led by Richard Allen, just down Sixth Street from Washington Square, and St. Thomas African Episcopal Church, led by the Rev. Absalom Jones, a block away on Fifth.

The importance of the Washington Square area to Philadelphia's black community continued for centuries to come. James Forten, a sailmaker who became one of Philadelphia's wealthiest African American leaders in the early nineteenth century, rallied the black community to the square to help defend the city when the British threatened during the War of 1812. Forten published a call in a local newspaper in September 1814 for blacks to gather at the

☞ Richard Allen

Richard Allen was one of the leaders who helped establish the area adjacent to Washington Square as the center of Philadelphia's free African American community in the years after the American Revolution. He was born February 14, 1760, to a family of enslaved African Americans who were owned by Benjamin Chew, Pennsylvania's colonial chief justice and one of the largest slaveholders in the Delaware Valley. In 1768, Chew sold Allen and his family to Stokely Sturgis, a middling-sort farmer who lived near the judge's Dover, Delaware, plantation. Enslaved people were subject to the economic and social instabilities of their masters; Sturgis sold Allen's mother and younger siblings, leaving three of the children at his farm.

Reverend Richard Allen (1760–1831), an engraving after a portrait by Rembrandt Peale.

The revolutionary era brought profound changes to Allen's life. His owner became a member of the emerging Methodist movement, and in 1780 Sturgis allowed Allen and his brother to work to purchase their freedom, swayed by his new religious convictions that slavery was wrong. By 1786, Allen himself had become a leading Methodist preacher to interracial audiences in the mid-Atlantic region. Francis Asbury, Methodism's founder, traveled the preaching circuit with Allen.

While the new Methodist Church supported abolition, racial equality was not among its beliefs. One Sunday, black and white members of St. George's Methodist Church on Fourth Street in Philadelphia knelt together in prayer. As the service began, white leaders ordered black congregants to go to the church's balcony. Absalom Jones, another leader of the black Methodists, "begged that the colored people might remain unmolested till the close of services," Allen recalled, but whites attempted to drag Jones, Allen, and other black worshippers from the spots where they were kneeling in prayer. This led to a walkout by black Methodists and eventually to the creation of the first African American churches in America: Jones's St. Thomas African Episcopal Church and Allen's Mother Bethel African Methodist Episcopal (AME) Church. St. Thomas's church relocated in the nineteenth century, but Mother Bethel's congregation remains on the same spot that Allen purchased in 1791. In 1793, Jones and Allen ☞

Interior of St. George's
Methodist Church.

☞ gained fame in the city during the yellow fever epidemic when they led their congregations to serve as nurses and helped bury the victims of the disease. Asbury ordained Allen a deacon in 1799, and he was consecrated a bishop of the Methodist Church in 1816. By the time of his death in 1831, the former slave was one of the most respected African American leaders in the world.

A late nineteenth-century edifice has replaced the small wooden building where Allen preached in the 1790s, but his remains are entombed in the crypt of the church, which also contains a museum that details his life and the history of the AME Church. ☜

square and march en masse to Fort Mifflin on the Delaware River, to build earthen works to protect their city.

By the end of the eighteenth century, the Southeast Square was transformed from its origins as a rural potter's field and grazing land. After the yellow fever epidemics and other health crises, Philadelphians grew squeamish about burials within the city limits, and the square's use as a cemetery came to an end. Developers saw the profit in parkside lots, and row houses rose on the land around the square. By the time Pennsylvania Hospital's center wing

was completed in 1804, the hospital sat amidst a growing residential neighborhood. The area is now called Washington Square West, in recognition of the former Strangers' Burying Ground, which was renamed to honor the military leader whose fallen men still rest under the city park's neat landscaped grounds.

Birch's 1799 engraving of the Walnut Street Jail, the noted Georgian-style building across from Independence Hall, also showed a work crew moving a simple two-story wooden structure south on Fifth Street. A longstanding belief holds that the building, once relocated, became the first Mother Bethel Church. Walnut Street Jail was torn down in the 1830s.

The restoration of Elfreth's Alley and its outstanding collection of "middling sort" houses had not yet begun at the time this photograph was taken in the early twentieth century. Numbers 126 and 128 Elfreth's Alley, at the center of this photo, are now a house museum interpreting three centuries of living on "America's Oldest Residential Street."

TWELVE

Old City

F OR RESIDENTS OF PHILADELPHIA'S Old City, the American Revolution became personal in the fall of 1777. Just over a year after the Continental Congress declared independence on the State House Square, the war was going very badly. American troops under General George Washington had suffered defeat after humiliating defeat. New York City had fallen to British forces, and had resumed its daily life, part colonial village, part occupied island, as it would remain for the rest of the war. Now, it seemed, the British command was setting its sights on another prize of war: the American capital, the city that contained the people and places most associated with the United States' formal break with the mother country.

Indeed, just days after George Washington's army was defeated along the Brandywine Creek

Philadelphia's Old City area was a world of busy riverside docks, crowded streets, and narrow alleys when Scull and Heap created this view in 1756. The area of Elfreth's Alley and Henry and Elizabeth Drinker's house were just to the right of the Presbyterian Church steeple (at far left), in this detail of Scull and Heap's "An East Prospect of the City of Philadelphia."

in southeastern Pennsylvania, the new nation's capital was captured by the enemy. We know the most about those stressful days through the pages of Elizabeth Sandwith Drinker's diary. As she looked west from her home on Front Street on September 26, 1777, the sight gave her heart pause: "Well, here are the English in earnest, about 2 or 3000, came in, through second street, without opposition or interruption, no plundering on the one side or the other." For a Quaker woman, thousands of men in uniform, bearing arms, must have been a chilling image.

The area that Philadelphians now call "Old City" was the mercantile, artisanal, and trade hub of the city in the eighteenth century. In this area—a space that stretched from the High Street Market through the northern border of the city at Mulberry (later Race) Street and from the Delaware River to the city's western edge around Sixth—a world of trade and work was carried on by "we, the middling People, the

Tradesmen, Shopkeepers, and Farmers of this Province and City," as Benjamin Franklin described himself and his neighbors in 1747.

The neighborhood that Elizabeth Drinker captured in her diary was a place of diversity in the eighteenth century, and each of these groups had to cope with the tumult caused by the coming of the American Revolution. The diary (which she continued to keep until just before her death in 1807) is the longest and one of the most complex pieces of literature produced by a woman in early America. Elizabeth Sandwith began her journal in October 1758, when she was twenty-three. When she was seventeen, she had lost both of her parents in a short span of time, and she and her sister, Mary, went to live with a fellow Quaker woman who was also a member of Philadelphia's Quaker meeting. It was at that meetinghouse at Second and Market that Elizabeth married Quaker merchant Henry Drinker, a widower, in 1761.

Elizabeth Drinker's domestic life, centered in her three-story brick home and garden on Front Street, filled the pages of her diary in the years to follow: the birth of her children, interaction with her unmarried sister (who lived with the Drinkers for the rest of her life), management of servants, and her husband's busy life as both a businessman and a leader of the Society of Friends' meeting. Indeed, world-changing events seem to have made little impression on her at first. She barely mentions the wars of empire that affected Pennsylvania's frontier, or the protests that followed Parliament's taxation of the colonies. Elizabeth Drinker left no record of the arrival of the Continental Congress, and her diary entries for July 1776 make no mention

Elizabeth Sandwith Drinker (1734–1807), like many Quakers, thought portraits to be a vanity, but as many of her contemporaries did, she sat for a silhouette cutter. Drinker's diary is an important source of information about daily life in Old City.

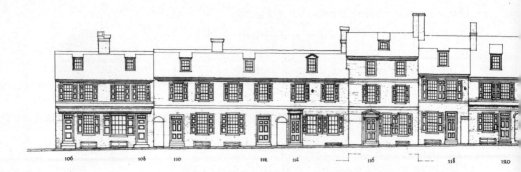

The historic facades of Elfreth's Alley's south side, drawn as part of the Historic American Buildings Survey in 1931. The street façade of number 128 was removed in the mid-nineteenth century when the building was used as a loading dock for the stove factory that stood behind it at the time, and houses 136 and 138 were destroyed not long after this drawing was made. Otherwise, the view remains much as it was when Philadelphia was the nation's capital from 1790 to 1800.

of the Declaration of Independence or its first public reading on July 8. Living just two blocks from Christ Church, she could not have avoided hearing the clamor of the church's bells calling the people of the city to hear that reading, but her diary never mentions it.

Instead, Drinker's diary notes the people and places that were central to her everyday life as a young Quaker woman, a bride, a mother, and a neighbor. Much of the physical world that Elizabeth Drinker and her Old City neighbors knew is now long gone. Nineteenth-century industrialization replaced the small shops of their contemporaries with factories that in turn have become loft apartments for modern-day city dwellers. The construction of Interstate 95 in the mid-twentieth century destroyed the blocks of the city closest to the Delaware River, including the site of the Drinkers' home, just north of Elfreth's Alley on Front Street. Yet with a careful look, and a bit of imagination, it is easy to see the world of these neighbors who experienced the transformations of the American Revolution, the "middling people" who watched British troops march into America's capital in 1777. Old City contains dozens of early American buildings, and they tell a story of

126 126 128 130 132 134 136 138

everyday Americans in far richer detail than per-haps any other neighborhood in the United States.

Outstanding examples of these "middling sort" houses survive all over Old City, with the greatest collection lining Elfreth's Alley, the fif-teen-foot-wide lane between Front and Second streets in the block bounded by Arch and Race. Blacksmith Jeremiah Elfreth and a neighbor opened the alley in 1702, cutting a lane along their property line to connect the busy area around Philadelphia's riverside port with Second Street, the road that led to the Northern Liberties, Germantown, and the Pennsylvania frontier beyond.

The oldest house on Elfreth's Alley—actually, two houses—is the structure containing num-bers 120 and 122, twin homes constructed around 1720. It was buildings like this that greeted young Benjamin Franklin when he arrived at Market Street wharf in 1723, and indeed, his friend William Maugridge lived in 122 Elfreth's Alley from 1728 to 1731. Along with ten other men whose shops sat in the blocks near the Delaware River docks, Franklin and Maugridge founded the Junto in 1727, the club that Franklin would later refer to as the

To be SOLD, TWO Houses in Sassafras street, between Second and Front streets, con-taining in Breadth on said Street 32 Feet, and in depth about 26 Feet; the Lot 51 Feet: And two Houses in Gilbert's Alley, the same Dimensions of the above. For further Information, apply to JEREMIAH ELFRETH, in Second street, Philadelphia.

—*Pennsylvania Gazette*, April 29, 1762

"best school" that then existed for middle-class Philadelphians to learn about literature, politics, business, and eventually science. The Junto began meeting in surveyor Nicholas Scull's tavern on Pewter Platter Alley in Old City, just across Second Street from Christ Church, in 1727. Each Friday, the dozen members would discuss what they had read, what ideas they had formulated, and what the conditions were for their businesses and lives in the colonial city. In 1731, Junto members spearheaded the founding of Franklin's Library Company of Philadelphia. In the decades to follow, these "philosopher mechanics" would help create the American Philosophical Society, the Academy and College of Philadelphia, Pennsylvania Hospital, and the Philadelphia Contributionship fire insurance company, among other schemes.

> The people of this province are generally of the middling sort, and at present pretty much upon a level. They are chiefly industrious farmers, artificers or men in trade; they enjoy and are fond of freedom, and the meanest among them thinks he has a right to civility from the greatest.
>
> —*Pennsylvania Journal*, 1756

Elfreth's Alley survives with an outstanding collection of thirty-two "middling sort" houses that date from the 1720s through the 1830s, and together, these buildings show the architectural history of early America. But beyond architecture, the alley also tells the story of early American artisans and their lives in a thriving urban space. They lived in close proximity to one another (some residences are separated by only one course of bricks or wood and a thin layer of plaster), and their shops dominated the front rooms of the buildings' ground floors, with goods and labor easily visible just inside the front windows.

The two houses that Jeremiah Elfreth built as speculative properties and sold in 1762 on "Gilbert's Alley" (the names Gilbert's and Elfreth's for the little street alternated during the early era) are now the Elfreth's Alley Museum, a

Pennsylvania founder William Penn's Quaker pacifism led to peaceful interaction with the Lenni Lenape. Almost a century later, Benjamin West celebrated this in his "Penn's Treaty with the Indians" (1771–1772). While historically inaccurate, the grand painting stressed the importance of the Penn family's increasingly controversial role to their supporters in pre-revolutionary Pennsylvania. *(Pennsylvania Academy of the Fine Arts)*

During the eighteenth century, Philadelphia grew from a small provincial village to the largest city in North America. Peter Cooper portrayed the town from the bank of the Delaware River (top) showing an optimistic view of the port, with more ships arriving than any day witnessed, and more steeples than the town actually had in 1720. (*Library Company of Philadelphia*) As Philadelphia grew, its citizens used architecture to define their rank, ambitions, and identity, an idea artist William Birch showed (above) in his view of the Market Street mansion merchant Robert Morris began, but never finished, due to his bankruptcy. (*Independence National Historical Park*) Throughout the era, Benjamin Franklin (right) played a key role in the changing nature of politics and society. Charles Willson Peale captured Franklin's active mind in his 1772 portrait (a copy of an earlier work, by David Martin), where he sits surrounded by books, letters, and a bust of Isaac Newton. (*American Philosophical Society*)

Sir Allan Ramsay captured King George III's majesty and splendor in his c. 1761 coronation portrait, which the Penn family had copied, intending this painting would hang in their colony's State House. The emerging revolutionary movement interrupted those plans, and the painting remained at the family's English estate until the nineteenth century. (*Pennsylvania Academy of the Fine Arts*)

In addition to being one of America's preeminent artists, Charles Willson Peale, strove to explain the wonders of the natural world as well as human development. Here, in his self-portrait "The Artist and His Museum," (1822) Peale pulls back a curtain in the Long Gallery in Independence Hall to reveal taxidermied specimens, a mastodon skeleton, and his gallery of notable Americans, portraits that now hang in the Second Bank of the United States. (*Pennsylvania Academy of the Fine Arts*)

Walking the streets of eighteenth-century Philadelphia afforded the opportunity to meet a diverse group of men and women, including political leaders like James Hamilton (right), propri-etary lieutenant governor under the Penn family, portrayed in this grand-manner portrait by Ben-jamin West in 1767; Mary White Morris (left) by Charles Willson Peale, c. 1782, whose elegant cos-tume represented her status as the wife of Robert Morris, a leading merchant and government leader in the new nation; Joseph Brant/Thayendanegea (upper right), also by Charles Peale, 1797, who came to the nation's capital to wage diplomacy during the Washington Administration (all, *Independence National Historical Park*); and the Reverend Absalom Jones (upper left), paint-ed by Raphaelle Peale in 1810, who rose from slavery to freedom and leadership roles in the city and Episcopal community. (*Delaware Art Museum*)

From an early date, Philadelphians understood their city's important role in the creation of the United States, and they preserved objects, spaces, and images connected with its colonial and revolutionary history. Sometimes, those memories were very personal, as when Bishop William White's family had John Sartain paint the bishop's study in 1836, an image that proved invaluable to National Park Service curators when the room was restored in the twentieth century. Later in the nineteenth century, history enthusiasts had turned the Assembly Room where the Declaration of Independence and U.S. Constitution had been signed into a national museum, with the walls filled by Charles Willson Peale paintings and later images of Penn, Lafayette, and the William Rush statue of George Washington, as well as the Liberty Bell, crowned by a stuffed American bald eagle, in this image by Max Rosenthal. (both, *Independence National Historical Park*)

☞ Architecture: Row Houses

When William Penn imagined the capital of his colony in 1681, he predicted a "greene, countrie towne" where Quaker farmhouses would sit in the center of large, country lots, dotting the landscape from the Delaware to the Schuylkill River. But Penn's dream remained just that. The colonists who arrived in Philadelphia immediately began constructing row houses, individual dwellings that shared a party wall with one or more neighboring buildings. Building houses as a row, a series of matching houses, dates back to medieval England. Philadelphia's English colonists began to copy that vernacular style by the 1720s, as builders saw the city's population doubling and doubling again. The architectural pattern that began by the early 1700s continued to shape Philadelphia's physical appearance for the three centuries to follow.

Housing for Philadelphia's expanding population had been a problem from the start, and the caves along the Delaware where some of the first settlers had taken shelter remained in use—if disreputably—as the colonial period wore on. Some of these small caverns, housing illegal "grog shops" or houses of ill repute, gave the area just north of Elfreth's Alley the nickname "Hell Town" in the late eighteenth century. William Penn actively encouraged builders to settle in his colony, and those men utilized the local building materials, including readily available lumber, marble for lintels and front stoops, and a rich vein of clay for bricks that ran directly under the city. ☞

The Rich-Truman house on Delancey Street is a fine example of an eighteenth century Philadelphia row house. Built in 1771 by plasterer John Rich, it was purchsed in 1774 by Richard Truman, a cabinetmaker.

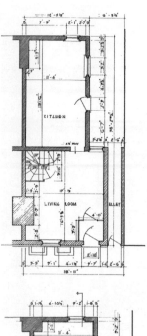

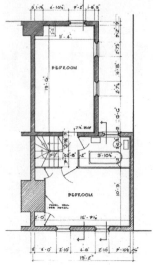

First- and second-floor plans of the Rich-Truman house, showing the main section of this "middling sort" row house facing Delancey Street, and the dependencies, at rear, holding the kitchen on the ground floor and sleeping quarters above.

The floor plan of middling sort row houses followed a common pattern repeated throughout the city: usually one room on the first floor, which served as either a family parlor or a shop area, or both. A winding stairway led to the second story, with sleeping quarters for the family there and in the space above, under the eaves. Some eighteenth-century row houses placed the kitchen in the basement, an area that could also be reached by a hatchway on the house's front, which allowed convenient delivery of large barrels of flour, vegetables, or other foodstuffs.

As the eighteenth century progressed, more and more Philadelphians moved their cooking facilities to the "L" in the rear of their houses, an area known as the home's dependency. Often (as in the case of many of the homes along Elfreth's Alley), these kitchens were connected to the main portion of the house by a "piazza," a small passageway that contained a staircase and access to the outside of the house. The "piazza"—an adaptation of an Italian architecture term for a deep, covered porch—became one of the eighteenth-century city's distinguishing architectural features. Servants, slaves, and apprentices often slept in the area above, reached by a small staircase or ladder.

As Philadelphia house builders rushed to build row houses to accommodate the city's exploding population, the style became a standard for the colonial city that would continue and develop in the centuries that followed. Benjamin Franklin, newly returned from a decade in Paris, incorporated the latest ideas from Britain and Europe when he built a row of rental properties along Market Street in the 1780s, including fire-stopping party walls and access to roofs, to stop chimney sparks from igniting shingles.

site that tells the stories of early American artisans and craftspeople and the immigrants and
workers who followed them to the street in the
centuries to follow. Mary Smith and Sarah
Melton purchased number 128 from Elfreth,
and it was in the house that Smith ran her business making mantuas—loose, flowing gowns—
until her death in 1766.

The inventory taken at the settlement of
Smith's estate at her death gives us a glimpse into
the lives of middling Philadelphians a decade
before independence. The £33.17 appraisal of
Mary Smith's estate reveals that the women had
a looking glass valued at £1, two oval tables, a
tea table and a stand all made of walnut, a dozen
rush bottom chairs where their customers could
sit while in the house for fittings, and a degree of
gentility, shown in the dozen cups and saucers,
china plates, and small china bowls that filled
their cupboards. But in addition to being a place
where the women entertained customers, this
house was also a workshop. Six candle stands
provided light for fine needlework, and a dough
trough, pewter dishes, a colander, and other
kitchen wares showed the daily living that went
on in the small kitchen.

When Mary Smith died, she left house 126 to
her "sister in Law" Sarah Melton. The relationship is confusing, as neither of the two married,
and thus "in-law" seems to have been part of a
wider family relationship. Sarah Melton continued to live here until her death in 1794. In the
decades the two women lived in this small row
house, they lived alongside diverse members of
Philadelphia's middling sort. Nearby, craftspeople made chairs, sewed, made pottery, baked,
and a carried out a variety of other crafts.

❧

The alley's population gives us a glimpse into just how diverse Philadelphia's Old City neighborhood was in the eighteenth century. The Drinker family members were "weighty friends," leaders of the Quaker meeting, while nearby Mary Smith, an Anglican, spent her Sunday mornings at Christ Church. Other neighbors practiced a variety of faiths. Just a few doors east of Smith and Melton's shop lived Moses and Esther Mordecai at number 118. Moses Mordecai was born in Bonn, Germany, in 1707, and moved to Philadelphia in 1758. He met his future wife, Elizabeth Whitlock, in England, and she changed her name to Esther when she converted to her husband's Jewish faith upon their marriage in 1761. By 1765, Mordecai had become one of the merchants protesting British taxation by signing the Non-Importation Agreement. He was a leader of Congregation Mikveh Israel, which met in private homes in the Old City area until construction of its first synagogue in 1780, about a block from Elfreth's Alley on Cherry Alley.

In the years after the American Revolution, the householders in the area became even more diverse. The revolution's message of liberty led to freedom for some enslaved African Americans, one of whom was Cuff, or Cophie, Douglass, who moved into house number 117 directly across Elfreth's Alley from the Mordecais' home. Douglass was born a slave, purchased his freedom, and in 1779 he married his wife, Phoebe, in Gloria Dei Church, a parish chosen by many poorer Philadelphians as a place for their marriages or funerals. During the five years they

Moses Mordecai and other members of colonial Philadelphia's Jewish community lie buried in Mikveh Israel Cemetery, located on Spruce Street, west of Eighth. The cemetery was established in 1740; the wall and wrought-iron gate date from 1803.

lived in house 117, Douglass assumed leadership roles in Philadelphia's emerging free African American community. In 1782, he joined a number of other free black men in seeking the right to fence in the African Burial Ground in the Strangers' Burial Ground, now Washington Square, to acknowledge the importance of that space for Philadelphia's newly free population.

Elizabeth Drinker's diary reveals that the American Revolution crept slowly into the lives of her friends and neighbors. In June 1776, she wrote that "two or 3 men call'd to look at our Window Weights," as the Committee of Safety had requisitioned that all lead weights in the city be collected to melt for bullets, but this delegation had "found them to be Iron." By July 16, things became more serious. "Friends Meeting-House at Market-Street Corner broke open by the American Soldiers, where they have taken up their Abode," she wrote. For the weeks that followed, the meetinghouse had the improbable cohabitation of the pacifist Friends with military men.

But Drinker's diary also shows the way the war affected the people of Old City, as its impact

This has been a day of Great Confusion to many in this City; which I have in great measure been kept out of by my constant attension to my sick Child. part of Washingtons Army has been routed, and have been seen coming into Town in Great Numbers; the perticulars of the Battle, I have not attended to, the slain is said to be very numerous—

became fully evident the following year. The Drinkers and their fellow members of the Philadelphia Friends Meeting had settled in the City of Brotherly Love to be able to follow their Quaker beliefs, and a cornerstone of their religious faith was opposition to violence of any kind and war in particular. As the Revolutionary War came closer and closer to the Quaker City, many of the non-Quaker leaders looked on the pacifist Friends with animosity and suspicion. The months that followed, with the war going badly for Washington's army, made matters worse. On January 25, 1777, Elizabeth Drinker recorded: "We had 5 American Soliders quartered upon us by order of the Counsel of Safty—the Soliders named Adam Wise, Henry Feating, these two stay'd 2 or 3 days with us, the rest went in an hour or two after they came." Quakers who had come to America to avoid warfare now had armed men in their houses.

The months following the Declaration of Independence grew more and more disconcerting for Elizabeth Drinker and her fellow Quakers, culminating with the revolutionary leaders' decision to arrest any Friends who refused to support the war effort or to swear a loyalty oath to the new government (an act doubly repulsive to Friends, who followed the biblical edict against swearing oaths). On September 2, 1777, as her husband, Henry, sat at his desk in their parlor recording information in the Friends' meeting minute book, "Wm. Bradford; one [Bluser] and Ervin, entered, offering a Parole for him to sign—which was refus'd." Two days later, the revolutionary leaders "took my Henry to the lodge—in an illegal, unpredesented manner." Henry Drinker joined numerous other leading Quakers in the Freemasons' lodge on Lodge Alley, near City Tavern, to await their fate.

The Quakers petitioned both the Pennsylvania Assembly and the Congress, but neither took the action they desired. On September 11, Elizabeth noted, "the Town is in great Confusion at present a great fireing heard below it is supos'd the Armies are Engaged." The cannon fire she heard to the south was the Battle of Brandywine, where George Washington and his Continentals engaged the British in one last battle to defend the national capital. The days that followed brought wounded soldiers, confusion, and panic to the city. Drinker recorded on September 19 that the British army was reputed to be approaching Philadelphia, and "Congress, Counsil &c are flown." Each of these events paled by comparison for the diarist, though. The revolutionary leaders had exiled her beloved husband and other leading Quakers to Winchester, Virginia. Henry Drinker and the others would be separated from their families until the end of April 1778.

Thus, Elizabeth Sandwith Drinker was a woman balancing personal and national crises when she watched the British army march into Pennsylvania's capital. Among the British who came to occupy Philadelphia that fall was Ambrose Serle. Like Drinker, Serle kept a careful diary of his experiences during the war, and the two texts allow us to see the two sides of the British occupation. Not himself a military man, Serle had learned the art of British bureaucracy in London, where he served as aide to the Earl of Dartmouth while that nobleman served as secretary of state for colonial affairs. In May 1776, Serle had sailed for the colonies in the service of

hundreds of their muskets laying in the road, which those that made off have thrown down—I was a little fluttered this Afternoon by hearing a Drum stop at our Door and a hard knocking succeed; it proved to be, men with orders for HD to appear or find a Substitute—there has been a meeting this Afternoon at the State-House, on what Account I know not.

—Elizabeth Drinker,
Diary,
September 12, 1777

Richard, Lord Howe, the British admiral whose career in Parliament had been marked by support for the American cause. But Lord Howe sided with the empire when the war began. In 1776, he led the naval forces sailing for North America to end that colonial rebellion; when Howe and Serle arrived in New York, they discovered that the colonies had declared that they were no longer colonies.

The problem was not just "corrupt" colonists who had duped or pressured their law-abiding neighbors into attacking British troops, Serle believed; it was the very system of colonialism itself. He noted, "These Colonies, and particularly the Northern, so far from being of the use that is pretended to G. Britain, have in several important & most essential Particulars been of great Disservice to her. Comparing the *political* Profit, as well as the *commercial*, and considering the Consequences of things to my dear Country, I almost wish that the Colonies had never existed."

Among his many observations on life in revolutionary America, Serle noted the discrepancy between words and reality when it came to race. As his ship sailed past Maryland's Eastern Shore, he wrote, "Scarce a white Person was to be seen; but negroes appeared in great abundance. These live in Huts or Hovels near the Houses of their Owners, they are treated as a better kind of Cattle, being bought and sold, according to Fancy or Interest, having no Property not even in their Wives and Children. Such is the Practice or Sentiment of Americans, while they are bawling about the Rights of *human Nature*, and oppose the freest Govt. and most liberal System of Polity known upon the Face of the Earth!"

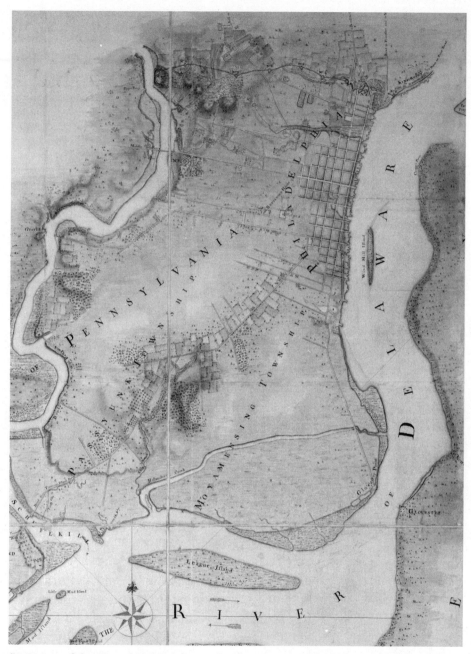

"A Survey of the City of Philadelphia and its Environs shewing the several Works constructed by his Majesty's Troop, under the command of Sir William Howe, since their possession of that city 26th September 1777" by British Chief Engineer John Montresor.

Serle was with Lord Howe off the American coast when the news from Brandywine arrived in September 1777. "News arrived of the Defeat of the Rebels, which great Loss to them both in Cannon & men," Serle recorded on September 13. "Mr. Washington is fled, & the Troops are on their march to Philadelphia. The Ships are now under sailing orders for the Delaware."

Soon thereafter, Serle followed British troops into the rebels' capital. "Walked early this morning about Philadelphia. It is finely laid out in a pleasant Situation upon the Banks of the Delaware. The Streets intersect each other at Right angles. There are some handsome public Buildings, and some Houses not inelegant, but the Generality of the last are rather mean Edifices, calculated more for the Reception of an industrious People in middling Circumstances, than for the Entertainment of the opulent and luxurious," Serle wrote, unimpressed by the "middling sort" nature of the town.

Serle's observations also show the toll that the war was taking on Philadelphia by the time he arrived there in November 1777: "There is but one market, wch is very large & built after the manner of the Fleet market in London: But I did not see one Piece of meat or a Fowl, and but very few Vegetables; all necessaries of Life being extremely dear, owing to the very small Extent of Country at this time under our Command." What Serle took to be the norm in Philadelphia was actually the result of what Elizabeth Drinker had been recording in her diary for many weeks: Pennsylvania farmers were either unwilling to bring their goods to the town's market, or were frightened of the American troops who were arresting anyone who was trying to get food or other commodities into the occupied capital. The result was inflation, hunger, and a lack of firewood that led inhabitants and their occupiers to burn fences, church pews, and other wooden objects.

As he was not impressed with the economic life of the city, Serle was likewise dismissive of the building where independence had been declared. "The Stadt-House, where formerly the assembly & lately the Congress held their meetings, is a large heavy Pile, & now converted into a Prison & Hospital for Rebels. This has been the Fate of some other public Buildings, wch were before employed in disseminating the Principles of Rebellion," his journal records.

From his first days in occupied New York City, Ambrose Serle had befriended American Loyalists, including some who had fled the revolutionary capital. Perhaps his closest companion in the months that followed was Joseph Galloway, the Philadelphia politician whose name appears frequently in the pages of Elizabeth Drinker's diary. A Maryland-born Quaker who had moved to Philadelphia while still a teenager in the 1740s, Galloway had begun to practice law, and married Grace Growden, a wealthy heiress who was a member of the Church of England (leading him to leave Quakerism). The years to follow had seen Galloway's political star rise. He was elected to the Pennsylvania Assembly in 1756, and became Benjamin Franklin's protégé and confidant in the movement to curtail the Penn family and their hold over the colony. Both men were defeated in the vicious political campaign of 1764, which had pitted supporters of the Penn proprietary group against opponents who were

Joseph Galloway (1731–1803), in a diamond-encrusted miniature by Thomas Day in London. Benjamin Franklin's onetime political protégé and speaker of the Pennsylvania Assembly is portrayed in the red coat of the British military, which he joined in December 1776 after having fled Philadelphia when it was discovered he was spying on the Continental Congress for the British.

Henry Dawkins's print "The Election, a Medley," one of America's first political cartoons, showed various segments of society expressing their views in the hotly contested Pennsylvania Assembly election of October 1, 1764.

lumped together in the "Quaker Party," although few were actually Friends. The next year, Galloway regained his seat in the Assembly elections, defeating John Dickinson, and the year that followed saw him become Assembly speaker. A member of the First Continental Congress, Galloway sought reconciliation with Great Britain, formulating a plan that would create an American congress that was a subsidiary of the Parliament in London. His plan was ignored by the congressmen. Refusing to serve in the second congress, and declining Franklin's attempts to persuade him to join the American cause, Galloway fled to British-held New York in late 1776. He would return to Philadelphia as General Howe's agent for maintaining public peace in the fall of 1777.

The British occupation of Philadelphia from the fall of 1777 to the spring of 1778 touched lives in every part of the city and colony, but perhaps the experiences of the Quaker residents of Old City relate the ways the revolution now became a civil war. Even before the occupation began, British officials were making plans to capture and keep the rebellious colonies' largest city. On the morning of April 4, 1777, Ambrose Serle went to visit Joseph Galloway in his rented rooms in New York, and found him "very uneasy, that a Person, whom he had employed to procure Pilots for the Delaware at Philadelphia, was confined to Prison & wd. probably be hanged." The capture, trial, and execution of James Molesworth was major news in the city and indeed in the new nation. In her diary, Elizabeth Drinker recorded, "a Young Man of the Name of Molsworth was hang'd on the Commons by order of our present ruling Gentr'y," a sarcastic jab at the revolutionary leaders by a Quaker woman who opposed the death penalty. But as Elizabeth Drinker and her fellow members of the Society of Friends struggled with the news of neighbors having neighbors put to death, James Molesworth's story was just beginning.

The *Pennsylvania Gazette* of April 2, 1777, gave an account of his punishment. "Monday last James Molesworth, a Traitor and a Spy, was executed on the commons near this city. It appears by sundry evidence and his own confession, that he had been sent from New York to procure pilots for conducting the British fleet up the river Delaware to this city." When Molesworth was caught spying, he was executed and buried. After his public execution, the Patriot leaders had given the spy the ultimate removal from their society: they buried him in the potter's field, the resting place of strangers or people without religious ties in the city.

But when Philadelphia fell to the British, Molesworth was on the move. Now with Loyalists in control of the local government, "a young woman nearly allied in kindred" successfully pleaded to have his body removed to the burial grounds of the Society of Friends, located at Fifth and Arch streets. The move outraged pro-revolutionary Philadelphians, and when the city once again was under their control, they ran the advertisement demanding the body be returned to its inglorious resting place. The *Pennsylvania Packet* of September 26, 1778, announced,

> To those Persons who were immediately concerned in removing the body of that infamous traitor, JAMES MOLESWORTH from the proper place of interment to the Quakers burying ground. YOU are desired immediately to remove the said body from the burying ground to the place from whence you thought proper to take it, and bring sufficient evidence of such removal for publication, within two weeks from this date, otherwise ample vengeance will undoubtedly fall on the heads of the delinquents.

The statement was signed simply "LEGION."

Thomas Harrison announced in the *Packet* of October 6, 1778, that he had "IMPRUDENTLY giving my personal attendance as one of the mourners when the body of James Molesworth was removed from the Potters Field to the Quaker burial ground, at the time the British army possessed this city, arose not from any party matter, nor particular respect to said Molesworth."

The strange postmortem travels of James Molesworth, British spy, do speak to one aspect of Philadelphia's revolution: the role of the

Society of Friends during the war for independence. Whether or not Molesworth was a member of the Quaker meeting is unclear. He may have been a former member, like Joseph Galloway, or the woman who pleaded for his reburial may have been a member. Or he may have been a non-Friend, whose only qualification for interment in the burial ground was that he was dead; Quakers did not discriminate on the basis of membership, unlike other religious groups in Philadelphia. But the Friends' tradition, that they were a people "set apart," added to the complexity of Philadelphia's story during the war.

For Elizabeth Drinker and her fellow Quakers, the revolution turned their normal lives into chaos. Drinker's diary records the panic and confusion as the city fell to the British, with Friends and others working to ensure the peace and safety of the town. Among those neighbors was Abraham Carlile, a Quaker house carpenter whose shop stood on the north side of Elfreth's Alley, very near Henry and Elizabeth's Front Street property. When the British took Philadelphia, Joseph Galloway placed Carlile in charge of a gate near his home on Front Street, monitoring who came in and out of the occupied city. "The poor people have been allow'd for some time past to go to Frankfort Mill, and other Mills that way, for Flour, Abraham Carlile who gives them passes, has his Door very much crouded every morning," Elizabeth Drinker wrote on November 24, 1777.

When the Americans retook Philadelphia, Carlile's name was among those associated with the British invaders, and he was subsequently

This detail of Benjamin Easburn's 1776 map of Philadelphia shows the close proximity of the burying grounds of the city's various religious sects, including the large Quaker plot along Fourth and Arch streets.

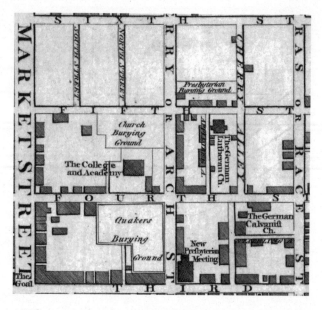

tried, sentenced to death by Judge Thomas McKean (a signer of the Declaration of Independence), and executed, despite petitions that numerous Patriots signed and presented to the new state government. Elizabeth and Henry Drinker visited their neighbor Ann Carlile, offering her solace prior to the execution. Elizabeth's diary for November 4, 1778, "they have actually put to Death; Hang'd on the Commons . . . an awful Solemn day it has been." The next day, Quaker diarist Jane Bonsall Clark recorded: "This day was buried Abraham Carlise of this City, who was executed the day before on the Commons; the Body was carried to his late dwelling, where his Afflicted wife and only son (& Child) Mournfully did the last offices of Love to his remains; the Funeral was large and many was deeply Afflicted by this Melancholy Case."

Elizabeth Drinker recorded the scene of Abraham Carlile's funeral in the Friends' burial ground: "Myself and 4 Children went . . . it was a remarkable large Funeral, and a Solemn time. George Dillwyn and S. Emlen spake at the grave, and the former, pray'd fervently." The Quaker burial ground on Arch Street between Third and Fourth was granted by William Penn in 1701 for use by the members of the Philadelphia meeting. For decades, the burial ground sat on the outskirts of town. The Friends' central meetinghouse—the building that Benjamin Franklin had dozed in on his first morning in Philadelphia—sat at the corner of Second and High streets. By 1772, the Philadelphia meeting divided into thirds, due to the growing number of residents in the city. The Drinkers attended "North Meeting" on Front Street, just yards from their home, while Quakers south of Dock Creek attended "South Meeting" on Pine Street in Society Hill, and those in the center of town continued to attend the meeting at Second and Market.

Perhaps no Quaker's life better shows the complexities of living through the American Revolution than Elizabeth Griscom Ross Ashburn Claypoole, or "Betsy Ross," as American legend has come to know her. Elizabeth Griscom was born January 1, 1752, the daughter of a Quaker carpenter and his wife. Betsy developed her sewing skills, both through her mother Rebecca's tutelage and as an employee in the workshop of John Webster, the noted Philadelphia upholsterer whose employees covered masterpieces like the Cadwalader family furniture, now among the most highly prized American furniture created in the colonial era.

Betsy Griscom married John Ross, an Angli-can, in 1773, and like other young Friends who married "out of meeting," she was disowned by the Quaker meeting. As with women of the colonial urban artisan class, Betsy Ross's economic and domestic lives were closely intermingled, doubly so because her first husband was an upholsterer, and her own skills were valuable to the family's economic life. But her world was violently altered when, in January 1776, John Ross died. Now a young widow, Betsy was left to carry on.

Those early details of the Betsy Ross story are easy to substantiate. More difficult to pin down is the legend of what happened in the year that followed, which made Betsy Ross an American folk hero. As the story goes, George Washington came to the Ross shop on Arch Street, seeking a seamstress who could make flags—standards that his troops could carry into battle. Congress had approved the design for the stars and stripes on June 14, 1776; and Francis Hopkinson, one of Philadelphia's most talented men of arts who was known locally for playing Christ Church's organ as well as for signing the Declaration of Independence, later remembered that he had supplied an early design, for which he requested payment from the Continental Congress of "a Quarter Cask of the public Wine" (a bill the congress declined to pay).

Betsy Ross told her story of the American leaders coming to her shop, and of the clever way she could fold a piece of fabric and cut it into a five-pointed star with one snip, remembering these events and recalling them for her grandchildren until she died in 1836. It was one of those grandchildren, William Canby, who

The Betsy Ross House, in a late nineteenth-century photograph when "The Birthplace of Old Glory" was squeezed between its neighboring, later buildings, and today, as restored and maintained by the city of Philadelphia.

shared the family story with a meeting of the Historical Society of Pennsylvania in 1870 and pushed the city of Philadelphia to preserve his grandmother's row house as a monument to the first American flag. Today, the Betsy Ross House is one of Philadelphia's most famous, and most visited, historic sites.

The question remains: did Betsy Ross really sew the first American flag, and if so, did she do it in that house? Both questions will probably never be answered definitively. But the story of Elizabeth Griscom Ross is far more interesting, and far more complex. Later generations could not be absolutely certain in which row house she lived: a persistent legend in Philadelphia is that the Rosses' shop was actually in the identical row house next door, where the museum's courtyard now sits (and where Betsy and her third husband were later reburied, in 1975).

Did Betsy Ross sew the first flag? That question is even harder to answer. Certainly, she sewed flags. The Pennsylvania naval board paid her £15 in May 1777 for providing flags for American ships. The confusion lies in the fact that, while the revolutionary leaders were busy

The Free Quaker Meeting House followed building styles used in earlier meetinghouses when it was constructed in 1783. It served as a house of worship until 1834, and was subsequently used for a variety of purposes including a school and a library. Now restored, it is the oldest remaining meetinghouse in Center City Philadelphia.

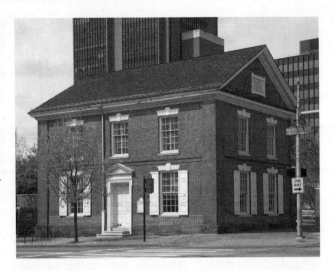

establishing a nation and winning a war, they had little time to delineate what that nation's flag should look like. Despite the mysteries that fill her story, the realities of Betsy Ross's life as a craftsperson in a revolutionary city disclose an equally fascinating chronicle.

Among the many revolutions Betsy Ross experienced was a split between the members of the Quaker meeting, and after John Ross's death, she was among the large number of disowned Friends who created the Free Quaker Meeting. Denied seats in other Friends' meetinghouses as well as burial in the Arch Street burial ground because they supported the revolutionary war effort, the Religious Society of Friends—commonly called "Fighting Quakers" or "Free Quakers," began meeting in 1781 and in June 1783 began plans to purchase land on which to build their own meetinghouse. Led by pro-independence leaders Timothy Matlack and Samuel Wetherill, the group purchased the land at Fifth and Arch streets on June 5, 1783, and plans were soon under way to construct the forty-eight- by thirty-six-foot meetinghouse.

Ironically, the Free Quaker Meeting House, founded because of its members' revolutionary break with Quaker peace tradition, is the oldest Friends meetinghouse in Center City Philadelphia. Constructed in a style that follows the neoclassical lines of late Georgian architecture while still adhering to Quaker beliefs that their worldly possessions be "of the best sort, but plain," the meetinghouse that Samuel Wetherill designed followed the plans of both the Society Hill meetinghouse and the Pine Street Presbyterian Church, which the builder studied and measured.

While the Friends and their neighbors had to contend with a variety of transformations brought by the revolutionary era, many of the city's old customs resumed once the war was over. Visiting Philadelphia from her native New

Old City in the last decade of the eighteenth century, as captured in an engraving by William Birch and sons. The image, showing the view from Fourth Street looking east toward the Delaware River, includes the brick façades of the row houses and their neat Pennsylvania marble steps. On the left is the Second Presbyterian Church, constructed between 1750 and 1753 at Third and Arch streets.

England in 1790, Judith Sargent Murray
observed,

> Philadelphia is indeed the Metropolis of the
> American World and, it is advancing for-
> ward to a state of high perfection—There is,
> however, a whimsical kind of singularity,
> remarkable in the Majority of the inhabi-
> tants of this Capital—For example, an ele-
> gant Carriage, superbly finished, and orna-
> mented in the height of the present taste
> drawn by beautiful horses, which are glitter-
> ing with the richness of their trappings—
> which carriage is attended, by servants, its
> complete livery, approaches, while the Lady
> issuing therefrom, exhibits in her dress, a
> perfect pattern of simplicity . . . it is only by
> their personal habiliments, that the Quaker
> can now be distinguished.

Elizabeth Sandwith Drinker would likely
have disagreed with Judith Murray's assessment
that only her clothing and the "thee and thou"
she used when speaking distinguished her from
her diverse neighbors near the Delaware River
port in the early national period, but she did see
a world around her that was changing, different
from the Quaker community into which she was
born. Even some of the most significant places
in that world were changing in the first years of
the new nation.

On June 18, 1797—the same day she recorded reading a British Quaker's published admoni-
tion to former president George Washington for
owning slaves—Elizabeth recorded attending
the family funeral of a one-day-old child in the
Quaker burial ground on Arch Street: "Went to
the funeral in our Carriage about 8 o'clock in

the evening. It was laid by Jacob Downings first child, with our family, as friends will not premitt anyone to dig in that part of the grave yard where Rhoadess and many other families lays, as it is that part which is laid out for a Meetinghouse, but cannot yet be brought to bare, as many are much opposed to it—it is not a pleasing thought to have the bones of our Ancestors disturbed."

The date stone below the roof peak of the Arch Street Friends Meeting House reads 1804.

Indeed, the growing population of Philadelphia, by 1797 the capital of the new nation, led Friends to sell their meetinghouse site at Second and Market and construct a new central meetinghouse on part of their burial ground. Construction on the main building of the Arch Street Meetinghouse—the largest Quaker meetinghouse in the United States—was completed in 1805, with a datestone reading 1804 placed above the building's main entrance. The building's final wing, on the west, was completed in 1811, and the historic Market Street building was sold and razed a short time later. The burial ground, which follows the traditional Quaker custom of not using headstones, holds the remains of many of Philadelphia's most prominent historical figures, including James Logan, Elizabeth Drinker and her family, and numerous victims of the yellow fever epidemic that raged through Philadelphia in 1793.

The National Constitution Center, located north of Independence Hall, celebrates the enduring legacy of the U.S. Constitution, written in Philadelphia from May to September 1787. The center's groundbreaking occurred on September 17, 2000, the two-hundred-thirteenth anniversary of the signing of the Constitution.

THIRTEEN

The National Constitution Center

ON SEPTEMBER 20, 1787, eighty-one-year-
old Benjamin Franklin wrote to his
younger sister, Jane Mecom, catching up with
his favorite (and last surviving) sibling on the
events of his life in the weeks and months just
past: "The Convention finish'd the 17th Instant.
I attended the Business of it 5 hours in every
Day from the Beginning which is something
more than four Months. You may judge from
thence that my health continues; some tell me I
look better, and they suppose the daily Exercise
of going and returning from the State house, has
done me good. You will see the Constitution we
have propos'd in the Papers. The Forming of it
so as to accomodate all the different Interests
and Views was a difficult task and perhaps after
all it may not be receiv'd with the same

Benjamin Franklin, the oldest delegate at the Philadelphia Convention of 1787, attended every day's meeting and pushed delegates to remember the people. Here, he is shown in an engraving of Charles Willson Peale's painting from the same decade.

Opposite, top: Detail of the Rising Sun Chair, purchased by the Pennsylvania State Assembly from craftsman John Folwell in 1779 and used by George Washington during the Philadelphia Convention.

Unanimity in the different States, that the Convention have given the Example of, in delivering it out for their Consideration." Summing the whole experience up, the months of work that he and the delegates from across the young United States had done, he confided "We have, however, done our best, and it must take its Chance."

Dr. Franklin and the other representatives to the convention, which met just a few blocks from Franklin Court from May 25 through September 17, 1787, participated in extensive discussions of the nature of government and citizenship, deciding on the fate of the American Revolution's ideals. In many ways, those four months were a culmination of Benjamin Franklin's political life. He had worked within Pennsylvania's State House walls almost from the moment the building was completed. A veteran of the political battles that marked colonists' maturing ideas of what it meant to be a people, he had risen from hired clerk to speaker of the colonial assembly in the building, and then seen his career "end" in the vicious election of 1764, pitting the Penn family and their supporters, who believed Pennsylvania was a personal fiefdom, against Franklin's Quaker Party, which advocated the rights of common people in the colonial government. Representing his colony in London for the next decade, he'd returned to advocate independence, and before he left for France in late 1776, helped draft his state's first constitution and the first draft of the Articles of Confederation.

The Articles, America's first system of national government, were finally adopted in 1781. They were a deliberately weak form of government that rested power in the individual states and in the people, satisfying revolutionary Americans' fear of an overpowerful central government. Each state had crafted its own constitution after the Declaration of Independence, ranging from Massachusetts' conservative frame that required legislators and the governor to own considerable wealth, to Pennsylvania's radical constitution of 1776, which gave unusually widespread voting rights to the free men of the commonwealth and restricted the terms and power of the state government. The government under the Articles had accomplished a great deal in the years they administered the United States: under the Articles, the new nation had waged war against the strongest military empire in the world; it had carried out diplomacy that brought foreign powers to recognize an independent America; and—in the Northwest Ordinances of 1785 and 1787—it had devised a plan that would allow the new nation's territories eventually to join an expanding republic as new states, not western colonies in an empire. Under the Articles of Confederation, Benjamin Franklin, John Adams, Henry Laurens, and John Jay had signed the Treaty of Paris in 1783, which secured America's independence from Great Britain.

But the years after the war had been trying ones for the United States of America. None of the states had ever been enthusiastic about funding the new national government, and money had always been a serious problem for the new nation. On June 21, 1783, those financial problems became very serious for the congress. Outraged American veterans, demanding back pay, surrounded the Pennsylvania State House. Congress' journal for that day related: "The

I have often and often in the course of Session, and the vicissitudes of my hopes and fears at its issues, looked at that [sun] behind the President without being able to tell whether it was rising or setting: But now at length I have the happiness to know that it is a rising and not a setting Sun.

—Benjamin Franklin,
September 17, 1787

Pennsylvania-born Benjamin West, by then living in London, attempted to paint the traditional, formal portrait of the peace commissioners negotiating the Treaty of Paris, which officially ended the Revolutionary War. West began the portrait of American delegates John Jay, John Adams, Benjamin Franklin, Henry Laurens, and Franklin's grandson, William Temple Franklin, but the painting was never completed, as British delegates refused to sit for a painting with men they considered traitors to their king.

authority of the United States having been this day grossly insulted by the disorderly and menacing appearance of a body of armed soldiers about the place within which Congress were assembled, and the peace of this city being endangered by the mutinous disposition of the said troops." The hours that followed grew more and more tense: "In the meantime the Soldiers remained in their position, without offering any violence, individuals only occasionally uttering offensive words and wantonly pointed their Muskets to the Windows of the Hall of Congress. No danger from premeditated violence was apprehended, But it was observed that spirituous drink from the tippling houses adjoining began to be liberally served out to the Soldiers, & might lead to hasty excesses. None were committed however, and about 3 O'C[lock]., the usual hour Cong. adjourned;

A R T I C L E S
OF

CONFEDERATION AND PERPETUAL UNION,

BETWEEN THE STATES OF

NEW-HAMPSHIRE,	THE COUNTIES OF NEW-CASTLE
MASSACHUSETTS-BAY,	KENT AND SUSSEX ON DELAWARE,
RHODE-ISLAND,	MARYLAND,
CONNECTICUT,	VIRGINIA,
NEW-YORK,	NORTH-CAROLINA,
NEW-JERSEY,	SOUTH-CAROLINA, AND
PENNSYLVANIA,	GEORGIA.

ART. I. THE name of this Confederacy shall be " THE UNITED STATES OF AMERICA."

ART. II. The said States hereby severally enter into a firm league of friendship with each other, for their common defence, the security of their liberties, and their mutual and general welfare, binding themselves to assist each other against all force offered to or attacks made upon them or any of them, on account of religion, sovereignty, trade, or any other pretence whatever.

ART. III. Each State reserves to itself the sole and exclusive regulation and government of its internal police in all matters that shall not interfere with the articles of this Confederation.

ART. IV. No State, without the consent of the United States in Congress Assembled, shall send any Embassy to or receive any embassy from, or enter into any conference, agreement, alliance or treaty with any King, Prince or State; nor shall any person holding any office of profit or trust under the United States or any of them, accept of any present, emolument, office or title of any kind whatever from any King, Prince or foreign State; nor shall the United States Assembled, or any of them, grant any title of nobility.

ART. V. No two or more States shall enter into any treaty, confederation or alliance whatever between them without the consent of the United States in Congress Assembled, specifying accurately the purposes for which the same is to be entered into, and how long it shall continue.

ART. VI. No State shall lay any imposts or duties which may interfere with any stipulations in treaties hereafter entered into by the United States Assembled with any King, Prince or State.

The Articles of Confederation and Perpetual Union, drafted between 1776 and 1777 by the Continental Congress and ratified by all thirteen states March 1, 1781.

the Soldiers, tho in some instances offering a mock obstruction, permitting the members to pass thro their ranks. They soon afterwards retired themselves to the Barracks." Fearing for the members' safety, Congress departed the building where the United States had been born seven years earlier, and never returned. Moving first to Princeton, New Jersey, then to Annapolis, Maryland, then to Trenton, New Jersey, the national government finally settled in New York City in January 1785, and it remained sitting there for the next five, difficult years.

Among the congressmen involved in the standoff in Independence Hall were men who would strongly influence the transformation of the national government in the next few years: Alexander Hamilton, representative from New York, and James Madison of Virginia both experienced the mutiny, as did John Dickinson, president of Pennsylvania's state government, which was meeting on the State House's second floor at the time. Congress fled Philadelphia, but these men and others carried the experience of that June into the years that followed. During that period, American nationalists, including Madison, Hamilton, and George Washington sought ways to make the American nation work, including calling a meeting at the general's Mount Vernon plantation in 1785 to discuss interstate commerce and then assembling a larger meeting the following year in Annapolis. Neither gathering accomplished much; Maryland, the state hosting the second meeting, didn't even bother to send delegates to it. The national congress seemed incapable of doing much, and elected congressmen often did not even show up for Congressional sessions.

But in 1786, American leaders witnessed an event that made the State House mutiny pale by comparison. Shays' Rebellion in Massachusetts, in which an army of 2,000 western farmers shut down local courts that were foreclosing on their neighbors' property and then nearly captured a federal arsenal, revealed the government's military weakness. Franklin, now returned from France and elected president of Pennsylvania's Supreme Executive Council, signed an order

An illustration from *Bickerstaff's Boston Almanack* of 1787 showing Daniel Shays and Job Shattuck, leaders of the Massachusetts "Regulators."

announcing his state's cooperation with Massachusetts to capture and try rebel leader Daniel Shays and his followers. Increasingly, American leaders became frightened that perhaps the revolution was dissolving into anarchy.

In February 1787, the Continental Congress in New York issued a call to each state to send delegates to a convention to be held in Philadelphia the following May "to devise such further provisions as shall appear to them necessary to render the constitution of the Federal Government adequate to the exigencies of the Union." As the delegates began to gather in Philadelphia, the *Pennsylvania Herald* of May 25 noted, "When indeed we consider the critical situation of the country, the anxiety with which every good citizen regards this *dernier resorte* [last resort], and the decisive effect it must have upon the peace and prosperity of America, though every thing should certainly be given to prudence and deliberation, not a moment can be spared to useless forms of profitable controversy."

Yet while many thought the American nation faced a critical moment without a government

Patrick Henry (1736-1799), one of independence's most strident advocates, had grave misgivings about the Constitutional Convention and refused to attend.

that could meet its needs, others saw any strong national government as a threat to liberty and refused to participate in the convention. "I smell a rat!" fumed Patrick Henry of Virginia. He was not alone; Philadelphian William Shippen wrote to his son on May 30, "much is hoped for from their wisdom & patriotism," but he looked on the delegates with suspicion: "Aristocracy is said to be the Idea of almost all of them—I shall not call it a Miracle if G^l W—n [Washington] is seen living in Philadelphia as Emporer of America in a few years—The eastern men hold these principles as strongly as the southern."

Becoming an American emperor was the farthest thing from George Washington's mind that spring. Indeed, the general—who had ceremoniously presented his retirement from the army to Congress at Annapolis four years earlier—was hesitant to attend, fearing that his fellow citizens might call him politically ambitious. As historians have long pointed out, Washington had the most to lose by attending the convention. He was wildly popular throughout the United States, and part of that admiration was based on his repeated habit of turning away from power when he could have taken it, making him a modern-day antithesis of Julius Caesar. But would he come to Philadelphia? Convention supporters added Benjamin Franklin to the already large number of delegates attending from Pennsylvania, in case Washington was not there to preside over the Federal Convention. Finally, Washington agreed to attend, arriving in Philadelphia to great fanfare in May. Franklin hoped to personally nominate Washington to be the convention's president, but bad weather forced him to stay home on May 25, and Robert

Morris of Pennsylvania made the nomination instead.

The convention's first task was gathering enough delegates to make a quorum to begin formal debates. Virginia delegate George Mason wrote to his son on May 20: "All the States, Rhode Island excepted, have made their appointments; but the members drop in slowly; some of the delegates from the Eastern States are here, but none have yet a sufficient representation, and it will probably be several days before the Convention will be authorized to proceed to business. God grant that we may be able to concert effectual means of preserving our country from the evils which threaten us."

But while Mason's days were spent meeting with his fellow Virginians, he quickly grew weary of the endless entertainments and formal protocol that the Constitutional Convention entailed. The revolution had removed the traditions associated with the hierarchy of English society, but how were Americans to organize themselves now? Some chose to become very formal, with bows, addresses, and social events that mimicked European courts, all in the setting of the new American republic. "I begin to grow heartily tired of the etiquette and nonsense so fashionable in this city. It would take me some months to make myself master of them, and that it should require months to learn what is not worth remembering as many minutes, is to me so discouraging a circumstance as determines me to give myself no manner of trouble about them," he wrote on May 27.

Finally, on May 25 delegates from enough states were present to begin work. In the months that followed—much to delegates' surprise, and

Wide-ranging respect for General George Washington led many delegates to attend the Philadelphia Convention and drew broad support from the people of the new nation. Portrait engraving by Charles Willson Peale, 1787, at the time of the Constitutional Convention.

I have news from America as late as July 19. Nothing had then transpired from the Federal convention. I am sorry they began their deliberations by so abominable a precedent as that of tying up the tongues of their members. Nothing can justify this example but the innocence of their intentions, & ignorance of the value of public discussions. I have no doubt that all their other measures will be good & wise. it is really an assembly of demigods.

—Thomas Jefferson, in Paris, to John Adams in London, August 30, 1787

in some cases disgust, the convention would not conclude its work until September 17, 1787. Fifty-five men from twelve of the thirteen United States met in the Pennsylvania State House, where they drafted the Constitution of the United States of America. The gathering included most of the leading names of American government and politics.

The delegates who gathered in Philadelphia held strong nationalist sentiments. Of them, forty-two had served in the Continental Congress or Congress under the Articles. Many others had been part of the Continental Army. Delegates were drawn from the ranks of wealthy merchants and planters; many were prosperous lawyers. They were well-educated, with twenty-six having graduated from college. Some, like James Madison, had made a lifetime practice of studying government, history, and politics. Washington and Franklin were undoubtedly the most famous men in America.

One of the first things the convention did was pass a collection of rules for members to follow, including adopting the policy on May 29 that all proceedings would be secret. The convention closed the windows of Independence Hall to avoid eavesdropping, stationed guards at their assembly room's door, and carefully monitored themselves and one another, to stop gossip about the meeting's action.

The Constitution that the delegates crafted was a collection of compromises in which each delegate and state had to give something to make the entire system work. Tempers flared often, and many men walked out of the hall; some did not return. The secrecy policy seems to have held, though. The *Pennsylvania Gazette* published a statement on July 18 (that was in turn reprinted in other newspapers), that "So great is the unanimity, we hear, that prevails in the Convention, upon all great federal subjects, that it has been proposed to call the room in which they assembly—UNANIMITY HALL." We are left to wonder how many delegates smirked at that suggestion.

Almost immediately, the delegates decided that revising the Articles of Confederation—the stated purpose of their meeting—would not go far enough. They scrapped the Articles in favor of creating something else. But what would that system be?

On May 29, Virginia Delegate Edmund Randolph laid out fifteen resolutions before the Convention that called for an entirely new system of government. Largely the work of James Madison, the plan called for a two-house legislature, where delegates would be apportioned based on either the taxes contributed or their population. The plan was somewhat vague on the roles of the executive and judiciary branches. Key factors such as the amendment and ratification of the government, and the admission of new states, were clearer than under the Articles. The day after the Virginia Plan was presented, the Convention agreed to support a new government that was "national and supreme," then spent the following two weeks debating the various aspects of Randolph's proposals.

The Virginia Plan was not the only proposal that delegates considered that summer. On June 14, William Paterson of New Jersey presented a starkly different plan, giving many of the nationalists present who wanted a new form of government reason for concern. The New Jersey

Though the particular arguments, debates, and decisions that take place in the federal Convention, are considered as matters of secrecy, we understand, in general, that there exists a very great diversity of opinion amongst the members, and that there has been already a wonderful display of wisdom, eloquence, and patriotism.

—*Pennsylvania Evening Herald,* June 13, 1787

We are at such a Distance from the present Head-Quarters of Politicks, that we know very little of the great things in Contemplation at Philadelphia. . . . The Clergymen begin to omit poor old Congress in their prayers and substitute instead thereof, the Convention. You know many of our political Ideas of New England have their Birth in the pulpit.

—Stephen M. Mitchell, in Wethersfield, Connecticut, to Charles Thomson, Secretary of Congress, in New York, June 6, 1787

Plan (actually prepared by delegates from New Jersey, Connecticut, Maryland, New York, and perhaps Delaware), called for retaining the national one-house legislature, with each state receiving one vote. But unlike the government under the Articles, the New Jersey Plan proposed a system wherein the government could raise funds through a stamp tax and import duties, regulate commerce, and force states to make their delinquent financial contributions. The plan called for a plural executive (rather than a single president) who would be selected by the Congress, and for a national judiciary. Acts of Congress and treaties were to be "the supreme law of the respective states."

The New Jersey Plan was soundly defeated, but it reminded delegates that American citizens were still apprehensive of strong national government.

On July 2, Roger Sherman of Connecticut called for a committee to be established to consider the issue of representation, which had drawn the convention to an impasse. Slavery was one of the most divisive issues of the Constitutional Convention. By 1787, the institution of slavery was dying in many or most of the northern states, but the South clung to a slave-based economy. Southern states demanded protection of the slave system, and part of that protection was counting enslaved blacks when enumerating the population for the sake of representation, but of course not granting any rights of citizenship, including voting, to those same slaves.

While the convention took a break for the Independence Day holiday, members of the Grand Committee met in Benjamin Franklin's home, where their host proposed the Connect-

☞ James Madison

James Madison arrived in Philadelphia three weeks prior to the opening of the Constitutional Convention, having spent months preparing for the debates that were to follow. While slight of body—he was once called "no bigger than half a piece of soap" by one colleague—Madison had an expansive mind that grasped history and political theory. His plan would shape the first weeks of debate over the Constitution; his notes would give us the best source we have about the events of the convention.

Virginia Delegate James Madison, in a life portrait by James Sharples, Sr., 1796–1797.

Madison was born March 16, 1751, at Port Conway, Virginia, the eldest of ten children. After an education at the College of New Jersey (now Princeton University), Madison entered politics in his native Virginia. He was elected to the Committee of Safety for Orange County at the outset of the revolution, and later to the governor's council in 1778. From 1780 to 1783, Madison represented Virginia in the Articles' Congress, meeting at Philadelphia, where he developed skill as a parliamentarian and political coalition builder. During these years, he also became concerned about the Articles' ability to serve and protect the new nation. Upon leaving Congress, Madison was elected to the Virginia House of Delegates, where he served until the end of 1786.

Upon returning to Virginia, Madison supplemented his longstanding interest in politics, government, and history by beginning a detailed study of the law, in part so he could have a profession so he could "depend as little as possible on the labour of slaves." While he contemplated freeing his slaves several times during his life, he never did so, instead becoming an advocate of colonization, the nineteenth-century scheme which would return free blacks to Africa. But Philadelphia's environment did affect his life as a slaveholder. Writing to his father in September 1783, near the end of his time in the Continental Congress, he stated, "On a view of all circumstances I have judged it most prudent not to force Billey back to Va. even if it could be done; and have accordingly taken measures for his final separation from me. I am persuaded his mind is too thoroughly tainted to be a fit companion for fellow slave in Virg[ini]a. The laws here do not admit of his being sold for more than 7 years. I do not expect to get near the worth of him; but cannot think of punishing ☞

All men having power ought to be distrusted to a certain degree.

—James Madison,
July 11, 1787

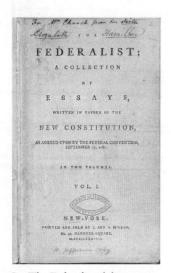

In *The Federalist*, delegates Alexander Hamilton and James Madison, along with politician and diplomat John Jay, argued for ratification of a strong federal government under the proposed Constitution. The eighty-five newspaper essays helped persuade at first reluctant New Yorkers, and then people across the nation to their views, once the essays were collected in book form in this first edition.

☞ him by transportation merely for coveting that liberty for which we have paid the price of so much blood, and have proclaimed so often to be the right, and worthy pursuit, of every human being." Billey Gardner, the slave Madison sold to a Philadelphia Quaker, died a free man while at sea a few years later.

During these years, Madison grew convinced that future American success depended on a united commercial policy that could overcome rivalries between the new states. To that end, he attended the Annapolis Convention in September 1786, which called for a convention of all the states the following year to remedy defects in the Articles of Confederation.

By the time James Madison came to Philadelphia to represent Virginia at the Federal Convention, he had made a careful study of ancient and modern republics and the reasons they failed. The result was his Virginia Plan, which called for a centralized government which could support American prosperity. Madison quickly established himself as a leader of the convention. Delegate William Pierce of Georgia wrote, "Mr. Maddison is a character who has long been in public life; and what is very remarkable every Person seems to acknowledge his greatness. He blends together the profound politician, with the Scholar. In the management of every great question he evidently took the lead in the Convention, and tho' he cannot be called an Orator, he is a most agreable, eloquent, and convincing Speaker. . . . The affairs of the United States, he perhaps, has the most correct knowledge of, of any Man in the Union."

Immediately after leaving the convention, Madison traveled to New York, where he, Alexander Hamilton, and John Jay wrote *The Federalist*, a group of essays that persuaded first that state, then others, to ratify the Constitution. Madison then helped lead the fight for his native state to ratify the Constitution, but his ambition to serve in the first United States Senate was blocked by Patrick Henry, who opposed the Convention from the start and had jousted with Madison for years over the separation of church and state. But Virginians elected Madison to the House of Representatives in 1788, where he served until 1797.

Madison returned to Philadelphia when the federal government moved to the city in 1790, and during his years in Congress he was acknowledged as one of the major authorities on the new Constitution, and leaders including President Washington turned to him for counsel. During this time he married Philadelphia widow Dolley Payne Todd. The combination of her personal popularity and vivacity and his cerebral, sometimes argumentative, nature formed one of the most important political partnerships of the young country.

Beyond Madison's Virginia Plan, beyond his persuasive Federalist essays and even beyond his service as a congressman, secretary of state, and later president, James Madison's role as a historian stands out as one of the most important contributions made by any of the Constitutional Convention delegates. For four months, James Madison took copious notes. After he died in 1836, Dolley Madison sold these papers to the government. They constitute the greatest record that survives of the debates that shaped the United States Constitution. ◁

icut Compromise. As presented to the full convention the next day, the Connecticut Compromise stated that representation in the lower house would be based on population, while each state would have an equal number of representatives in the upper. The Connecticut Compromise introduced the "federal ratio" into the United State Constitution, resolving the question by counting enslaved African Americans as three-fifth of a human being when tallying the states' populations to apportion members of the House of Representatives or votes in the electoral college that would elect America's presidents. The measure passed on July 16, finally removing the main point dividing the states, large and small, north and south. But the "Great Compromise" came at a price to

Pennsylvania delegate James Wilson (1742-1798) brought an impressive legal mind to the Philadelphia Convention, and crafted the actual wording of the Constitution of 1787. President Washington would appoint him one of the first associate justices of the Supreme Court in 1789.

millions of Americans. The final compromise protected the slave trade until 1808 and provided for a national fugitive slave law. The slavery issue would have profound long-lasting ramifications in the political and social history of the century to follow, and for the citizens—white as well as black—of the new nation.

Once the issue of representation was decided, with the three-fifths compromise firmly in place, the Convention's Committee on Detail drafted the Constitution itself. Led by John Rutledge of South Carolina with Pennsylvania's James Wilson as its most active participant, the committee created a list of specific powers granted to the president and judiciary, and noted what powers were denied to the states. The federal government would have the power to tax and borrow money, to regulate commerce, make war, and establish inferior courts. The president was given independent power to make war and carry out diplomatic efforts. The Constitution established a national judiciary, with a supreme court and federal judges, with details to follow once the federal government was in place.

On the last day of the Federal Convention, Benjamin Franklin asked to be allowed to make some final comments to the assemblage. Franklin was often uncomfortable at that time, suffering from gout and gallstones, and though he was present that day he opted to have James Wilson read his speech. Many suspected that Franklin, far more liberal than many delegates, would reject the Constitution. Nineteen of the delegates had already left the meeting, protesting one part of the document or another.

Instead, Franklin called for acceptance: "I confess, that I do not entirely approve of this

❧ James Oronoko Dexter and His Neighbors

On July 16, 1787—the same day that the secret convention meeting in the Pennsylvania State House formally adopted the Connecticut Compromise—James Oronoko Dexter of Philadelphia met with representatives to certify his freedom before the Pennsylvania Abolition Society.

"Oronoko" was born sometime prior to 1749. His unusual name probably came from the transatlantic world of letters: *Oroonoko or, The Royal Slave in London* was a popular English novel written by Aphra Behn in 1688. When his owner, Henry Dexter, died in 1749, his will granted "Oronoke" to his son, James Dexter. James planned to free "Oronoko royal Slave" upon his death in 1767, but he died in debt, and Oronoko remained in slavery. In 1787, Quakers Isaac Zane and James Pemberton testified to his free status, relating that, "when young and in Slavery," Ononoko "was hired by his master to the Keeper of a Tavern in this City and being of an obliging behavior gained the good will of those who frequented the house so that by presents he Renewed from them in the space of four years he had saved to the amount of fifty Pounds."

Attaining his freedom, Oronoko "being desirous of settling in life, and inclining to marry . . . fixed on a young woman of reputation" named Priss. He "obtained the Consent of her possessor who held her in so high estimation that he rated the price of her redemption from Slavery at so great a rate that Oronoko could not comply with the terms, and therefore for some time declined further proceeding." Finally, a friend prevailed upon Priss's owner to accept £50 instead. "Noke" had been able to save £30 already; friends loaned the other £20 to secure the bride's freedom.

By the 1780s, James Oronoko Dexter (who, as a free man, adopted his former master's name) was supporting himself as a coachman and had become a leading member of Philadelphia's free African American community. Isaac Zane noted Dexter's "humanity in assisting and Relieving those of his own Colour and difficulty . . . as far as is in his power which with his conscientious principles rendering him a Truly worthy Character." In 1782, he joined with his fellow freeman Cuff Douglas and four ❧

☞ other men to petition Pennsylvania's governor to allow them to fence off part of the Strangers' Burying Ground (now Washington Square) as a designated African burial ground, a petition the state government refused.

James Dexter was among the first members of Philadelphia's Free African Society, and in December 1792 he hosted the first meeting of the African Episcopal Church of St. Thomas congregation in his home at 84 North Fifth Street. Dexter and his second wife, Sarah, lived in the small, rented two story house from the time of its construction in 1791. His neighbors included other members of Philadelphia's community of artisans and working people, white and black.

Elizabeth Drinker, who lived just four blocks from the Dexters during the 1790s, mentioned in the pages of her diary his work as a coachman employed by her friend Hannah Pemberton. She recorded that he went into the city during the crisis of the yellow fever epidemic in the summer and fall of 1793, perhaps traveling into the town because of the widespread (but ungrounded) belief that African Americans could not catch yellow fever. Drinker's diary provides James Dexter's epitaph: on August 10, 1799, she recorded, "Oronoko is dead, our Jacob went to his funeral, many a pleasant ride have I taken with his Mistress under his care and protection, poor Noke." "Our Jacob," as Drinker called him, was an African American free man who worked in the Drinker household. Her men-

In the James Dexter archaeological site plan, archaeologists meticulously plotted each "Feat."—features that included filled water wells and the privy pits from long-gone outhouses. These spaces revealed aspects of James Oronoko Dexter's life on North Fifth Street, land that is now part of the National Constitution Center block.

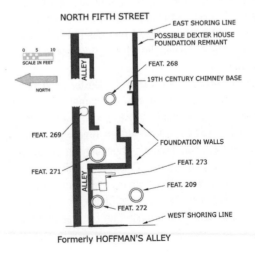

NORTH FIFTH STREET
EAST SHORING LINE
POSSIBLE DEXTER HOUSE FOUNDATION REMNANT
FEAT. 268
19TH CENTURY CHIMNEY BASE
0 5 10
SCALE IN FEET
NORTH
ALLEY
FEAT. 269
FOUNDATION WALLS
FEAT. 273
FEAT. 271
FEAT. 209
ALLEY
FEAT. 272
WEST SHORING LINE
Formerly HOFFMAN'S ALLEY

tion of him attending the funeral makes it likely that James Dexter's final resting place was the African burial ground in the Strangers' Burial Ground at Washington Square, joining members of the city's black community in their unmarked, and still unfenced, last resting place.

The Constitution of 1787 largely forgot the plight of James Oronoko Dexter and the people like him who longed to translate the American Revolution's message of freedom into freedom from slavery, too. Ironically, the National Constitution Center's construction in the early years of the twenty-first century led to the unexpected consequence of bringing Dexter's life to national attention. Federal law required that archaeological analysis be conducted on the "footprint" where the new building would sit, along with extensive historical research on the people who had lived on the site. National Park Service historians discovered that Dexter had lived on the block, and expanded the dig plans to explore his yard's remaining artifacts. This dig uncovered artifact deposits that revealed the experiences of "Noke" and members of his community in the first years of the new nation. Studied and conserved by NPS archaeologists, these artifacts are now on display in the Constitution Center, which celebrates the legacy of a living constitution that finally ended slavery with ratification of the Thirteenth Amendment in 1865 and removed the three-fifths compromise as part of the Fourteenth Amendment, ratified in 1868. ◁

Constitution at present; but . . . I am not sure that I shall never approve it; for, having lived long, I have experienced many instance of being obliged, by better information or fuller consideration, to change my opinion even on important subjects, which I once thought right, but found to be otherwise," Franklin wrote. "It is therefore that the older I grow, the more apt I am to doubt my own judgment of others. . . . In these sentiments . . . I agree to this Constitution, with all its faults, if they are such; because I

Philip Syng, a noted Philadelphia silversmith, crafted this inkstand, with pen holder and sand shaker used to help dry wet ink, for the Pennsylvania colonial Assembly in 1752.

Thus I consent . . . to this Constitution, because I expect no better, and because I am not sure that it is not the best. The opinions I have had of its errors I sacrifice to the public good. I have never wispered a syllable of them abroad. Within these walls they were born, and here they shall die.

—Benjamin Franklin, September 17, 1787

think a general Government necessary for us."

Franklin took pen in hand and, using the silver ink stand that his old friend Philip Syng had made for the Pennsylvania Assembly years earlier, signed his name to the Constitution of the United States.

Later, as he led the delegates out of the State House to City Tavern, Franklin encountered his neighbor Elizabeth Willing Powel, awaiting news of the results of the four-month secret convention. When Mrs. Powel asked what kind of government the Convention had created, he offered a memorable response: "You have a republic, if you can keep it."

Page one of the Constitution of the United States of America, signed by thirty-nine delegates representing twelve of the states on September 17, 1787, and sent to the nation for ratification.

We the People of the United States, in Order to form a more perfect Union, establish Justice, insure domestic Tranquility, provide for the common defence, promote the general Welfare, and secure the Blessings of Liberty to ourselves and our Posterity, do ordain and establish this Constitution for the United States of America.

—The Preamble, written by Pennsylvania delegate Gouverneur Morris

Edward Savage's *The Washington Family*, painted between 1789 and 1796, showed the president, his wife, and Martha Washington's grandchildren, Eleanor Parke Custis and George Washington Custis. The African American servant in livery at right cannot be identified. This engraving, copying the original, nine-foot wide painting, was distributed throughout the United States in the decades that followed.

FOURTEEN

The President's House

T HE WASHINGTON FAMILY'S carriage rolled north toward Philadelphia in the last days of November 1790 as the result of one of the new nation's first major political compromises. The fifty-eight-year-old president of the United States, his wife, her grandchildren, and the enslaved servants who saw to their daily needs entered the new nation's new capital with relative peace and quiet that day. Philadelphians— who had grown very accustomed to giving the general rousing receptions during the preceding ten years—had celebrated their new residents and their city's return to national status as the capital the previous September. Loud cheers and receptions celebrating the federal government had taken place then, but the president had left, spending time at Mount Vernon and in the

South. Now, as the last decade of the eighteenth century dawned, the Washingtons were traveling to their new home at 190 Market Street, as part of the experiment in federal government.

When the United States government began to organize under the new Constitution twenty months earlier, Philadelphia had long since lost its role as the nation's capital. After the rebellious mob of unpaid American soldiers frightened Congress into fleeing the State House Square in 1783, it seemed the city would not regain the seat of power. Despite arguments, pleas, and persuasions, the capital remained in New York as the last Congress under the Articles of Confederation finished its work, and a new government—the first elected under the federal Constitution—was elected by the first eleven states (North Carolina did not ratify the Constitution until November 1789, and Rhode Island not until May 1790). The newly elected congressmen traveled to New York to take their oaths of office in the spring of 1789, and Washington swore his oath on the front balcony of Federal Hall there on April 30. But Philadelphians had never lost hope that when tempers cooled, the national government might return.

The following June, just a year after the new government convened, one of its first major compromises resulted in the capital's return to Philadelphia. President George Washington had appointed his first cabinet, and Secretary of the Treasury Alexander Hamilton was seeking congressional approval for the new economic system to control the massive American national debt. By 1789, America's credit was destroyed, its commerce struggling. Under Washington's

George Washington took the oath of office for the first time on April 30, 1789, at Federal Hall. Originally built as New York's city hall, the building had been remodeled by Pierre-Charles L'Enfant, who would later design Washington, D.C. The building was razed in 1812. Engraving by Amos Doolittle.

orders, Hamilton crafted a plan: the federal government would assume responsibility for the $21 million in debts that the individual states had acquired during the revolution, then sell bonds to finance the debt. Doing so, Hamilton reasoned, would strengthen the new federal government by tying the interests of the wealthy men who held government bonds to the future of the country. Hamilton—a canny politician as well as a skilled economist—knew that he would need the support of southern planters as well as northern merchants and financiers (his staunchest allies) if he hoped to pass his reforms.

Among those who disagreed with Hamilton's plan were Congressman James Madison and Secretary of State Thomas Jefferson, both from Virginia, and both leery of linking the new government to the men of finance who surrounded them in New York City. An unexpected meeting, outside President Washington's rented home on Cherry Street in New York, led Jefferson to invite Hamilton to a dinner where they could discuss their differences. At that dinner, Hamilton and Jefferson crafted a compromise that would placate both of their factions. Jefferson and his southern colleagues would support Hamilton's program, and in exchange Hamilton agreed to support a plan to move the federal capital away from New York, his home, and presumably away from the influence of northern financiers. Under the Residency Act of 1790, President Washington would find a location for the permanent capital close to the geographic center of the country, and the government would move there no later than 1800. For the ten years in between, the federal government would move to Philadelphia.

In 1790, Philadelphia was the largest city in the United States. With a population of over 42,000 that would increase by another 19,000 in the next decade, it was the country's economic, cultural, and intellectual center. Proud of their preeminence, and hoping to recover the lost commerce that the city had suffered after the national government had fled, Philadelphians had been pushing the government to return for years. New York City was still tainted by memories that it had been held by the British for the entire Revolutionary War. Philadelphians touted their patriotism, their climate, even their entertainments as they pleaded to be the capital city again. Not everyone was impressed. Representative Fischer Ames of Massachusetts called the competition for the capital "a despicable grog-

Cong. fs Embark'd on board the Ship Constitution of America bound to Conogocheque by way of Philadelphia.

shop contest, whether the taverns of New York or Philadelphia shall get the custom of Congress." But in July, both houses of Congress narrowly passed the act.

The government's decision to move with little advanced notice created a scramble for housing, servants, and supplies as the three branches prepared to reconvene in Philadelphia in December 1790. The national government was very small, of course, with only a few hundred men serving in its various offices and branches. Congress and the judiciary moved into quarters on State House Square, the only time in American history when one city block held the governments of a city, county, state, and nation.

As the government prepared to relocate, George and Martha Washington set about establishing their household in Philadelphia. The president stopped in Philadelphia on his way to Mount Vernon, and with the assistance of his secretary Tobias Lear, began making plans to

New Yorkers did not let the government leave without a fight, as shown in this anti-relocation political cartoon of 1790, "Cong-ss embark'd on board the ship Constitution of America bound to Conogocheque by way of Philadelphia." Philadelphia's distinctive grid plan is at left, but the ship *Constitution* (which has, as one passenger is pointing out, a masthead of a goose rather than an eagle) nears the Delaware River's falls, with Satan coaxing the group forward, saying "This way, Bobby" to Robert Morris, one of the move's main supporters.

George and Martha Washington took up residence at 190 High Street, a house owned by Robert Morris, one block from State House Square.

move into the house at 190 High Street that Philadelphia's city council was renting for him, a mansion owned by Robert Morris, not far from State House Square. "The arrangements which are made with respect to Mr Morris' house appear to be such as will render it a more commodious and eligible dwelling than you had reason to expect on your first settlement in Philadelphia. The people here appear pleased with the prospect of your being so well accommodated," Lear wrote to Washington on September 12. In the weeks that followed, the president's aide oversaw painting, furnishing, and preparing the Morris house for the first family's arrival, including construction of a three-story bow room on the house's south side, to create a larger, more elegant space in which the presidential couple would entertain. When the Washingtons arrived, the Philadelphia town house would hold all of the ceremonial, residential, and office functions of the president and his family.

The president knew the location of his new residence very well. When he had first arrived in Philadelphia as a Continental Congressman

In East View of GRAY'S FERRY, near Philadelphia, with the TRIUMPHAL ARCHES, &c. erected the Reception of General Washington, April 20th 1789.

PHILADELPHIA, *December* 1.
On Saturday laſt at eleven o'clock, A. M.
GEORGE WASHINGTON, President of the United States, with his Lady and Family, arrived in this city.

Above, newspaper notice of the arrival of President George Washington from New York. Left, "An East View of Gray's Ferry, near Philadelphia, with the Triumphal Arches, & c. erected for the Reception of General Washington, April 20th, 1789." Charles Willson Peale created the image, as well as the actual elements of the celebration, for America's first president as he traveled to New York to be inaugurated.

from Virginia in 1775, the house next door at the corner of Sixth and Market had been the home of Joseph Galloway, a leading Philadelphia politician. At the outbreak of the revolution, Galloway had become a Tory, fled to New York, and then reentered the city with the invading British in 1777. He left his elegant home for the last time in 1778, when he evacuated Philadelphia with the British Army. The next year, Charles Willson Peale and revolutionary leaders confiscated the building, and the American patriots physically removed Mrs. Galloway from the premises.

Next to the Galloway house was the town house built by Mary Masters about 1767, a wedding present she gave to her daughter Polly when she married Richard Penn, William Penn's grandson. The Penns moved to England at the outbreak of hostilities, and the Masters-Penn house saw much activity during the war, used at various times by Washington's opponent, General William Howe, then by his friend-turned-traitor, Benedict Arnold.

After the war, Robert Morris purchased the Penn home, which had been badly damaged by

Charles Willson Peale captured this grand manner portrait of Robert Morris, "financier of the revolution," in 1782. Within a few years, Morris would be a U.S. Senator, leading proponent of the federal government's relocation to Philadelphia, and bankrupt, the victim of unstable financial times and overextending himself in investment and building an even grander house.

a fire, and rebuilt it into a grand city house. Morris, "the financier of the revolution," was a Philadelphia businessman who helped secure independence through his keen financial strategies; he hosted Washington in the house many times, including a four-month stay during the Constitutional Convention in 1787. In 1790, he agreed to rent his mansion to serve as the president's house, and the Morrises moved next door, into the former Galloway house, which he also owned. Thereafter, the Morris house came to be known as the President's House.

Robert Morris was born in Liverpool, England, in 1735 and immigrated to Maryland with his father twelve years later. He moved to Philadelphia in 1747 and became apprentice to Charles Willing, a leading merchant in the city. After the elder Willing's death, Morris and Willing's son Thomas established the firm of Willing and Morris, and the firm's interests came to span the Atlantic World. In 1769, Morris married Mary White.

Morris became a leader in the nonimportation movement protesting British taxation policies, but he was reluctant initially to support independence from Britain. As a delegate from Pennsylvania he did sign the Declaration, and helped lead the new nation during its first years. He managed the government's finances and personally loaned money to feed and equip George Washington's troops. After he left office in 1784, the Willing and Morris firm sent Philadelphia's first merchant ship to China, opening a highly lucrative trade. Morris was elected again to the Pennsylvania Assembly in 1785, attended the Annapolis Convention in 1786, and pushed for a stronger national government as a delegate to the Constitutional Convention.

By the 1790s, Morris was the richest man in America, but that status did not save him from tumultuous financial times and overextending his credit to build a larger, more elegant house. He went bankrupt in 1798 and spent three years in the debtors' prison on Walnut Street, sometimes hosting George Washington in his quarters there when the former president would bring tea to his old friend. Morris was released under provisions of America's first bankruptcy law in 1801, and he died in 1806. He is buried in a borrowed grave, part of the family plot of his wife's brother, Bishop William White, at Christ Church.

As the Washingtons settled into the President's House, they positioned themselves at the center of a social circle of supporters of the new national government, known to contemporaries as the Republican Court. Washington was extremely sensitive to allegations that he behaved in a too-regal manner, or that he had royal pretentions. Yet the court, which followed the behavior of royal courts even as it celebrated being part of a new republic, did draw criticism, particularly over the formality of the weekly levees the president and first lady hosted, and the members' decision to celebrate the president's birthday, much the same way colonists had celebrated monarchs' in earlier generations.

The Washingtons' Tuesday afternoon levees, held in the President's House from three to four, were moments of solemn formality. The president stood in the house's first floor parlor, with his back to the newly added bow window. One visitor, who recalled the scene decades later,

Mrs. Washington her-
self made tea and cof-
fee for us. On the table
were two small plates
of sliced tongue, dry
toast, bread and but-
ter, etc. but no broiled
fish, as is the general
custom. Miss Custis,
her grand-daughter, a
very pleasing young
lady, of about sixteen,
sat next to her, and her
brother, George
Washington Custis,
about two years older
than herself. There
was but little appear-
ance of form: one ser-
vant only attended,
who had no livery; a
silver urn for hot
water, was the only
article of expense on
the table.

—British visitor
Henry Wansey,
June 6, 1794

observed "the manly figure of Washington clad in black velvet; his hair in full dress, powdered and gathered behind in a large silk bag; yellow gloves on his hands holding a cocked hat with a cockade in it, and the edges adorned with a black feather about an inch deep. He wore knee and shoe buckles; and a long sword, with a finely wrought and polished steel blade, and appearing from under the folds behind." The president's guests were ushered in by a secretary, formed a circle around the walls of the room, and Washington greeted each one. After he had made the circuit of his guests, Washington returned to his place in the room's bow window, and each guest bowed to the chief executive and departed. "By four o'clock this ceremony was over," William Sullivan recalled.

Resettling into Philadelphia did bring some domestic concerns to the families who arrived in 1790. Abigail Adams, the wife of the vice president, discovered that her best gowns were ruined when the ship the family was taking to Philadelphia sprung a leak; she also learned that Bush Hill, their rented country home north of the city, required numerous servants to maintain it and large amounts of firewood to heat it. And like many of the women who employed servants in the post-revolutionary period, Mrs. Adams was learning that the much-touted democracy of the new nation had bad effects on her domestic help. One Philadelphia servant lasted only three days before she was fired for drunkenness. She quickly concluded that hiring free African American servants was a better bet.

The Washingtons' solution to the need for domestic help led to one of the most criticized aspects of their lives and his presidency. George and Martha Washington brought as many as eight or nine enslaved African Americans with them to the President's House. Slavery had of course existed in Philadelphia for more than a century. But by 1790, slavery's future in the northern states was questionable, at best. Pennsylvania had led the way in challenging the establishment of slavery during the revolution. On March 1, 1780, the Pennsylvania Assembly passed the Act for the Gradual Abolition of Slavery, a law that denied any further importation of slaves into the state and declared any children born to slaves from that date onward free. Amendments to the act in 1788 disallowed anyone from transporting enslaved pregnant women out of state, so their children would be born slaves, and it required that any enslaved person brought to Pennsylvania be freed after six consecutive months of residence.

Martha Dandridge Custis Washington (1731–1802), wife of America's first president, as painted by Charles Willson Peale in 1795.

That act, and the Pennsylvania Abolition Society's petition to Congress in early 1790—signed by the group's dying president, Benjamin Franklin—preyed on both Washingtons' minds when they moved to Philadelphia. The Washingtons' solution was to make sure that none of their enslaved servants stayed in the capital city long enough to qualify for freedom. They would transport their servants out of the state before the six months were up, and then return them to the President's House—and life-long slavery—a short time later.

George Washington's domestic life and slave ownership were more complicated than was usual. In 1759, the twenty-six-year-old military hero had married Martha Dandridge Custis, one of Virginia's wealthiest widows. While husbands immediately took possession of their wives' property in eighteenth-century Anglo-America, the property of deceased fathers was held in trust for their children. This was the case for the Custis-Washington family, and one of the reasons that we know so much about their domestic life is because Washington was required to keep a careful record of any expenditures that would affect his stepchildren's inheritance.

When the President and Mrs. Washington moved to Philadelphia in 1790, they brought with them some people whom George Washington owned and some who were owned by his wife and her children. Washington kept a careful account of his slaves, and who owned them, writing to Tobias Lear on April 12, 1791: "As all except Hercules and Paris are dower negroes [belonging to Martha Washington's children], it behoves me to prevent the emancipation of them, otherwise I shall not only loose the use of them, but may have them to pay for."

As part of their plan to keep their slaves enslaved in spite of Pennsylvania law, the Washingtons attempted to keep news of what they were doing from both the general public and their enslaved African Americans. As the first six-month time mark neared, the first couple planned to take Hercules, their enslaved cook, on a trip to their Virginia plantation. "I mentioned that Hercules was to go on to Mount Vernon a few days after that," Lear wrote to Washington.

When he was about to go, somebody, I presume, insinuated to him that the motive for sending him home so long before you was expected there, was to prevent his taking the advantage of a six months residence in this place. When he was possessed of this idea he appeared to be extremely unhappy—and altho' he made not the least objection to going; yet, he said he was mortified to the last degree to think that a suspicion could be entertained of his fidelity or attachment to you, and so much did the poor fellow's feelings appear to be touched that it left no doubt of his sincerity—and to shew him that there were no apprehensions of that kind entertained of him, Mrs Washington told him he should not go at that time; but might remain 'till the expiration of six months and then go home—to prepare for your arrival there. He has accordingly continued here 'till this time, and tomorrow takes his departure for Virginia.

Hercules, the enslaved servant at the center of this correspondence between the president of the United States and his secretary, was one of the most notable characters in the Washington household. He had been chief cook at Mount Vernon for four years, and when the capital relocated to Philadelphia, he was brought north to serve in the kitchen at 190 High Street. Washington's letter to Lear on November 22, 1790, as he departed for the new national capital, noted that "Austin & Hercules goes on in this days Stage, & will, unquestionably arrive several days before us," in Philadelphia. Hercules's son, Richmond, joined his father in the president's household, as a kitchen worker. Hercules's skill was noted by visitors and family members alike, and the Washingtons prized his cooking enough to allow him the unusual reward of being allowed to sell leftovers from the presidential table and keep the profits.

PHILADELPHIA,
March 5.
Yesterday, 4th March,
1793, our beloved and
venerable GEORGE
WASHINGTON,
came to the Senate
Chamber of Congress,
and took the usual
oath of office, which
was administered to
him by Judge Cushing,
at noon, in the pres-
ence of an immense
concourse of his fellow
citizens, members of
both houses of the
United States,
Legislature, and
several foreign minis-
ters consuls, &c—
There was likewise an
assemblage of ladies,
attending on this
solemn occasion, and
the day was extremely
serene; for Providence
has always smiled on
the day of this man,
and on the glorious
cause which has ever
espoused, of LIBER-
TY AND EQUALI-
TY. . .

As the Washington family settled into a rou-
tine in Philadelphia, the president was mindful
of setting precedents that future chief executives
would follow. In his clothing, governing, and
even entertaining, he attempted to strike a balance between the formality befitting a head of
state and the democratic customs of a republic.
Even a moment of national mourning was not
without this debate. When word reached New
York in April 1790 that Benjamin Franklin had
died, the House of Representatives immediately
went into formal mourning, on the motion of
Congressman James Madison. Thomas Jefferson
recommended that the executive branch follow
the House's lead, but Washington demurred,
fearing setting a precedent. Jefferson countered
that the American people put Franklin and
Washington on one side of a line, everyone else
on the other, but Washington refused. The
Senate also refused to go into mourning, as two
of Franklin's old political foes blocked the
motion. Pennsylvania Senator William Maclay
fumed that the inaction was "really insulting."

One of the precedents that Washington was
most anxious to set was that presidents were not
elected for life. He planned to retire after one
four-year term and return to Mount Vernon permanently, fearful that, should he die in office,
no future president would retire from office. By
1792, differing views of government were
already leading to the split that created the first
American party system. Washington's supporters
pressured him to run again, in order to use his
personal popularity to strengthen the national
government. Elizabeth Willing Powel, a close
friend of both George and Martha Washington
who was not above giving him the benefit of her

usual frank opinions, wrote, "The antifederalist would use it for an argument for dissolving the union, and would urge that you, from Experience, had found the present system a bad one, and had, artfully, withdrawn from it that you might not be crushed under its Ruins."

Under pressure from Powel and many others, the president agreed to run for a second term, and once again he was unanimously elected. Washington's second inaugural address, administered this time in the Senate Chamber in Congress Hall, lasted only a few minutes. The moment was both a personal honor for Washington and a sign that the new Constitution worked. But almost immediately, Washington's honors became mixed with hurled insults, and his second term proved full of unforeseen difficulties.

Foreign affairs caused great strife during Washington's second term. America's old ally, France, was in the midst of a bloody revolution of its own. Many, including Secretary of State Jefferson, saw France's revolution as the logical continuation of America's. But soon the excesses in Paris, particular the mass executions epitomized by the guillotine, led many Americans to say that their government should distance itself from France. To further complicate matters, war broke out between England and France in 1793. Now the question posed itself: should America feel bound to its old ally, or side with its former mother country, who controlled the seas and was a valuable trading partner?

Philadelphia had welcomed a new ambassador from revolutionary France, Edmond Charles Genêt, in 1793. Citizen Genêt had arrived in Charleston, South Carolina, that April in the

After taking the oath, the President retired, as he had come, without pomp or ceremony, but on his departure from the house, the people could no longer refrain obeying the genuine dictates of their hearts, and saluted him with three cheers.

—*The Diary or Loudon's Register*, New York, New York, March 6, 1793

midst of his country's war with Britain. Many, including Genêt, expected the American government to support its former ally, but Washington sought to remain neutral in the European war. Genêt disregarded President Washington's statements of neutrality and did everything he could to bring the United States into the conflict, including fitting out privateers from American ports to raid British ships and ports. Genêt went so far as to threaten that he would go around Washington and appeal directly to the people for support. John Adams would later write of "the terrorism excited by Genêt in 1793, when ten thousand people in the streets of Philadelphia day after day threatened to drag Washington out of his house, and effect a revolution in the Government, or compel it to declare war in favor of the French revolution."

In the midst of international crises and a widening divide between the members of his own cabinet, George Washington and his fellow residents of Philadelphia faced a cataclysmic event: the yellow fever epidemic of 1793. The disease drove the government from Philadelphia, killed some five thousand people, and crippled the city in the months that the fever raged (see Chapter 15). Congress reconvened on December 5, 1793, only once it was again safe to meet in Philadelphia, as frost and cold weather had killed the mosquitoes that carried the disease.

Many forces were trying to pull the United States into war, but the president's neutrality policy held. He devoted most of his 1793 address to Congress to explaining the causes for his having made the Neutrality Proclamation during Congress' recess. He also submitted documents detailing Genêt's improper behavior and demanded that the minister be recalled. But the government of France had shifted, and with the radical Jacobins now in power, Genêt feared for his life if he returned home. The minister asked for and received asylum in the United States; he eventually received U.S. citizenship and married the daughter of New York Governor George Clinton.

Edmond Charles Genêt, minister plenipotentiary from the newly proclaimed French Republic.

Foreign policy problems did not cease with the end of the Genêt crisis. As Washington's second term progressed, the political factions that grew around Alexander Hamilton and Thomas Jefferson were identified, in part, by their ideas of foreign alliance. While Hamilton favored close ties with England in order to maintain the commercial successes of his supporters, Jefferson saw perpetual ties to France as the key to American foreign policy. As he prepared to resign late in 1793, Jefferson submitted his "Report on the Privileges and Restrictions on the Commerce of the United States in Foreign Countries" supporting ties to France, while his ally James Madison submitted propositions to the House that demanded England treat the United States with justice and respect.

The threat of war with England continued. Despite Washington's efforts to maintain his policy of neutrality, the British repeatedly treated the United States as a belligerent nation. Britain seized American vessels trading in the French Caribbean and enlisted Barbary pirates to attack American shipping, and British troops continued to occupy the American Northwest Territory, in violation of the 1783 treaty that ended the Revolutionary War. Anti-British sentiments, both in Congress and throughout the

United States, seemed to show that another war would be inevitable. In 1794, Washington sent Chief Justice John Jay to England to attempt to gain reparations for seized American vessels, to gain a commercial treaty with Britain, and to end British occupation of the Northwest Territory. When Washington called the Senate into special session to ratify the treaty that Jay secured, deep divisions were evident. Jay had received a guarantee of most favored nation status with Britain, as well as an agreement that the British would leave the Northwest forts by 1796. But he had not secured an agreement that Britain would respect America's right to neutrality. This outraged the Jeffersonian Republicans and caused a serious rift with France. The Senate approved the Jay Treaty by a vote of 20 to 10, exactly the two-thirds required by the Constitution, and Washington signed the treaty into law, but the public uproar continued.

Washington was adamant that he would not seek a third term in office. In 1796, he published in Philadelphia's newspapers his farewell address, a document that he had crafted with the assistance of James Madison and Alexander Hamilton. That fall, the United States underwent its first contested presidential election, in which John Adams narrowly defeated Thomas Jefferson to be the nation's second president. The Washingtons began to prepare to leave the President's House, packing the furnishings they had acquired and planning the futures of the enslaved servants they had brought with them.

Ona Judge was not the only member of the Washington household to declare independence as the first president's term of office came to an end. In March 1797 Hercules, the presidential

☞ Ona Judge

Ona "Oney" Judge was born at Washington's Mount Vernon plantation, sometime around 1773, to Betty, an enslaved woman who was one of the eighty-five dower slaves who were part of Martha Washington's first husband's estate, and Andrew Judge, a white indentured servant working as a tailor on the plantation.

As a young girl, Ona was taken into servitude in the plantation house, to serve and play with Nelly Custis, Martha Washington's granddaughter. By 1789, Ona was personal servant to the first lady, and she moved to New York, dressing Martha Washington's hair each day, seeing to her clothing, and sitting with her, doing needlework. In November 1790, she moved with the presidential household into the President's House in Philadelphia.

Ona Judge was constant companion to Mrs. Washington, and—as one of the dower slaves—was one of the president's primary concerns under the Pennsylvania Abolition Law. Thus, Tobias Lear wrote to his employer on May 15, 1791: "Mrs Washington proposes going over to Jersey for a few days—she makes her visit to Mrs ☞

Ten Dollars Reward.

ABSCONDED from the houſehold of the Preſi-
dent of the United States, on Saturday afternoon, ONEY JUDGE, a light Mulatto girl, much
freckled, with very black eyes, and buſhy black
hair—She is of middle ſtature, but ſlender and deli-
cately made, about 20 years of age. She has many
changes of very good clothes of all ſorts, but they
are not ſufficiently recollected to deſcribe.

As there was no ſuſpicion of her going off, and
it happened without the leaſt provocation, it is not
eaſy to conjecture whither ſhe is gone—or fully,
what her deſign is; but as ſhe may attempt to eſcape
by water, all maſters of veſſels and others are cauti-
oned againſt receiving her on board, altho' ſhe
may, and probably will endeavour to paſs for a free
woman, and it is ſaid has, wherewithal to pay her
paſſage

Ten dollars will be paid to any perſon, (white or
black) who will bring her home, if taken in the
city, or on board any veſſel in the harbour; and a
further reaſonable ſum if apprehended and brought
home, from a greater diſtance, and in proportion to
the diſtance.   FRED. KITT, Steward.
    May 24   ‖3

The Washingtons placed several advertisements seeking Ona Judge's return, including this one in *Claypoole's American Daily Advertiser*, on May 24, 1796. This ad noted the runway's build, age, complexion, and amount of clothing, though it was "not sufficiently recollected to describe."

☞ Dickinson. . . . Mrs Washington takes the children with her & Christopher & Oney. I shall have the honor to attend her on horse back." Martha Washington was guaranteeing that Judge would not live for six consecutive months in Pennsylvania, and thus that she would remain a slave.

As the president's second term neared an end, Martha Washington informed Ona Judge that she was giving her to her granddaughter as a wedding present, an action that would guarantee that Ona would never gain the freedom she was determined to have. Instead, Judge decided to run away.

"Whilst they were packing up to go to Virginia, I was packing to go, I didn't know where," she told a writer almost a half century later, "for I knew that if I went back to Virginia, I should never get my liberty. I had friends among the colored people of Philadelphia, had my things carried there beforehand, and left Washington's house while they were eating dinner." Eventually, she escaped the capital aboard ship, and settled in Portsmouth, New Hampshire.

Martha Washington was furious when she learned about Ona Judge's escape. The president—who popular culture would later record was incapable of telling a lie—violated national law and government ethics by pressuring

cook renowned for his food as well as his style of dress, ran away, too. Sources are unclear as to where Hercules departed from, some indicating he had already been returned to Mount Vernon, others that he departed from 190 High Street. Former president Washington wrote to his steward Frederick Kitt on January 10, 1798: "We have never heard of Herculas our Cook since he left this; but little doubt remains in my mind of his having gone to Philadelphia, and may yet be found there if proper measures were employed to discover (unsuspectedly, so as not to alarm him) where his haunts are."

the federal port agent in Portsmouth to help capture the runaway, using his government position to help regain personal property. The New Hampshire man refused to do it.

In the months to follow, the situation grew more complicated: Ona Judge married a sailor named Jack Staines in New Hampshire, and while she was expecting their first child, the Washingtons learned that—should she be recaptured—they would be the owners of both her and her child. In August 1799, the now former president sent instructions along with his wife's nephew to capture Judge and get her onboard ship, heading for a southern port. The nephew, Burwell Bassett, stayed with Senator John Langton and his family in New Hampshire. The Langtons were old friends of the Washingtons, and their daughter was the one who had informed the first lady of Ona's location, after seeing the former slave on the street in Portsmouth. But Senator Langton was mortified when he heard of the plot to recapture and ship the pregnant woman back to slavery. While hosting Bassett at dinner, he sent a message to Ona to hide or risk reenslavement. She went into hiding and escaped the slave catchers who were looking for her.

Ona Judge Staines lived a free woman for the rest of her life, dying in New Hampshire in February 1848. ⌁

The Washingtons were never able to locate the former cook. Hercules, as the property of Washington himself, was freed by the terms of the late president's will. His wife and children, as property of Martha Washington and her heirs, remained enslaved.

John Adams arrived at Congress Hall on the morning of March 4, 1797, dressed in a gray suit that Benjamin Franklin Bache's *Aurora* praised for its "Republican plainness." The second president stood out in contrast to his pred-

John Adams, second president of the United States, as portrayed by Charles Willson Peale, c. 1791. Like his predecessor, Adams sought to portray "republican simplicity" in his style of dress, but his opponents found him brusque and aristocratic.

ecessor, being considerably shorter and more plump than either Washington or Thomas Jefferson, who earlier that morning had been sworn in as vice president. In his inaugural address, the new president noted he had been:

Employed in the service of my country abroad during the whole course of these transactions, I first saw the Constitution of the United States in a foreign country. Irritated by no literary altercation, animated by no public debate, heated by no party animosity, I read it with great satisfaction, as the result of good heads prompted by good hearts, as an experiment better adapted to the genius, character, situation, and relations of this nation and country than any which had ever been proposed or suggested. In its general principles and great outlines it was conformable to such a system of government as I had ever most esteemed, and in some States, my own native State in particular, had contributed to establish.

"What other form of government, indeed, can so well deserve our esteem and love?" Adams asked the crowd gathered in the House chamber. Describing the ceremony to his wife Abigail, Adams wrote of the now-former president: "Me thought I heard him think, 'Ay! I am fairly out and you are fairly in! See which of us will be the happiest!'"

Indeed, John Adams had few days of celebrating in the three years that he lived in Philadelphia's President's House. The United States found its neutrality policy almost leading itself into war with its former ally a short time later. France, angered by the ratification of the Jay Treaty and also by the election of a president

from the emerging Federalist Party, began a policy of seizing American ships.

The president's attempt to lessen the tension actually made matters worse. Adams sent three commissioners to France to attempt to solve the problems between the two nations, but these negotiations were far from successful. In the spring of 1798, Adams sent his commissioners' dispatches to Congress, documents that revealed that members of the French Directory were attempting to extort large amounts of money from the United States as the basis for any treaty. This event, known as the XYZ Affair (the three letters were used as substitutions for the French officials' names), outraged members of Congress and the public. Expecting the French to declare war, Adams began a policy of armed neutrality: America had not had a navy since at least 1784, but now the Department of the Navy was raised to full cabinet rank; the United States Marine

William Birch's print of Washington's funeral procession passing the High Street Market, December 26, 1799. While the first president had been buried days before at Mount Vernon, local and national leaders conducted a state funeral, with Virginia congressman "Light Horse Harry" Lee intoning, "First in war, first in peace, and first in the hearts of his countrymen."

Corps were revived; and three new frigates were built. Congress appropriated money for arms and defense, and the army was enlarged. For the following two years, the United States was in a state of Quasi-War with France.

The fear of foreigners that grew out of the Quasi-War had dramatic implications for American domestic policy. In 1798, Congress passed the Alien and Sedition Acts. Ostensibly to curtail the actions of new arrivals in the United States, these acts were also used to harass foreign-born Jeffersonian Republicans. The Alien Act expanded the time requirement for immigrants to become citizens and gave the president the power to expel foreigners. The Sedition Acts levied heavy fines on anyone speaking against the government or any of its officials. Thomas Jefferson and James Madison secretly penned the so-called Virginia and Kentucky Resolutions, questioning the constitutionality of both acts. This restriction of the rights of the people led to the discrediting of the Federalist Party and finally to the election of Thomas Jefferson as president in 1800.

While war with France was narrowly avoided, the Adamses' last winter in Philadelphia was marred when news arrived that George Washington had died at Mount Vernon on December 14, 1799. "I feel myself alone, bereaved of my last brother," John Adams wrote in a message to the Senate. On December 26, Philadelphia conducted a day of mourning, with the bells of Christ Church tolling, the city and its people draped in black. After a formal ceremony, hundreds of people crammed into the President's House, in what would be one of its last major functions as the executive mansion.

The following May, Abigail Adams returned to their farm in Quincy, Massachusetts, for the summer, and on May 27, President Adams departed for the new capital, Washington, D.C., and its still-unfinished White House. There, he would live for the remaining months of his presidency, losing his bid for reelection to his vice president, Thomas Jefferson. Abigail Adams did not stay in the capital to watch the rejoicing at her husband's defeat. As she traveled through Philadelphia while returning to Massachusetts, she was angered by the celebrations surrounding Jefferson's election, writing to her husband on February 21, 1801, "I have heard some of the democratic rejoicing such as Ringing Bells and fireing cannon. What an inconsistancy said a Lady to me to day, the Bells of Christ Church ringing peals of rejoicing for an *Infidel President!*"

The Deshler-Morris "Germantown White House," completed in 1773 as an addition to an older structure at its rear. The five-bay Georgian house was the residence of General Howe after the Battle of Germantown in October 1777, and of President Washington during the summers of 1793 and 1794.

FIFTEEN

The Germantown White House and Its Neighbors

GEORGE WASHINGTON and the members of the first federal government faced many challenges in the decade the government sat in Philadelphia. Establishing precedents, figuring out the separation of powers that divided the three branches, and writing and interpreting new laws all filled their hours. But the crisis that had the single most profound impact, that filled every heart with dread and eventually led the government to flee the capital and temporarily resettle in a village outside the city, was a mosquito-borne disease that could turn a healthy person into a feverish, vomiting victim in a matter of hours. The yellow fever epidemic would shake Philadelphia, the capital of the United States, to its foundations in 1793, and the disease would continue to affect the city and its people for the years to follow.

They are Dieing on our right hand & on our Left, we have it oposit us, in fact, all around us, great are the number that are Called to the grave. . . . To see the hurst go by, is now so common, that we hardly take notice of it, in fine we live in the midst of Death. When I see the Metropolis of the United States depopulated, it is too distressing and afecting a sean, for a person young in Life to bear.

—Isaac Heston, September 19, 1793, written ten days before his death from yellow fever

The yellow fever epidemic that raged in Philadelphia from August to November 1793 was one of the most devastating medical emergencies to occur in eighteenth-century America. Early Americans were accustomed to disease, and widespread outbreaks, including the smallpox epidemic that raged during the revolution, as well as a host of others, had affected Philadelphia from its founding. But the 1793 yellow fever outbreak was different: it was debilitating, spread quickly, and carried off far more people than anything citizens had experienced before. "Tis a sickly time now in Philada. And there has been an unusual number of funerals lately here," Elizabeth Drinker recorded in her diary on August 16. The epidemic had just begun. As with the British occupation of Philadelphia in 1777–1778, Drinker's diary provides us with the best glimpse of the city's people at a moment of extreme crisis. Drinker and her family would ride out the storm of sickness in Germantown, about seven miles from the city, receiving regular updates as life in Philadelphia turned to panic and chaos.

The first cases struck along Water Street near Elfreth's Alley and the Drinkers' house on Front Street, close to the Delaware River. In the months that followed, that square block would have the largest number of yellow fever fatalities. The area had become home to white refugees from the French colony of Santo Domingo, where slaves had declared a revolution against their masters, eventually creating the new nation of Haiti. In addition to bringing linguistic and cultural changes to the nation's capital, these French expatriates brought the yellow fever virus to Philadelphia.

Many believed that foul air was the cause of disease. Certainly, Philadelphia's air quality was not one of the city's better attributes. Garbage collection was intermittent at best, and carcasses of rotting animals floated in Dock Creek and the Delaware River. Initially, many believed that a shipment of rotting coffee beans left on a dock was causing the illness by making the air putrid.

Today, we know that yellow fever is transmitted by the bite of *Aedes aegypti* mosquitoes. Females of the species transmit the blood from infected people to others. Philadelphia had experienced a warm winter and dry summer that left only murky standing water that was ripe for mosquito breeding. In addition, Philadelphians kept household water supplies in rain barrels, which became brackish and allowed mosquitoes to propagate. But eighteenth-century science was still years away from germ theories or knowledge of blood transmittal, and doctors had little idea of what was happening to their patients, how to stop the disease's spread, or how to treat those already infected.

Dr. Benjamin Rush (1746–1813), one of Philadelphia's most eminent men of science, whose medical training left him ill-prepared for the devastation the yellow fever epidemic of 1793 brought. Portrait by Charles Willson Peale (1818), after an original by Thomas Sully.

Panic began to sweep the city. Wealthy families who owned country houses fled the town, leaving unlucky servants to care for city residences. As the Washingtons prepared to leave the capital for Mount Vernon, the couple invited their close friend Elizabeth Powel to join them on their journey to Virginia. On August 9, she wrote to thank them, but declined the offer: "After a long conversation with him [Samuel Powel, who was now the president of the Pennsylvania State Senate], I collected that he saw no Propriety in the Citizens fleeing from the only Spot where Physicians conversant with the Disorder that now prevails could be consulted, nor does he appear to be impressed with the degree of Apprehension that generally pervades the Minds of our Friends—however he wished me to follow my own Inclination and the Dictates of my own Judgement in a Matter that may eventually affect my Life and his Happiness—this has thrown me into a Dilemma the most painful. The Conflict between Duty and Inclination is a severe Trial of my Feelings; but as I believe it is always best to adhere to the line of Duty. . . . The Possibility of his being ill during my Absence & thereby deprived of the Consolation and Aid, he might derive from my Attention to him would be to me a lasting Source of Afflictions." Samuel Powel would die of yellow fever on September 29 at his country house west of the city.

At the end of August, Dr. Benjamin Rush estimated that 325 people had already died. Of the 50,000 people who resided in the city, approximately 5,000 would die by the time the epidemic ended, a staggering 10 percent of the population. Hundreds more caught the disease and felt its devastating effects, but survived. Everyone in Philadelphia, regardless of wealth or position, would feel its consequences for years to come, in experiences ranging from the loss of loved ones to the changed political atmosphere of the city. Between August 1 and December 25, 1793, 1,426 burials were recorded in the Strangers' Burying Ground in Washington Square. Though that number reflected a massive increase in the number of people interred there, it was quite likely a vast underestimation on the part of the sexton and clerks of Christ Church and St. Peter's Parish, the men charged each year with tallying Philadelphia's dead.

Bill of Mortality, Philadelphia, 1793. Matthew Whitehead and John Ormrod, members of the United Congregation of Christ Church and St. Peter's, were charged with tallying the results of Philadelphia's baptisms and deaths in 1793. In the right-hand column, they recorded 5,019 deaths since August 1, 1,426 in the Strangers' Burial Ground alone.

When the full effects of the epidemic hit Philadelphia, most of the social institutions which made the city function collapsed. The governments of the city, county, state, and country—all headquartered in buildings on the State House Square—shut down, as officials from councilmen to the president of the United States abandoned the city. President Washington departed on September 10, and Vice President John Adams, Secretary of State Thomas Jefferson, and leaders of the congress left, too. Secretary of the Treasury Alexander Hamilton contracted yellow fever and recovered with the help of a physician who had known the disease while living in the Caribbean, but he found it

Bush Hill, once the country estate of Andrew Hamilton, the Philadelphia lawyer and politician intimately connected with the design of Independence Hall, was later a rental home for John and Abigail Adams. In 1793, it was pressed into service as hospital for the numerous victims of the yellow fever epidemic.

BUSH-HILL,

difficult to return to his home in New York to recuperate, due to the spreading panic around the nation. Churches, clubs, and philanthropic organizations all saw similar flights of their leaders, or worse, their sudden deaths from the mysterious disease.

The yellow fever epidemic brought out the worst in some of the people of Philadelphia. As the churches' burial grounds and the pit graves of the Strangers' Burying Ground at Washington Square filled up, fear crippled most people's sense of duty or kindness. Spouses abandoned their fatally ill partners for fear of contracting the disease. Neighbors ignored the plight of orphans left alone in houses with their dead parents lying nearby.

But it also brought out the very best in others. Dr. Rush and other physicians worked exhausting hours, using the best techniques they could muster to treat their patients. Mayor Matthew Clarkson stayed in the city despite the risk to his own health. In the years immediately following the revolution, the position of mayor had been one with relatively little power, a remnant of a fear of strong executives that remained from the revolutionary era. But Clarkson proved himself to be willing to ignore those restraints when the crisis demanded it, and he rallied citizens to establish a hospital at Bush Hill north of the city, care for the sick, and assume other tasks.

With so much of society in turmoil, Mayor Clarkson turned to Philadelphia's black community, and specifically to the leadership of the Free African Society, for help. Common belief of the time held that African Americans were immune to yellow fever. While incorrect, this idea may have had some grounding in fact: the disease spread with such force because it had been almost unknown in the northeast, and residents had not built up resistance to it, whereas slaves imported from Africa or the Caribbean had been exposed earlier, and therefore did not catch it. But Philadelphia's black population in 1793 was largely native-born and had never been exposed to the disease. They were as likely to contract it as white people were. But Philadelphia's civic and medical leaders, and the leaders of the Free African Society, did not know this, and the myth would cost a number of lives.

Founded in 1787 as a nondenominational group to assist newly freed men and women with their economic, spiritual, and social concerns, the Free African Society provided the heroes who came to the aid of their city in 1793, believing that their resistance to the awful disease imparted some responsibility to help their suffering neighbors. Absalom Jones and Richard Allen, two former slaves who were leaders of Philadelphia's new free African American community, stepped forward to organize blacks to nurse the sick of all races during the epidemic; William Gray agreed to see to the burial of the dead.

Absalom Jones and Richard Allen co-authored *A Narrative of the Proceedings of the Black People during the Late Awful Calamity in Philadelphia in the Year 1793, And a Refutation of Some Censures, Thrown Upon Them in Some Late Publications*, published in 1794. The same white Philadelphians who had fled the city for their own safety were willing to cast aspersions on the African Americans who had stayed in the city to help the sick and dying, charges the two ministers refuted.

When the people of colour had the sickness and died, we were imposed upon and told it was not with the prevailing sickness, until it became too notorious to be denied, then we were told some few died but not many. Thus were our services extorted at the peril of our lives, yet you accuse us of extorting a little money from you.

—Richard Allen and Absalom Jones, *A Narrative of the Proceedings of the Black People During the Late Awful Calamity in Philadelphia in the Year* 1793

The society met on September 5, and immediately sent members out in pairs to survey the situation. Allen and Jones later published an account of their efforts during the epidemic, and the scene they recalled was chilling: The first home they visited was on Emsley's Alley, where they found two young children in a house alone with their dead mother and dying father. By the end of the day, the two men had visited and cared for over twenty families. Soon, the society established a corps of three hundred nurses to care for the sick. Allen and Jones wrote: "Thus were many of the nurses circumstanced, alone, until the patient died, then called away to another scene of distress, and thus have been for a week or ten days left to do the best they could without sufficient rest, many of them having some of their dearest connexions sick at the time and suffering for want while of their husband, wife, father, mother have been engaged in the service of the white people."

While this epidemic raged in his capital, President Washington pondered what he could do, and how far he could go in calling the federal government back to work. The constitution allowed the president to call a special meeting of Congress but did not grant him the authority to change the capital's location. Still, as he received news of the crisis, Washington decided that he must convene at least the executive branch, and he opted to join many of Philadelphia's other refugees in Germantown, seven miles north of the city.

Germantown was first established by German Quaker settlers in 1683, the result of William

William Rittenhouse, a Dutch immigrant, founded Rittenhouse Town in 1690. The seven remaining buildings along the Monoshore Creek, near the modern Lincoln Drive, display the evidence of traditional German building techniques in structures that were once the first paper mill in British North America.

Penn's invitation to settle in his new colony that guaranteed religious freedom. The grant of land Penn gave to Francis Daniel Pastorius drew settlers who were members of other dissenting religious sects, too, including the forerunners of today's Mennonite, Church of the Brethren, and Amish religious groups. Taking up residence along the Indian path known as "the great road" (today's Germantown Avenue and Road), these settlers established a diverse, thriving community by the early eighteenth century. Few of the buildings from the first generations of German settlement survive, or they have been radically altered as use or styles changed. But nearby, along the Wissahickon Creek in Fairmount Park, Rittenhousetown preserves domestic and work spaces that date back to the 1690s. There, Dutch immigrant William Rittenhouse produced the paper that William Bradford used in his Philadelphia print shop, the same shop young Benjamin Franklin entered on his first Monday in Philadelphia in October 1723. David Rittenhouse, who was born in the Rittenhouse dwelling house in 1732, would become one of Franklin's scientific protégés and

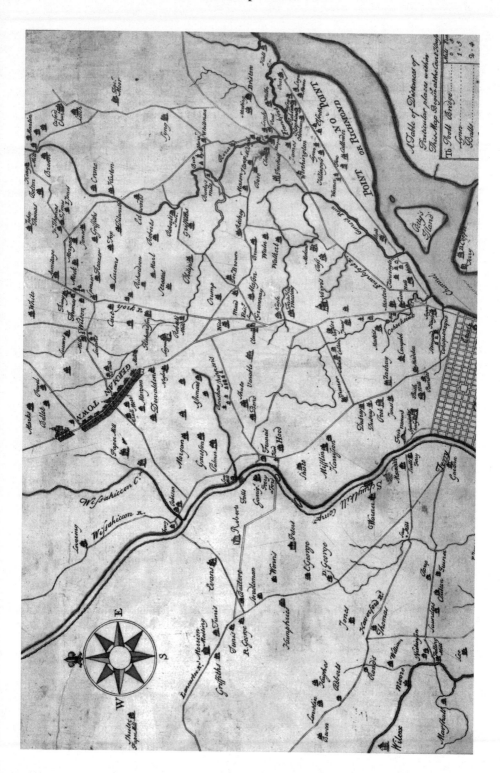

succeed him as president of the American Philosophical Society.

The village of Germantown grew in the first decades of Pennsylvania settlement, with numerous houses built of local stone lining Germantown Road. By the 1720s, the village and its outskirts took on a new role as wealthy Philadelphians bought land to build country houses. James Logan, the Irish-born Quaker who came to Pennsylvania in 1699 as William Penn's personal secretary, built his country house Stenton around 1728 on his 500-acre farm, declaring, "I am about purchasing a plantation to retire to for I am heartily out of love with the world." Logan's rise to success and wealth mirrored the colony that he served for most of his adult life.

Years later, Logan told Benjamin Franklin of his voyage to the colony with William and Hannah Callowhill Penn: while at sea, the ship on which they were traveling was approached by a suspected pirate ship. The captain ordered all noncombatants below deck, and Penn and his family took shelter there. Logan, however, chose to remain on deck, helping the crew prepare for an impending attack. It turned out that the ship approaching them was not a threat, however, and when the young secretary went below to inform his employer that they were safe, Penn sternly chastised him in front of other Friends for his military actions. Angered, Logan said "I being thy servant, why did thee not order me to come down? But thee was willing enough that I should stay and help to fight the ship when thee thought there was danger." Logan's life revealed the complexity of Quaker beliefs and actions in

Opposite, "German Town," located seven miles northwest of Philadelphia, as depicted in Nicholas Scull and George Heap's 1777 "A Plan of the City and Environs of Philadelphia" (detail). James Logan's Stenton is shown just south of the village, to the right of the Germantown Road. The Rittenhouse family's paper mill is to the left, along Wissahickon Creek.

Stenton, James Logan's plantation house located four miles northwest of central Philadelphia, was built between 1727 and 1730. Owned by the Logan family for six generations, it is one of the most intact and authentic colonial homes in the United States.

the changing world of eighteenth-century Pennsylvania.

James Logan had been a dedicated employee and friend to the Penns over the decades that witnessed his rise in Pennsylvania colonial politics as well as acquiring wealth in land and fur trading. By 1730, when he moved to Stenton, he was following the English custom of owning a finely appointed country house that removed him from the noise and dirt of the city, but was near enough that he and his visitors could return in a short ride. Stenton sat far back from Germantown Road, south of the village itself.

In the years that followed, other prosperous Philadelphians began to purchase country houses in or near Germantown. Philadelphia's leaders, including William Allen, who built his estate Mount Airy north of Germantown near the village of Chestnut Hill, and Benjamin Chew, the chief justice of Pennsylvania who presided over the colonial courtroom in the

Pennsylvania State House, and built Cliveden, set the tone for spending winters in the city but summering in the countryside.

George Washington's return to Germantown on November 1, 1793, must have conjured some odd memories for the first president of the young country. As he settled into the house he rented from Colonel Isaac Franks, he was just a short distance down the Germantown Road from Cliveden, where he had suffered defeat by the British army on October 4, 1777, during the Battle of Germantown. Chief Justice Chew's elegant Georgian country estate proved to be more than just ornamental: its cut stone walls deflected American musket balls when British troops barricaded themselves into the house, turning it into a fortress. Today, the splendid exterior still shows the marks of shot and cannon fire, as the American army made a futile attempt to stop the British invasion of Philadelphia. Defeated, Washington's army moved to winter quarters at Valley Forge. The memories of bitter cold and starving soldiers without shelter or clothing probably gave little comfort to the former commander, who now faced another crisis of equally great proportions.

During that battle, General Sir William Howe had used the house that Washington now rented as his headquarters. Franks's house had been built by David Deshler, a Quaker merchant, along the Germantown Road beginning in 1752. Like many Philadelphia houses, the one the president now occupied had started as a smaller structure, which had grown over time as the owner's wealth allowed. The original small house, with four rooms, became the house's service wing, or "dependency," when Deshler

William Allen (1704–1780) was one of the staunchest supporters of the Penn family's proprietorship, and he made a sizable fortune in land investments through that support. In 1750, he built Mount Airy, a country house along the Germantown Road between Germantown and Chestnut Hill, helping to establish the fashion of wealthy families summering in the area. The Allen family became Loyalists, and the house was confiscated during the American Revolution and razed in the nineteenth century. Portrait by Robert Feke (1746).

On October 4, 1777, Washington's army suffered a defeat on the front lawn of Cliveden, country house of Chief Justice Benjamin Chew, when British troops barricaded themselves within the house's sturdy cut stone walls (*see page 196*). Scars of the battle are still visible on the building's façade.

I have taken a house in Germantown . . . commodious for myself and the entertainment of company.

—George Washington, 1793

added an elegant five-bay Georgian front wing in 1772, facing the Market Square and Main Street, as Germantown Avenue was then known. Deshler finished his English-style house just in time for it to be invaded by the British. After the American defeat at Germantown, General Howe stayed two more weeks in the Deshler house.

Isaac Franks bought the house after Deshler's death in 1792 and twice played landlord to the president of the United States. The house's time as the presidential residence in 1793 was brief but eventful. Just before the yellow fever epidemic had begun, Edmond Genêt, France's new ambassador, had aroused rioting in the capital. At the cabinet meetings held in his Germantown house, Washington listened to Alexander Hamilton and Thomas Jefferson debate the country's policy on neutrality in the war between France and England, as Secretary of War Henry Knox argued for war against France. And the president continually monitored the situation in Philadelphia, where death tolls rose daily during the yellow fever epidemic.

Philadelphia's refugees remained in Germantown well into November, until cold weather finally killed off the infected mosquitoes, and it became safe to return to the city. On November 13, Elizabeth Drinker awoke to find "it was snowing fast, ye houses and trees covered. How much more beautiful the appearance than in the City! and what in ye country is not?" Two days later, with the crisis seemingly over, she asked her friend James Pemberton if she could borrow the services of James Oronoko Dexter, the African American coachman and leader of the free black community whom Drinker had grown to know well and trust. The next day, Dexter drove Elizabeth and her son back to their home on Front Street. "We are all through mercy . . . highly favored," she wrote. "Most of ye Philadelphians are returned to ye City."

The president of the United States and his cabinet returned in the days that followed. On November 24, George Washington wrote to Burgess Ball from Germantown, reporting, "The malady with which Philadelpa has been sorely afflicted, has, it is said, entirely ceased; and all the Citizens are returning to their old habitations again. I took a house in this town when I first arrived here, & shall retain it until Congress get themselves fixed; altho I spend part of my time in the City." Congress returned to the city the following month, and the Washingtons took up residence at the President's House once again.

Sir:

On my return from Lancaster, I found, that Major Franks had agreed to let you have his house. But the terms are excessive; being no less than 150£ per annum, or for a shorter period, not under six months, at the same rate. Except a looking-glass or two, and a few pictures, he will not suffer any of the furniture to remain; tho' I have prevailed upon his agent to permit a couple of beds and some chairs and tables to continue, until you can accommodate yourself from some other quarter. But I have made no conclusive bargain; leaving this . . . free for your choice.

—Attorney General Edmund Randolph to President George Washington, Germantown, October 22, 1793

ᴥ Architecture: Country Houses

A public health emergency drove George Washington to move to Germantown in late 1793, but when the president rented the same house the following summer, he was part of a rising trend among elite, urban Americans to leave the city for healthier climates in the hottest months of the year. The American country house was a new phenomenon of the eighteenth century, a reaction to the increasing crowdedness of colonial port cities and the resulting diseases, as a rising number of city dwellers could afford to keep a summer residence outside major cities like New York, Charleston, and Philadelphia. In the South, wealthy owners may have lived and done business in the cities, but their plantations had defined the planters' world for more than a century; in the North, however, country houses were devoted to summer recreation and health, rather than centerpieces of a plantation economy. Philadelphians did use their rural land for more modest food production: Samuel Powel's account books for Powelton, his land along the Schuylkill River west of Philadelphia, record crops and livestock production that would fill the table of his Third Street mansion, for example.

James Logan was not the first Philadelphian to venture into the surrounding countryside when he built his country seat, Stenton, in the late 1720s. By the time Logan moved into the elegant new estate, Samuel Preston had built Bellair, southwest of Philadelphia, and Isaac Norris had constructed Fairhill, not far from Germantown Road south of Stenton. In each of these country houses, these colonial leaders and their families could entertain, enjoy fresh air, and avoid the crowds, dirt, and noise that filled the heart of the nearby city.

Bellair (right) was the rural house of provincial treasurer Samuel Preston, built between 1714 and 1720. With its Flemish bond brick pattern and symmetrical bays of entrance door and windows, it signaled Philadelphians' move to adopting Georgian architecture in their country places. Later, more elaborate Georgian country estates included Woodford (top) and Mount Pleasant (middle), two grand country villas located near the Schuylkill River, on land that is now part of Fairmount Park.

In the years leading up to the American Revolution, Philadelphia country houses became architectural masterpieces, as well as places for leisure and recreation. Woodford, built by Benjamin Franklin's fellow Junto member William Coleman in the late 1750s and expanded by David Franks and his family in 1772, survives as one of the outstanding Georgian country houses in the city. Not far from Woodford on the banks overlooking the Schuylkill River is Mount Pleasant, built in 1763 by Captain John Macpherson, who had made his fortune during the Seven Years' War. He hired Philadelphia master builder Thomas Nevell to create an outstanding Georgian country estate, which John Adams described as "the most elegant seat in Pennsylvania."

During the last years of the eighteenth century, these country houses would serve as centers of entertainment for leaders of the new national government, and their papers often tell of excursions to the country estates along the Schuylkill, in West Philadelphia, or near Germantown. Ironically, as many of these country estates helped Philadelphians survive the yellow fever epidemics of 1793, 1794, and 1798, yellow fever also helped many of the Schuylkill villas survive. In the early 1800s, concerned that a fresh water supply was essential for the city and conscious that disease-carrying mosquitoes bred in stagnant water, the city of Philadelphia bought up the country estates along the river to guarantee the purity of their drinking water, creating Fairmount Park. Today, many of these country houses have been restored and are open to the public. ✄

Isaac Norris's Fairhill, one of the earliest examples of a country estate built by a wealthy Philadelphia Quaker, was located north of the city. The residence included a cupola atop its roof and a walled forecourt (items that historians now believe were copied, and later lost, at James Logan's Stenton). British troops burned Fairhill during the American Revolution.

William Birch's 1800 view of State House, or Independence Square, shows the formal landscape added after the revolution, the flattened roof installed after the original wooden portion of the bell tower rotted, and the Federal-style Philosophical and Library Halls in the distance. Birch often included illustrations of American Indian diplomatic delegations in his images of Philadelphia.

SIXTEEN

Philadelphia
as the
Nation's Capital

W HEN THEY ARRIVED in the City of
Brotherly Love in late 1790, the members of the first government serving under the
United States Constitution could immediately
see a host of reasons why Philadelphia could call
itself the metropolis of America. Philadelphia's
economy had begun to revive from its postwar
slump, and the shops were now full of merchan-
dise, buildings were undergoing repair, and the
port on the Delaware River was busy again.

Just west of Independence Hall, congressmen
encountered the newly constructed county
courthouse, now redubbed Congress Hall,
where they would meet. Congress Hall had considerably less space than Federal Hall, the legislative branch's New York quarters from 1789 to
1790. But members of the House of Represen-

The rapid growth of this City is wonderful—It is little more than a Century, since it was the residence of untutored Nature. . . . Now, Arts, Science, and all the variety of their improvements flourish here— Philadelphia is indeed the Metropolis of the American World and, it is advancing forward to a state of high perfection.

—Judith Sargent Murray, July 3, 1790

tatives could step out of their chamber's eastern door and stroll around the transformed State House Square. The land where the Declaration of Independence had its first public reading on July 8, 1776, had often been used as a dumping ground or storage yard by colonial officials, filled with old munitions and a large, multiseat privy. Now, it was laid out and landscaped in the style of a London square. Judith Sargent Murray described it in June 1790 as a "garden . . . tastefully and elegantly arranged, the whole being disposed in enchanting, and various order—the gravel walks are, alternatively, in a direct line, or pursue a serpentine course. . . . Interjacent Lawns delight the eye, a great variety of well pruned trees shade, and beautify. . . . These walks, and the surrounding views, are indeed charming, and perhaps they want only to be more spacious to equal any, prominades which our globe can exhibit."

In addition to gardens, the new national capital boasted a score of cultural venues and attractions in the 1790s: Charles Willson Peale's museum had moved into nearby Philosophical Hall in 1791; Library Hall, whose façade sported a marble statue of the recently deceased Benjamin Franklin, held one of the most impressive collections of books in the nation; and the University of Pennsylvania was not far away. Numerous amusements were available, from the elegant salons hosted by wealthy ladies to Philadelphia's rambunctious circus performances. The city's diverse religious denominations flourished under Philadelphia's freedom of religion, which the Bill of Rights would guarantee for the whole nation the next year.

And for those willing to risk the scandal, Philadelphia had a theater. "'The Play house is a school for vice,'" Philadelphians repeatedly told Judith Murray, she reported in a letter to her sister, bemoaning that she would not at last have the opportunity to attend a play during her visit in 1790. Murray was in town with her husband, a founder and clergyman of the Universalist Church, and thus she feared the gossip if she were seen in the theater. But the Murrays' new friends persuaded the minister's wife that it would be alright, and on July 10, 1790 (wearing a dark bonnet and shawl to mask her appearance), she attended a performance of Royal Tyler's play *The Contrast*—the 1787 comedy that had been the first American play to be performed by a professional company.

Chestnut Street Theatre sat just west of Sixth Street, a few steps from Congress Hall (left). The playhouse provided Philadelphians and their visitors with the latest plays from London, to the delight of some but the mortification of Quakers and others who thought theaters were "a school of vice."

Behind it [the State House] is a garden, which is open for company to walk in. It was planned and laid out by Samuel Vaughan, Esq. a merchant of London, who went out a few years ago, and resided some time at Philadelphia. It is particularly convenient to the House of Representatives, which being on the ground floor, has two doors that open directly into it, to which they can retire to compose their thoughts, or refresh themselves after any fatigue of business, or confer together and converse, without interrupting the debate.

—Henry Wansey's Journal, June 7, 1794

In addition to entertainments, Philadelphia's leaders offered every possible incentive to welcome—and, they hoped, keep—the national government in their city: they established a lottery to pay for a City Hall, east of Independence Hall, where the United States Supreme Court could hold its twice-yearly sessions; they convinced financier Robert Morris to rent his High Street mansion for the temporary president's residence; they made plans to build an even more elegant executive mansion three blocks away; and Philadelphia prepared its new County Courthouse to welcome the two elected houses of the national legislature.

When congressmen arrived in December 1790, they found themselves in elegant surroundings. Philadelphians had been planning to build city and county buildings to join the complex of buildings around the State House since 1737. Construction of the county courthouse began in 1787, but Pennsylvania decided to convert the building for the Congress' use instead. Philadelphia craftsmen were renowned furniture-makers, and state leaders commissioned one of the city's best to furnish Congress Hall. Thomas Affleck made banks of elegant mahogany desks and black leather armchairs for the House of Representatives, set in a curve that faced the House Speaker's chair. For the Senate chamber on the second floor, he made individual desks and red leather chairs. Congress brought only books, papers, and the House of Representatives' mace with them from New York.

The democratic beliefs of the revolutionary generation led to the first major alteration to Congress Hall: the addition of an observation

Philadelphia's new County Court House, renamed Congress Hall, housed the U.S. Senate on the second floor and House of Representatives on the first from late 1790 to early 1800.

gallery in the House of Representatives chamber. At the north end of the room, facing the Speaker's chair, this "very capacious gallery" could seat 300 to 400 people. While other legislatures in Britain and its American colonies had been open to visits from the "better sort"—special guests of legislators—observing the United States Congress was to be more democratic. As members of the House debated, this area was often filled to capacity. Congress rivaled circuses, bear baiting, and musical events as a lively entertainment for Philadelphians and their visitors.

A growing country soon resulted in another major change to Congress Hall. In 1790, the federal government conducted the first federal census, and learned that the population of the United States was much larger than they had estimated. The 1793 reapportionment increased

The chambers of the two houses of Congress: the House chamber, restored to reflect its appearance after the 1790 U.S. Census showed a far larger population requiring a greater number of representatives in Congress, and the Senate chamber. The "upper house" had a more elaborate decorative style, and its members received individual desks.

Finding the Congress was still sitting, and expected to adjourn every day, I lost no time in going to hear the debates. . . . On entering the House of Representatives, I was struck with the convenient arrangement of the seats for the members. The size of the chamber was about one hundred feet by sixty. . . .

the House from 69 to 105 members. To accommodate them, the building was expanded by an additional twenty-six feet to the south (an addition that is still noticeable in the brick façade facing Independence Hall). The speaker's dais was moved from the south to the west wall of the building.

From the moment they first met in New York City, the members of the executive and legislative branches under the new Constitution realized that their actions might become precedents for the nation to follow in the future. Pennsylvania Senator William Maclay quickly grew weary of the self-awareness of his colleagues in the government, comparing them to a bunch of youths being trained by a dancing master. John Adams, the first vice president and presiding officer of the Senate, struggled with the question of how to welcome President-elect George Washington for his 1789 inauguration. "Gentlemen," Maclay recorded Adams saying, "I feel great difficulty how to act." Maclay developed an intense dislike of Adams, a great suspicion of Alexander Hamilton, and eventually a disgust with President Washington.

When Congress began meeting in Philadelphia in December 1790, it arrived with a host of issues under debate, primarily the series of financial reform programs that Alexander Hamilton was presenting. While in Philadelphia, Congress would create the Bank of the United States and the U.S. Mint, centralizing finance and currency in ways unheard of in colonial America. But finance was not the only issue they faced. In February 1791, following the guidelines set by the Northwest Ordinance of 1787, which stated that the United States would not become an empire with colonies, Congress welcomed Vermont as the fourteenth state, entering the union in complete equality with the original thirteen. Congress would admit delegates from the new states of Kentucky in 1792 and Tennessee in 1796 while meeting in Congress Hall.

While many of the precedents Congress set during its decade in Philadelphia held long-lasting benefits to future generations of Americans, others were detrimental. One of the most controversial was the passage of the Fugitive Slave

The seats in three rows formed semi-circles behind each other, facing the speaker, who was in a kind of pulpit near the centre of the radii, and the clerks below him. Every Member was accommodated for writing, by there being likewise a circular writing desk to each of the circular seats. Over the entrance was a large gallery, into which were admitted every citizen, without distinction, who chose to attend. . . . Over the door I observed a bust of Dr. Franklin, the great founder of their liberties, and the father of their present constitution.

—Henry Wansey's Journal, June 5, 1794

Old City Hall, completed in 1791, housed the sessions of the United States Supreme Court during the decade the federal government met in Philadelphia, an era when the court was still establishing its role within the new nation.

Act on February 12, 1793. The Constitution supported the institution of slavery, counting enslaved people as only three-fifths of a person in the census in apportioning membership in the House or presidential electors. While Article 4, section 3 of the Constitution guaranteed the rights of slave owners to recovery runaways, the 1793 act allowed any master or slave catcher to capture and transport any African American person after giving oral testimony to a state or federal judge claiming that the person was a runaway. The alleged runaway was denied trial by jury, and the judge's ruling was final. The law fined any free person who attempted to help an alleged runaway $500. Northern states, fearing that the law would lead to the kidnapping of free blacks, began to pass Personal Liberty Laws. In 1842, in the case of *Prigg v. Pennsylvania*, the U.S. Supreme Court ruled these liberty laws unconstitutional. With Congress' passage of the

☞ William Maclay

"Ceremonies endless ceremonies the whole business of the day," Senator William Maclay recorded in his diary on Saturday, April 25, 1789. He had just assumed his duties as one of the first members of the United States Senate, representing Pennsylvania alongside Robert Morris, "the financier of the Revolution," as the new government met in New York City.

William Maclay was perhaps the least famous man to take a seat in the first Congress, and perhaps one of the least lucky. He drew an unfortunate lot and was one of the men whose term was to be just two years (the Senate divided into thirds, each group drawing a term of two, four, or six years, so a third of the senators would face re-election every two years in the years to follow), and the Pennsylvania Assembly did not reelect him in the spring of 1791. But Maclay's short two years in the Senate were very productive in one sense: he kept a diary, a document that gives detailed if opinionated observations on the actions of the federal government in its first meetings.

Pennsylvania's William Maclay (1734–1804), the least famous member of the first U.S. Senate, whose diary tells us the most about the body's debates.

William Maclay was born July 27, 1734, in Chester County, Pennsylvania, the son of an Irish immigrant. Maclay fought in the Seven Years' War, worked for the Penn family as a surveyor prior to the revolution, and then supported the revolutionary cause. During and after the war, he assumed leadership roles in Pennsylvania.

The state assembly chose William Maclay to be one of its first senators for several reasons (senators would not be directly elected by the people until after the Seventeenth Amendment was ratified in 1913): he was a westerner, living in Harrisburg, the town his father-in-law John Harris had founded along the Susquehanna River, and he supported agrarian interests, while still having experience and contacts in Philadelphia. Perhaps Pennsylvania's state legislators had learned their lesson; when they chose delegates to the Constitutional Convention in 1787 they had appointed only men from Philadelphia County, angering rural men who subsequently threatened to oppose the document's ratification. Maclay would be a western voice in the United States Senate, if not always a very happy one. ☞

In my usual round in the royal square, from Congress hall to the house of state, in which placed the wise akers of America are framing laws for the citizens of these United States, I carelessly sauntered into the city court house, where the federal supreme court was sitting. I had been there but a few minutes, when I was accosted, by a plain, decent, elderly looking man, thus; "canst thou tell me, friend, whether those servants of the people on yon elevated seats, dressed in party coloured robes of livery, cannot pass sentence according to law, on right or wrong, without being cloathed in that Harlequin dress?" I replied, "I had heard they could not." He shrugged his shoulders and said, "Poor Americans! . . .

☞ "Mr. Maclay possesses great talents for government . . . in his manners he is a perfect republican," Dr. Benjamin Rush wrote. Still, Abigail Adams reported that her husband "did not like pensilvana's chusing a man who had never been heard of before, he might be a good man, but he wanted those men in office whose fame had resounded throughout all the states," a sentiment that seems to have been typical of others' reactions to Maclay.

Maclay's diary, which was not published until 1880, reveals the intricate discussions and debates that took place during Congress' first two years. Congressmen argued about how much the two houses should follow Parliament's traditions; how the United States should react to Barbary pirates kidnapping American sailors in the Mediterranean; and how the federal government could solve the economic problems that had plagued the country for years. Maclay was particularly upset that the Senate met in secret and twice attempted to pass legislation to open the debates to the public, something that did not happen until 1795, four years after he left office.

Maclay's days following the Congress's arrival in Philadelphia in December 1790 were filled with jockeying to convince members of the state assembly to reelect him to his Senate seat, an event he quickly realized would be unlikely. Pennsylvania legislators, sharply divided over support for their own new state constitution as well as national events, could not come to a decision of who should have the seat, and instead left it vacant for the years to follow. After his short term in the Senate, William Maclay returned to Harrisburg, where he remained active in state politics until his death in 1804. ◁

Fugitive Slave Law of 1793, African Americans saw their dreams of freedom destroyed in courtrooms across the new nation, including the ones surrounding Independence Hall.

❧

In the decade that the U.S. Supreme Court met on Independence Square, it likewise worked to clarify its role in the new nation. Of the three branches of government created by the Constitution, the judiciary was the least defined. The federal government laid out the parameters of the nation's courts in the years to follow, but it would be almost a generation before the Court took on a strong role in the government.

New York's John Jay, a skilled diplomat and administrator, was appointed by President George Washington as the first chief justice of the United States.

Article III of the Constitution states: "The Judicial Power of the United States shall be vested in one supreme Court, and in such inferior Courts as the Congress may from time to time ordain and establish." Opinions varied on what the role of the courts should be. Many founders—including James Madison—believed that the Articles of Confederation's lack of a national judiciary was one of the key disadvantages of that system; others remembered Britain's colonial judges as arbitrary tyrants.

The Judiciary Act of 1789 established that there would be a chief justice and five associate justices (as compared to the eight associates who now serve). Immediately, President Washington nominated six geographically diverse men to the court in September 1789, including New York's John Jay as chief justice. By the time the justices of the Supreme Court reached Philadelphia for their February term in 1791, their role in the national government was still vague, and they had accomplished relatively little. They had met twice in New York in 1790, had sworn in lawyers to practice before them, and adjourned without deciding any cases. The Court made no rulings in its first two years in Philadelphia, and would hear only eighty-seven cases prior to its 1801 term.

If that is the case, your independence has not mended your condition much, your liberty is but a shadow indeed, when you carry the badges of European slavery on your backs to your seats of justice."

—*Dunlap's American Daily Advertiser*, February 9, 1793

Oliver Ellsworth (1745–1807) was nominated by Washington to be chief justice on March 3, 1796, following John Jay's resignation and the Senate's failing to confirm John Rutledge for the post. His brief tenure helped define the court's role, including rulings on judicial review and the separation of powers. Like Jay, he carried out diplomatic missions during his time as chief justice.

Several factors contributed to the court's identity problem. The 1789 act required justices to travel throughout the country serving as the federal Circuit Court as well, and they complained bitterly. The first justices were also distracted by nonjudicial roles at times. Chief Justice Jay took on diplomatic duties for President Washington, crafting the massively unpopular treaty with England that bore his name, before he resigned to run for governor of New York in 1795. Justice James Wilson of Pennsylvania made unwise investments in shady land deals, fled the capital, and died in North Carolina in 1798. Of George Washington's first six appointees to the court, only one remained in office past 1800.

But beyond the Court's problems, the justices' limited court rulings point to a major difference between the modern Supreme Court and its eighteenth-century beginnings. In the colonial period, judges were seen as knowledgeable, experienced leaders of the community, not necessarily legal experts. Chief Justice John Jay was a former president of the Continental Congress and a diplomat, but not a judicial authority. Others on the court had more legal experience in their careers, like Justice Wilson, who was a professor of law at the University of Pennsylvania and who had crafted much of the final draft of the Constitution. But, like colonial judges before them, the first Supreme Court justices carried out duties that went far beyond interpreting the law. Congress requested that the justices oversee the first U.S. Census in 1790. Oliver Ellsworth, appointed chief justice after Jay resigned and John Rutledge failed to receive confirmation by the Senate, led a diplomatic

ᴋ⤳ Architecture: The "Federal Style" and Philadelphia Public Buildings

The two Philadelphia buildings that held the legislative and judicial branches of the United States government in the 1790s, Congress Hall and City Hall, are outstanding examples of the changing American tastes following the Revolution, tastes that created the Federal style in architecture.

There was usually a timelag between styles becoming fashionable in the mother country and their gaining popularity in the colonies, and this was certainly true of late Georgian architecture, as the British called it. In fact, by the time the style crossed the Atlantic, the colonies had declared and gained their independence from Great Britain, and the style was renamed Federal in the United States.

Federal style was strongly influenced by architect Robert Adam in Britain, who continued to use the classical patterns of Georgian buildings while he added his personal interpretations of ancient Roman decorative elements to them. Adamesque style replaced the richness of Georgian style with more restrained lines. Pilasters, pillars, and moldings became more flat or narrow; use of ovals, including oval rooms like the ones in Philadelphia's Lemon Hill in Fairmount Park along the Schuylkill River and the White House in Washington, D.C., became fashionable. Windows narrowed, and delicate wooden muntins connected the panes. ᴋ⤳

Federal-style, also known as late Georgian, architecture became highly fashionable in the last years of the eighteenth century. The never-occupied President's House, at Ninth and Market streets used aspects of this neoclassical design: elaborate windows, entrances, and stone pilasters.

The William-Hathurin House, an example of Federal domestic architecture on Spruce Street, was constructed by Philadelphia carpenter William Williams in 1791, during the decade Philadelphia served as the nation's capital.

☞ The Federal style reached Philadelphia just as the city was becoming the new nation's capital in 1790, and its use in prominent government buildings gave the Roman-style architectural pattern a uniquely American tone. In addition to Old City Hall and Congress Hall, the Federal style is also apparent on several other public structures built in these years, including Library Hall and Philosophical Hall, the center wing of the Pennsylvania Hospital, and the Head House at New Market. But the Federal style was also extremely popular in domestic architecture. Both small and large homes embraced the new style. Visitors today can stand in the center of Elfreth's Alley and juxtapose the colonial houses that dominate the lane's south side with the Federal, which are predominantly on the north side. But craftspeople's smaller homes were not the only ones to embrace the new style. Senator William Bingham of Pennsylvania built the grandest Federal house in the capital on south Third Street near Spruce, a building that was razed in the mid-nineteenth century. But many others survive, including the Bishop White House, Physick House, and the Woodlands and Lemon Hill, country houses along the Schuylkill River west of Center City Philadelphia.◁

mission to France in 1799 at the request of President Adams, grew ill while traveling, and resigned by letter from Europe.

The Supreme Court's major judicial decision during its years in Philadelphia was *Chisholm v. Georgia*, in 1793. In the case, the justices ruled 5-1 (with Justice James Iredell of North Carolina dissenting) that citizens of South Carolina could sue the state of Georgia. It was an inauspicious beginning for the court's legal rulings. States complained vociferously that the ruling could destroy them economically. In 1798, the Eleventh Amendment overturned the *Chisholm* ruling.

It was not until after the federal government moved to Washington, D.C., that the Supreme Court established itself as a branch equal to the Congress and presidency, with power to review all laws in the United States. The roots of that transformation took place in Philadelphia, though. Among the attorneys who took the oath of office to practice before the high court in Old City Hall was John Marshall of Virginia, who would eventually lay the foundations for the modern United States Supreme Court.

As Americans divided into the first two political parties while the government was headquartered in Philadelphia in the 1790s, Marshall sided with the Federalist Party—whose leaders included George Washington, John Adams, and Alexander Hamilton—rather than the Democratic-Republicans, led by his distant cousin Thomas Jefferson and James Madison. Adams appointed Marshall secretary of state in May 1799, and in January 1801—as one of his last acts as president—appointed Marshall to be chief justice, to replace the ailing Oliver Ellsworth. Marshall became chief justice on February 4, 1801, serving in both his cabinet post and judicial role until Adams left office on March 4. The second president later wrote: "My gift of John Marshall to the people of the United States was the proudest act of my life."

President-elect Thomas Jefferson was infuriated by Adams's last-minute appointment of Marshall and other judges, saying that the incoming president should fill open judicial spots, rather than allowing lame-duck presidents and congresses to appoint "midnight judges." Yet the appointment stood, and Jefferson and Marshall crafted the modern idea of separation

John Marshall (1755–1835) served in Congress in Philadelphia and then as John Adams's secretary of state prior to his appointment as the third chief justice of the United States in 1801.

of powers between these two branches. In 1809, in Marshall's *Marbury v. Madison* decision, the Court set forth one of its most important rulings: the Supreme Court would have the full power of judicial review, having the final say over the constitutionality of acts by Congress or the president. That idea was one of the most important—and controversial—foundations of American federalism.

The political controversy that divided cousins John Marshall and Thomas Jefferson in the 1790s was not unusual. Increasingly, as the decade wore on, ideological divisions led to animosity in the halls of Congress and in the streets of Philadelphia, and to the creation of the first American political parties.

The emotional pitch of these congressional divisions was perhaps best explained by the strange events of January 30, 1798, and the days that followed. The House of Representatives was in the middle of debating an act of impeachment against Senator William Blount of Tennessee. Blount, it seemed, had attempted to incite Cherokee and Creek Indians to aid British military forces to attack Spanish West Florida. A copy of Blount's letter on the subject had reached President John Adams, and Congress now debated what to do with a senator accused of treason.

On January 30, Irish-born Democratic-Republican Representative Matthew Lyon, known for his hot temper and mean-spirited rhetoric, turned to fellow congressman Roger Griswold, a Federalist, and spat in his face. The reason? Lyon had been in the middle of a loud diatribe on the House floor, saying he could travel from his state of Vermont to Griswold's

"Congressional Pugilists," a 1798 political cartoon depicting the fight that broke out on the House floor in Congress Hall, between representatives Matthew Lyon and Roger Griswold, included the inscription "He in a trice struck Lyon thrice/Upon his head, enrag'd sir,/Who seiz'd the tongs to ease his wrongs,/And Griswold thus engag'd sir."

home state, Connecticut, and after establishing a Democrat-Republican press and newspaper there, convince the people of Connecticut to join his party in six months. More than that, Lyon said, he knew the people of Connecticut, he'd fought them in the past. "Mr. Griswold asked," the *New-York Post and General Advertiser* reported on February 6, "if he fought them with his wooden sword," a reference to the Vermonter's having been court-martialed during the revolution, and made to wear a wooden sword as an embarrassing punishment.

Spitting wasn't the end of the discussion. On February 15, Griswold entered the House chamber and began to beat Lyon with his walking stick. Lyon grabbed a nearby pair of fireplace tongs, and a fight ensued. Congressmen from both parties pulled the two men apart, and—

after the House threatened each of them with expulsion for fighting—they apologized. Lyon received the distinction of being the first congressman in history to be brought up on charges before the House Ethics Committee. Griswold was among the Federalist congressmen to call for dissolving the American union in 1803, following President Thomas Jefferson's purchase of the Louisiana Territory, which they believed threatened the power of northeastern states.

Both Griswold and Lyon were reprimanded, and both were blasted in the press, but usually in different newspapers. By 1798, American newspapers were already entrenched in the heated, sometimes nasty, and occasionally violent world of American party politics. Indeed, the federal era was marked by a return of the tradition of dueling that had disappeared generations before. On June 14, 1804, Alexander Hamilton—the man who had been at the center of many of the factious political debates during Philadelphia's decade as the nation's capital—was killed in a duel over his alleged political slanders. His opponent was Aaron Burr, the vice president of the United States, who soon thereafter returned to his seat presiding over the United States Senate despite the fact that he was facing charges for murder in New York State.

But by the time those events unfolded, the government had left the banks of the Delaware River for the Potomac. On May 14, 1800, Congress fulfilled the terms of the Residency Act that Jefferson and Hamilton had negotiated ten years before, finishing its business in Philadelphia and agreeing that, when they reconvened, they would meet in the new capital city in the District of Columbia. That day, the Senate

"Resolved that the thanks of the Senate of the United States be presented to the Commissioners of the City and County of Philadelphia, for the convenient and elegant accommodations furnished by them for the use of Senate, during the residence of the National Government in this City." It was the end of an era for Philadelphia. The state government had departed for Lancaster the year before, and now the city's role as the federal capital was over, too.

The federal government finished its business in the "convenient and elegant accommodations" on State House Square in May 1800, departing for their summer recess and then to Washington, D.C., the new national capital. William Birch's 1800 print shows the still-busy building, with a crowd of men on Congress Hall's steps.

The Liberty Bell.

SEVENTEEN

The Liberty Bell

FOR ALMOST TWO CENTURIES, the small, cracked, 2,080 pound Liberty Bell, which once hung in the tower of the Pennsylvania State House, has been used as a dramatic physical reminder of the lofty ideals of the Declaration of Independence that was signed in the assembly room below it. Longstanding myths told the inaccurate tale that the bell had rung at the moment the Second Continental Congress voted independence on July 4, 1776. That story was untrue, but the Liberty Bell rang for many significant events, happy as well as sad, during the era of America's founding. The bell began its time in Philadelphia as an integral part of the transforming city, witnessed some of the most important events in the city's history, and then— retired, broken, and eventually reclaimed—has grown to symbolize some of America's central

The Declaration was yesterday published and proclaimed . . . in the State house Yard, by whom do you think? By the Committee of Safety! the Committee of Inspection, and a great Crowd of People[.] Three cheers rended the Welkin. The Battalions paraded on the common, and gave us the Feu de Joy, notwithstanding the scarcity of Powder. The Bells rung all Day, and almost all night. Even the [Christ Church] Chimes, chimed away.

—John Adams,
July 9, 1776

ideas. Like many symbols, the bell became something very different from what it had originally been, and its true origins are often obscured by the myths that have grown around it over the centuries.

When the members of the Pennsylvania Assembly ordered a bell for their State House in 1751, they had no idea that their purchase would one day become a worldwide symbol. Instead, they were heralding the prosperity and success of their colony. At last, the State House was finished, its original building along Chestnut Street now joined by a south wing capped by a bell tower. The State House was still on the outskirts of the town in 1751, and so the Assembly wanted a bell to communicate with the citizens of Philadelphia.

Bells had been used for centuries for just such purposes. Their peals announced political gatherings and warned of impending dangers; when muffled by bags of sand attached to their lips, tolling bells mourned the dead. Before Benjamin Franklin made his startling electrical experiments in 1752, they were even believed to prevent lightning strikes.

Pennsylvania politicians saw their world full of good news for a new bell to announce. Their colony had a unique source of liberty, they believed: the key to Pennsylvania's growing population and commercial wealth lay in the freedoms that William Penn's 1701 Charter of Privileges had given to the people of his colony. Large numbers of men could vote, and religious freedom was guaranteed. Penn's just laws had drawn new and diverse communities of people to the colony, and by 1750 Philadelphia was the largest city in British North America.

On November 1, 1751, Isaac Norris, Thomas Leech, and Edward Warner, members of the Pennsylvania Assembly and superintendents of the State House, ordered the bell. In their letter to Robert Charles, their agent in London, they requested a 2,000 pound bell, for which they expected to pay £100 sterling:

Let the Bell be cast by the best workmen & examined carefully before it is Shipped with the following words well shaped in large letters round it vizt
BY order of the Assembly of the Povince [sic] of Pennsylvania for the State house in the City of Philad^a 1752
and Underneath
Proclaim Liberty thro' all the Land to all the inhabitants thereof
Levit. XXV.10.

Americans have long wondered why Norris and the other superintendents chose this passage from the Old Testament for their State House bell. The full passage describes God's instructions to Moses: "And ye shall hallow the fiftieth year, and proclaim liberty throughout all the land unto all the inhabitants thereof: it shall be a jubilee unto you; and ye shall return every man unto his possession, and ye shall return every man unto his family." The year 1751 was the fiftieth anniversary of William Penn's granting the Charter of Privileges to the colony. Was Norris commemorating Penn's charter? No definitive answer to that question exists, but it is possible in light of the complex nature of Pennsylvania politics in the 1750s.

Norris and his fellow members of the Assembly fiercely stood by the belief that

Thomas Penn (1702–1775), William and Hannah Callowhill's second son, inherited the proprietorship of Pennsylvania with his brothers at their father's death in 1718, and became the chief proprietor upon the death of his brother John in 1746. He spent his adult life trying to make a profit on his father's investment in the colony, and asserting his authority over its elected legislature.

An engraving from Denis Diderot's *Encyclopédie* shows eighteenth-century bell casters at work, using a molded board to shape the bell's exterior.

William Penn had promised them unusual and valued liberties, liberties that they strove to preserve sometimes in opposition to Penn's heirs, who now governed the colony. Norris may have been thinking that celebrating the fiftieth anniversary—or "jubilee" year—of Penn's charter might be one more way to push the version of the founder's memory favored by Norris's party before Penn's sons' eyes.

Thomas Penn and his family were not enthusiastic supporters of the newly built State House. They saw the colonial assembly's financial support of that building project, as well as the Library Company, the Pennsylvania Hospital, and the Academy of Philadelphia, as extravagances, money that could be flowing into the proprietary coffers rather than building up the colonial capital. In essence, Thomas Penn was a dissatisfied landlord who took little delight in civic improvements in his family's colony. Thomas was far more aligned temperamentally with his grandfather Admiral Sir William Penn's aristocratic, courtly life than the simplicity his parents' Quaker beliefs demanded. Indeed, Thomas's marriage to Lady Julianna Pomfret brought his identification as a Quaker and attendance at Friends religious services to an end. The proprietor was feeling less and less compassion for the leaders of Pennsylvania's colonial assembly.

When the bell finally arrived from England, it immediately cracked. It may have been damaged in transit, or it may have been defective from the start, or perhaps overly enthusiastic citizens had broken it. But in any event, the leaders of the Pennsylvania Assembly now had a very large chunk of metal that didn't work. After much discussion, local craftsmen John Pass and John Stow melted the bell down to recast it, but these amateur bellmakers added metal and changed the composition of the bell, resulting in a "clang" that was painful to the townspeople's ears. So it was back to the drawing board for Pass and Stow, and back to the melting pot for the bell. On the third try, Pennsylvania finally had a State House bell that worked, for a while.

Once hung in the State House tower, the bell announced moments of celebration and sadness to Pennsylvania's citizens, including increasing strife on Pennsylvania's frontier during the Seven Years' War and Pontiac's Uprising in 1764, and growing tension between the mother country and the colonies in the years that followed. Parliament's passage of the Stamp Act, which

Metalsmith John Stow's mark on the reverse of a drawer pull's escutcheon, a more typical product of the amateur bellmaker's work.

The Bell rings, and I must go among the Grave ones, and talk Politicks.

—Benjamin Franklin to Catherine Ray. October 16, 1755

would tax paper, playing cards, and even death certificates, led to riots throughout the colonies. When John Hughes, Deborah Franklin's kinsman, received an appointment as commissioner of stamps, the appointment did not go as he planned: "On Saturday the 5th of October last, the State-house and Christ-church bells were rung muffled. . . . In consequence whereof, a large number of people was raised and assembled at the state-house, where it was publicly declared (as I am informed), that if I did not immediately resign my office, my house should be pulled down and my substance destroyed."

Hughes accepted the threat, and quit his job. Parliament rescinded the Stamp Act, and on May 20, 1766, Philadelphia's bells rang once more, this time in celebration of their freedom from taxation without representation.

The State House bell remained a working tool, a way for the people of Philadelphia to communicate with one another, in the years leading up to independence. At times, the bell's somewhat unusual tone was as welcome to the State House's eighteenth-century neighbors as blaring car alarms are to people today. The neighbors tried to fight the noise pollution, as on September 17, 1772, when the Assembly recorded: "A Petition from divers Inhabitants of the City of Philadelphia, living near the State-House, was presented to the Chair and read, setting forth, that they are much incommoded and distressed by the too frequent Ringing of the great Bell in the Steeple of the State-House, the Inconvenience of which has been often felt severely when some of the Petitioners Families have been afflicted with Sickness, at which Times, from its uncommon Size and unusual

Sound, it is extremely dangerous, and may prove fatal." The Assembly ignored the request, and the bell tolled on.

Perhaps those same neighbors were outraged on July 8, 1776, if the Liberty Bell was one of the chimes that John Adams recorded hearing summoning the people of Philadelphia to the State House Square for the first public reading of the Declaration of Independence. The tower was already experiencing structural failure by early 1775, but it seems unlikely that the State House bell was silent on that noisy, celebratory day.

The revolution unleashed a series of events that would turn the Liberty Bell into one of the most-traveled bells in history. The bells of Philadelphia rang on July 4, 1777, to celebrate the first Independence Day celebration, but the American defeat at Brandywine on September 11 that year made the invasion of Philadelphia seem imminent. On September 14, the Continental Congress requested that Pennsylvania's Supreme Executive Council arrange for all the city's bells to be removed, to keep the British from melting them into cannon balls that they could turn on the Americans. Over the days that followed, Christ Church's seven bells, two bells from St. Peter's, and two from the State House (the Liberty Bell and the clock bell, which hung in another part of the building) were removed and whisked out of town just before the British invaded, eventually hiding in a church basement in Allentown, Pennsylvania. Tory Robert Proud wrote that the "rebels" had carried "off almost every Thing, which they thought might be of use to the English Army, besides what they apprehended might be wanted by themselves, which they chiefly took from

Yesterday being the King's birthday, when he entered His Twenty Ninth Year, the Honorable Assembly dined with his Honor the Governor, by Particular Invitation. . . . Our Bells were rung; the Ships in the Harbour displayed their Colours; and other Demonstrations of Loyalty and Joy were shown on the happy occasion.

—Pennsylvania Gazette, June 3, 1766

the Quakers, and such as lest favoured them; as Blankets, Carpets, Cloathing, etc. they likewise took away all the Lead and Leaden Pipes, and all the Bells, in the City, except one."

By the time the Treaty of Paris ending the revolution was signed in 1783, the bell was back in the State House. The wooden portions of the State House's tower, decaying from lack of maintenance, were removed in the spring of 1781, but the bell was hung in the room at the top of the brick section of the tower, directly under the new, flatter roof, for the decades to follow. When the federal government moved to Philadelphia in 1790, the bell called congressmen to session from that room, announced public celebrations, and rang to welcome new states into the union. The state government left Philadelphia in 1799, and the federal government departed in 1800. The old bell, now deprived of its original purpose serving the Assembly, was left behind. When the state sold the old State House to the city in 1818, the Liberty Bell remained in place, perhaps forgotten like an old piece of office equipment.

The bell's story would change significantly in the decades that followed.

Two factors led to the Liberty Bell becoming famous in the early nineteenth century: a growing feeling that recording and preserving history was an important way to connect with the ideals of the past, and a rising, controversial movement that held that the Declaration's statement that "all men are created equal" should encompass all people.

Interest in the old State House grew starting in the 1820s, driven by the loss of the revolutionary generation, and by the Marquis de

Lafayette's 1824 visit to the nation he had fought for as a young man. Two Philadelphia newspapers published items that described the bell and its inscription that year. In 1828, city leaders hired architect William Strickland to re-create the wooden section of the bell tower, missing since 1781, and a new bell crafted by John Wilbank was hung in it. The old State House bell remained below in the upper level of the original brick portion of the tower. In 1841, British writer James Silk Buckingham visited, and wrote, "This bell though no longer used for general purposes, still occupied the place in which it was originally hung, and, like the great bell of St. Paul's in London, [is] used on special occasions such as the anniversary of the Declaration of Independence and visits of dis-tinguished visitors such as Lafayette . . . it will no doubt be preserved as a national treasure."

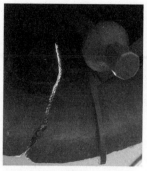

The Liberty Bell undergo-ing a recent stress test. The bell had been drilled out in an attempt to correct the vibrating noise caused by its crack, and was secured with a metal framework, or "spider," in the early twentieth century.

Sometime during this period, on one of those special occasions, Pennsylvania's old State House bell cracked. For decades to follow, long after the bell became world famous, elderly Philadel-phi-ans would recall one date or another as the moment when the bell first cracked—the British Parliament's passage of the Catholic Relief Act in 1829; the celebration of George Washington's one hundredth birthday in February 1832; the death of Charles Carroll, the last living signer of the Declaration of Independence, later that year; or—as a persistent, inaccurate myth, said—the death of former chief justice John Marshall in July 1835.

It is possible that the bell, always fragile and of a brittle metallic composition, actually cracked slowly, over time. Frequent mentions of the bell having an odd tone could substantiate this. Whenever the cracking started, by 1846, Philadelphia's leaders saw it as a serious problem. On February 12 of that year, the city's Select and Common Councils asked the mayor to "cause the Independence Bell to be rung" to celebrate George Washington's birthday. In an attempt to repair the bell, the superintendent of the State House had it drilled and the crack filed out to separate the two sides from vibrating against each other and causing a buzzing sound. The drilled hole might keep the crack from worsening, craftsmen thought. Superintendent William Eckel understood the bell's historic, almost mythic quality: the city had most of the filed metal shavings collected, melted down, and recast into a small bell that they presented to the Historical Society of Pennsylvania for safekeeping.

The attempted repair didn't work, however. The *Public Ledger* of February 26, 1846 announced: *"The Old Independence Bell.* This venerable relic of the Revolution rang its last clear note on Monday last . . . and now hangs in the great city steeple irreparably cracked and forever dumb. It had been cracked long before, but was put in order for that day. . . . It gave out clear notes and loud, and appeared to be in excellent condition until noon, when it received a sort of compound fracture in a zigzag direction through one of its sides, which put it completely out of tune and left it a mere wreck of what it was."

The reporter noted that he had been "lucky to get a small fragment" of the now silent bell, and would "keep it sacred, in memory of the good and glory achieved by the old herald of Independence in times long past, and ever to be remembered." Plans were already being considered, the paper reported, to melt the bell down and recast it.

At the same time that Americans were developing a sense of the importance of their history, some also grew increasingly concerned that the promises of the Declaration of Independence were being denied to millions of people who were held in slavery. The 1830s witnessed the birth of a widespread, well-publicized effort to abolish slavery from the United States of America. By that decade, human slavery had become the "peculiar institution" of the American South. All northern states had either outlawed it by the turn of the nineteenth century or seen slavery simply cease to exist within their borders. The British Empire had made slavery illegal in its remaining colonies in 1834. How, some northern reformers asked, could America be a free nation when millions were held in bondage?

The American Anti-Slavery Society was founded in Philadelphia in 1833. The society followed the ideas expressed by Boston abolitionist William Lloyd Garrison, who inaugurated his movement on January 31, 1831, with the first issue of his newspaper the *Liberator*, in which he announced "I am in earnest, I will not equivocate, AND I WILL BE HEARD."

Garrison's was one of several reform movements springing up across the country, seeking the end of slavery as well as improvement of a host of social ills ranging from the consumption of alcohol to education for the poor, and advo-

The abolitionist must be put down, or the Union of these states will be dissolved.

—Samuel Breck, 1838

cating expanding the rights of women, and better treatment for prisoners, the mentally ill, and immigrants. Numerous Philadelphians, many of them members of the Society of Friends, were drawn to the reform movements in general and to the abolition movement in particular. Among the most prominent of these antislavery crusaders were Lucretia Mott and her husband, James.

But in fact the majority of Philadelphians and Americans opposed the work of the abolitionists. Andrew Jackson, a president celebrated for his democratic beliefs, called abolitionism unconstitutional and said in an 1835 message to Congress that their antislavery activities should be broken up by mobs. Although the 1830s are often considered a time of expanding democracy, it was also the era in which a new Pennsylvania State Constitution of 1838 explicitly denied African Americans the right to vote, a right freemen had held since the writing of the Pennsylvania Constitution of 1790.

Racial hatred grew throughout the nation, including in the City of Brotherly Love. Many of the wealthy white Philadelphians who had been the firmest supporters of philanthropic institutions for the poor and for African Americans discontinued their support.

Increased racial fears led to increased violence. On August 12, 1834, a scuffle broke out between white and black Philadelphians near the Flying Horses, an early carousel, on South Street. The fight quickly turned into a riot, and angry whites began storming nearby streets and alleys, the heart of Philadelphia's black neighborhood. The white rioters destroyed houses and their furnishings, dragged residents from their

A mob destroyed Pennsylvania Hall on May 17, 1838, a key event in the rising tide of anti-abolitionist sentiment that was gripping Philadelphia and parts of the nation.

dwellings and beat them, and damaged two churches. Financially prosperous blacks were particularly singled out by the mob.

On May 17, 1838, flames ripped through the elegant new Pennsylvania Hall. The Greek Revival building on Sixth Street, a few blocks north of Independence Square, had just been completed, built by the members of the growing American Anti-Slavery Society. The ranks of anti-abolitionists were also growing, and their influence had made it difficult for the society to find a meeting place. To celebrate the hall's opening, the members of the Anti-Slavery Convention of American Women walked into the new building with linked arms, black and white members together. Outraged racists looked on in fury. That night, a mob attacked the building and burned it to the ground.

Why were the 1830s so turbulent? Historians agree that the social and political upheaval taking place at the same moment as significant economic changes, including the worldwide economic depression that followed the "killing" of the Second Bank of the United States, led to these outbreaks. At the same time, then, that Philadelphia was becoming a center of antislavery activity, and that the Liberty Bell and the Declaration of Independence were gaining widespread recognition as symbols of what the American dream could be, Philadelphia's black citizens were facing widespread violence and racism, victims of a new economic order, the brunt of anger of white Americans and new immigrants who felt they had been denied a dream themselves.

Abolitionists first adopted the Liberty Bell as a symbol of American freedom in 1835, in a pamphlet published in Boston by the Friends of Freedom. Their image of the bell was somewhat idealized, but the biblical inscription "PROCLAIM LIBERTY TO ALL THE INHABITANTS" was clearly there. The accompanying poem, "suggested by the inscription on the Philadelphia Liberty Bell," stated:

It is no tocsin of affright we sound,
Summoning nations to the conflict dire;—
No fearful peal from cities wrapped in fire
Echoes, at our behest, the land around:—
Yet would we rouse our country's utmost bound.

By the middle decades of the nineteenth century, Americans were debating exactly what their founding fathers' legacy was. Some saw the right to property, including the right to own other people, as the greatest liberty that was guaranteed by the men who met in Independence Hall to create the nation. Others saw that "liberty" meant freedom for all Americans, including those African Americans who were held in chains. The debate grew violent in Philadelphia and other northern cities throughout those decades.

The adoption of the Liberty Bell as a symbol of the revolution it had helped ring in began in these years. In 1848, Benson J. Lossing, a popular if sometimes inaccurate historian, pondered the bell and the history it had witnessed. Lossing gave to Americans the long-surviving myth of a young boy running up the State House stairs to tell an old man "Ring! Ring!" at the moment independence was declared. The bell had not really rung that evening, but the name "Liberty Bell" that he gave to it, as well as some of the myths he invented, would survive.

An 1856 edition of *The Liberty Bell*, an American Anti-Slavery Society publication that ran from 1839 to 1858.

By 1852, when delegates from the original thirteen states gathered in Philadelphia to consider erecting a monument to the signers of the Declaration of Independence, the Liberty Bell had been removed from its perch in Independence Hall's tower and moved to the building's first floor assembly room, allowing visitors to see it more conveniently. There, the bell became a more central part of the story of American Independence. Prints from the time show the bell surrounded by visitors, sitting upon its thirteen-sided platform. As the years passed, the bell moved around the hall, into the central passage, then the Supreme Court chamber, and eventually hung from a thirteen-link chain from the ceiling of the tower room. More safety-conscious heads prevailed, and the bell was placed in a glass enclosure on the floor of the tower room.

The Liberty Bell, hanging from a thirteen-link chain in the stair tower of Independence Hall, in the late nineteenth century. Patriotism, combined with new methods of transportation, made the hall and bell a major tourist attraction in the era.

Like many symbols, the meaning of the Liberty Bell has been reinterpreted by many people over the years. In the twentieth century, protesters gathered around it to use its message of liberty to support their causes. Celebrants have gathered at the bell to celebrate America and its history. And visitors from around the globe, world leaders and common citizens alike, have made pilgrimages to this bell that has become the symbol of people continuing to strive for freedom and liberty.

The bell was sent across the country several times after the Civil War, as a unifying symbol of the shared revolutionary heritage of the North and South. The bell went to New Orleans by rail car in 1885 for the World Industrial and Cotton Exposition there. As it traveled into the former Confederacy, the tangible reminder of the Revolution was treated as a nearly religious icon when people journeyed to see it, touch it, or kiss it in reverence. One historian recorded that Jefferson Davis, the Confederacy's former president, left his sickbed to see the bell and said: "I believe the time has come when reason should be substituted for passion and when we should be able to do justice to each other. Glorious old Bell, the son of a revolutionary soldier bows in reverence before you." When the Liberty Bell returned to Philadelphia, it was given a citywide welcome that befitted an international celebrity.

In the years to follow, the Liberty Bell crossed the country several times, again acting as a unifying symbol of the United States: trips to Chicago in 1893, Charleston, South Carolina,

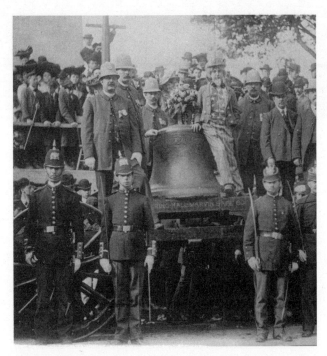

The Liberty Bell made several cross-country voyages in the late nineteenth and early twentieth centuries, including this visit to Bunker Hill in Boston in 1903.

in 1902, Boston in 1903, and later that year to St. Louis to honor the anniversary of the Louisiana Purchase. In 1915, the Bell travelled to San Francisco for the Pan-Pacific Exposition, and in 1917, citizens paraded the bell through the streets of Philadelphia to raise patriotism and money when America entered World War I.

Numerous groups used the bell as a symbol of their fight for equal liberty in the United States. Suffragists created their own bell, the Justice Bell, in 1915, chaining its clapper so it could not be rung until women gained the right to vote, which the Nineteenth Amendment secured in 1919. By World War II, efforts to preserve the Liberty Bell from bomb attacks like those that devastated English and European historic sites drew national attention, and these ideas led to the founding of Independence National Historical Park in 1948.

Women demanding the right to vote created the Justice Bell, using the national symbol in much the same way that earlier feminists had based their 1848 Declaration of Sentiments, which argued for women's equality in phrases based on the Declaration of Independence. The Justice Bell's clapper was chained, silencing the bell, until the passage of the Nineteenth Amendment in 1919.

The original Liberty Bell announced the creation of democracy, the Women's Liberty Bell will announce the completion of democracy.

—Katherine Ruschenberger, *New York Times,* March 31, 1915

The Liberty Bell continued to be a tangible symbol of American freedom and reform in the mid-twentieth century. Protesters staged a sit-in around it in 1965 to demand civil rights for all Americans. Advocates for gay rights, the abolition of the death penalty, and numerous other causes have used the bell's symbolic message in recent years, much as antislavery advocates did in the mid-nineteenth century.

To accommodate the increasing number of visitors to the Liberty Bell, the National Park Service moved it to a small glass pavilion as the Independence Hall clock struck midnight on January 1, 1976, and the bell remained in that building for the decades to follow. On October 6, 2003, the bell made its most recent move, to the newly completed Liberty Bell Center, directly across Chestnut Street from Independence Hall. At sunrise on that day, workers

The Rev. Dr. Martin Luther King, Jr., laid a wreath at the Liberty Bell, then located in the stair tower of Independence Hall, on February 2, 1959.

slowly moved the bell from its home of twenty-seven years as an interpreter playing Thomas Jefferson intoned the statement the third president wrote to commemorate the United States' fiftieth birthday, just days before he and John Adams died, hours apart, on July 4, 1826:

> The general spread of the light of science has already laid open to every view the palpable truth, that the mass of mankind has not been born with saddles on their backs, nor a favored few booted and spurred, ready to ride them legitimately, by the grace of God. These are grounds of hope for others –for ourselves, let the annual return of this day forever refresh our recollections of these rights, and an undiminished devotion to them.

Overleaf: The Liberty Bell moved to its newly constructed Liberty Bell Center on October 6, 2003, just across Chestnut Street from Independence Hall.

Notes on Sources

INTRODUCTION

Lord Adam Gordon's observations may be found in Newton Mereness, ed., *Travels in the American Colonies* (New York, 1916), 410; Dr. Alexander Hamilton's are in Carl Bridenbaugh, ed., *Gentleman's Progress: The Itinerarium of Dr. Alexander Hamilton, 1744* (Chapel Hill, 1948). Stephanie Grauman Wolf's *As Various as Their Lands: The Everyday Lives of Eighteenth-Century Americans* (New York, 1993), provided both the description of early American's cacophony as well as a host of information that shaped this study. Numerous works study the rise of Philadelphia by the eighteenth century, including Carl and Jessica Bridenbaugh, *Rebels and Gentlemen: Philadelphia in the Age of Franklin* (New York, 1942); Frederick B. Tolles, *Meeting House and Counting House: The Quaker Merchants of Colonial Philadelphia, 1682–1783* (New York, 1948); American Philosophical Society, *Historic Philadelphia: From the Founding Until the Early Nineteenth Century* (Philadelphia, 1953); Carl Bridenbaugh, *Cities in Revolt: Urban Life in America, 1743–1776* (Oxford, 1955); Gary B. Nash, *The Urban Crucible: Social Change, Political Consciousness, and the Origins of the American Revolution* (Cambridge, MA, 1979); Russell F. Weigley, ed., *Philadelphia: A Three-Hundred-Year History* (New York, 1982); Michael Zuckerman, ed., *Friends and Neighbors: Group Life in America's First Plural Society* (Philadelphia, 1982); Thomas M. Doerflinger, *A Vigorous Spirit of Enterprise: Merchants and Economic Development in Revolutionary Philadelphia* (Chapel Hill, 1986); Susan E. Klepp, *Philadelphia in Transition: A Demographic History of the City and Its Occupational Groups, 1720–1830* (New York, 1989); and Toby L. Ditz, "Shipwrecked; or, Masculinity Imperiled: Mercantile Representations of Failure and the Gendered Self in Eighteenth-Century Philadelphia," *Journal of American History* 81, no. 1 (June 1994), 51–80.

Many studies of the material culture of early Pennsylvania have informed and influenced this study, including Martin P. Snyder, *City of Independence: Views of Philadelphia Before 1800* (New York: 1975); Bernard L. Herman, *Town House: Architecture and Material Life in the Early American City, 1780–1830* (Chapel Hill, 2005); Jack L. Lindsey, ed., *Worldly Goods: The Arts of Early Pennsylvania, 1680–1758* (Philadelphia, 1999); Emily T. Cooperman and Lea Carson Sherk, *William Birch: Picturing the American Scene* (Philadelphia, 2011); Margaretta Lovell, *Art in a Season of Revolution: Painters, Artisans, and Patrons in Early America* (Philadelphia, 2005); Edgar P. Richardson, Brooke Hindle, and Lillian B. Miller, eds., *Charles Willson Peale and His World* (New York, 1982); and Doris Devine Fanelli and Karie Diethorn, *History of the Portrait Collection, Independence National Historical Park* (Philadelphia, 2001).

On the restoration and interpretation of the Independence area, see Freeman Tilden, *Interpreting Our Heritage* (Chapel Hill, 1957); Constance M. Greif, *Independence: The Creation of a National Park* (Philadelphia, 1987); George

Tatum, *Philadelphia Georgian: The City House of Samuel Powel and Some of Its Eighteenth-Century Neighbors* (Middletown, CT, 1976); Gary B. Nash, *The Liberty Bell* (New Haven, 2010). This book would not have been possible without the outstanding works exploring each aspect of Independence National Historical Park's restoration and interpretation found in the park's library and archives, including the historic structure and historic furnishings reports.

Chapter 1: Welcome Park and William Penn

Voltaire's thoughts on Quakerism are found in the first four letters of François-Marie Arouet de Voltaire, *Letters on the English* (*Lettres Philosophiques*) (New York, 1914); Susan Klepp gives the best recent succinct overview of Pennsylvania's early settlement in "Encounter and Experiment: The Colonial Period," in Randall Miller and William Pencak, eds., *Pennsylvania: A History of the Commonwealth* (University Park, PA, 2002); on William Penn, see Richard S. Dunn and Mary Maples Dunn, eds., *The World of William Penn* (Philadelphia, 1986); Richard S. Dunn and Mary Maples Dunn, eds., *The Papers of William Penn*, 4 vols. (Philadelphia, 1981–87); Catherine Christie Dann, "'Governments, Individuals and Old Houses': The Slate Roof House of Philadelphia" (M.A. thesis, Winterthur Program, University of Delaware, 2000); James D. Kornwolf, *Architecture and Town Planning in Colonial North America*, 3 vols. (Baltimore, 2002); Alexander Graydon's recollections are found in *Memoirs of a Life, Chiefly Passed in Pennsylvania Within the Last Sixty Years* (Harrisburg, 1811); on Hannah Penn, see Alison Duncan Hirsh, "'Instructions from a Woman': Hannah Penn and the Pennsylvania Proprietorship" (Ph.D. diss., Columbia University, 1991); Sophie Hutchinson Drinker, *Hannah Penn and the Proprietorship of Pennsylvania* (Philadelphia, 1958).

Chapter 2: Gloria Dei Church and Southwark

On the New Sweden colony, see Ruth L. Springer and Louise Wallman, "Two Swedish Pastors Describe Philadelphia, 1700 and 1702," *PMHB* (April 1960), 193–218; Richard Hulan, *The Swedes in Pennsylvania,* Pennsylvania Historical and Museum Commission Peoples of Pennsylvania series, vol. 5 (Harrisburg, 1994). The Nicholas Collin letter related to Benjamin Franklin is in the *Papers of Benjamin Franklin* online edition, franklinpapers.org. On the church and its surroundings, see Penelope Hartshorne Batcheler, "Gloria Dei–Old Swedes Church: Getting to Know the Building," presented at the American Swedish Historical Museum, March 18, 2000, copy in the archives of Independence National Historical Park; Margaret B. Tinkcom, "Southwark: A River Community: Its Shape and Substance," *Proceedings of the American Philosophical Society* 114, no. 4 (1970), 327–42; Billy G. Smith and Susan E. Klepp, "The Records of Gloria Dei Church: Burials, 1800–1804," *Pennsylvania History* 53, no. 1 (1986), and Klepp and Smith, "The Records of Gloria Dei Church: Marriages and 'Remarkable Occurrences,' 1794–1806," *Pennsylvania History* 53, no. 2 (1986); Whitfield J. Bell, Jr. "Nicholas Collin's Appeal to American Scientists," *William and Mary*

Quarterly 13, no. 4 (1986), 519–50; the Moreau de St. Méry quotation is in Kenneth Roberts and Anna M. Roberts, *Moreau de St. Méry's American Journey* [1793–1798] (Garden City, NY, 1947); Adolph B. Benson, ed., *Peter Kalm's Travels in North America: The English Version of 1770,* 2 vols. (New York, 1937). Little physical evidence of Philadelphia's pre-settlement period exists within the city, largely due to three centuries of digging and building, but the story of the Lenni Lenape is vital to the city's history. See Daniel K. Richter, *Facing East from Indian Country: A Native History of Early America* (Cambridge, MA, 2001), and Amy C. Schutt, *Peoples of the River Valleys: The Odyssey of the Delaware Indians* (Philadelphia, 2007).

CHAPTER 3: MARKET STREET AND CHRIST CHURCH

For Franklin's recollections of his arrival, see Leonard W. Labaree et al., eds., *The Autobiography of Benjamin Franklin* (New Haven, 1964). On Pennsylvania religious freedom, see Dunn and Dunn, eds., *Papers of William Penn,* vol. 2; Frank Lambert, *Inventing the Great Awakening* (Princeton, 1999); William Pencak, "Beginning of a Beautiful Friendship: Benjamin Franklin, George Whitefield, the 'Dancing School Blockheads,' and a Defense of the 'Meaner Sort,'" *Proteus* 19, no. 1 (2002). On the market, see J. D. Schoepf, *Travels in the Confederation, 1783–1784* (Philadelphia, 1911); *Minutes of the Common Council, 1704–1776* (Philadelphia, 1847); *Watson's Annals of Philadelphia* (Philadelphia, 1857), vol. 2. On Christ Church, see Deborah Mathias Gough, *Christ Church, Philadelphia: The Nation's Church in a Changing City* (Philadelphia, 1995); Charles E. Peterson, Nicholas Gianopolos, and Bruce Cooper Gill, *The Building and Furnishing of Christ Church Philadelphia* (Philadelphia, 2001); on Robert Smith, see Peterson, *Robert Smith: Architect, Builder, Patriot, 1722–1777* (Philadelphia, 2000); Hubertis Cummings, *Richard Peters: Provincial Secretary and Cleric, 1704–1776* (Philadelphia, 1944). For accounts of Philadelphia during the era, see Jacob Duché, *Caspipina's Letters; Containing Observations on a Variety of Subjects, Literary, Moral, and Religious. Written by a Gentleman who Resided Some Time in Philadelphia. To which is added, the Life and Character of Wm. Penn, ... In two volumes* (Dublin, 1792); William Duane, *Extracts from the Diary of Christopher Marshall: Kept in Philadelphia and Lancaster, During the American Revolution, 1774–1781* (Albany, 1877); L. H. Butterfield, Marc Friedlaender, and Mary-Jo Kline, eds., *The Book of Abigail and John: Selected Letters of the Adams Family, 1762–1784* (Boston, 1975); Butterfield, ed., *Diary and Autobiography of John Adams,* 4 vols. (Cambridge, MA, 1964). On Alice, see Gary B. Nash, *Forging Freedom: The Formation of Philadelphia's Black Community, 1720–1840* (Cambridge, MA, 1988). I am especially grateful to Susan Klepp for sharing her recent research on Alice with me.

CHAPTER 4: FRANKLIN COURT

For Franklin's writings, see Labaree et al., eds., *The Autobiography of Benjamin Franklin,* and Labaree et al., eds., *The Papers of Benjamin Franklin,* 39 vols. to date

(New Haven, 1959–), now available online through franklinpapers.org. On Franklin Court, see Edward M. Riley, "Franklin's Home," in *Historic Philadelphia: From the Founding Until the Early Nineteenth Century*; Claude-Anne Lopez et al., *Benjamin Franklin's "Good House": The Story of Franklin Court* (Washington, D.C., 1981) Barbara Liggett, *Archeology at Franklin's Court* (Philadelphia, 1973); John L. Cotter, *The Buried Past: An Archaeological History of Philadelphia* (Philadelphia, 1993); Greif, *Independence*; Bonnie Hurd Smith, ed., *From Gloucester to Philadelphia in 1790: Observations, Anecdotes, and Thoughts from the Eighteenth-Century Letters of Judith Sargent Murray* (Cambridge, MA, 1998). On Franklin and his family, see Claude-Anne Lopez and Eugenia W. Herbert, *The Private Franklin: The Man and His Family* (New York, 1975); Sheila L. Skemp, *William Franklin: Son of a Patriot, Servant of a King* (New York, 1990); David Waldstreicher, *Runaway America: Benjamin Franklin, Slavery, and the American Revolution* (New York, 2004); Keith Arbour, "One Last Word: Benjamin Franklin and the DuPlessis Portrait of 1778," *PMHB* 118, no. 3 (July 1994). J. A. Leo Lemay's unparalleled grasp of Franklin's life and work is found in his Benjamin Franklin: A Documentary History (http://www.english.udel.edu/lemay/franklin/) and in the three volumes of his proposed seven-volume biography of Franklin, completed at the time of his death in 2008.

Chapter 5: The Second Bank Area

The founding of the Library Company of Philadelphia is disclosed in the organization's minute books, dating back to November 1731, archives of the Library Company of Philadelphia; I trace this story and other aspects of Philadelphia's Enlightenment in George W. Boudreau, "The Surest Foundation of Happiness: Education and Society in Franklin's Philadelphia" (Ph.D. diss., Indiana University, 1998); see also Jean O'Neill and Elizabeth P. McLean, *Peter Collinson and the Eighteenth-Century Natural History Exchange* (Philadelphia, 2008). On the American Philosophical Society, see Whitfield J. Bell, *Patriot-Improvers: Biographical Sketches of Members of the American Philosophical Society*, 3 vols. (vol. 3 with Charles B. Greifenstein; Philadelphia, 1997, 1999, 2010); and Edward G. Carter, *"One Grand Pursuit:" A Brief History of the American Philosophical Society's First 250 Years, 1743–1993* (Philadelphia, 1993); Joyce E. Chaplin, *The First Scientific American: Benjamin Franklin and the Pursuit of Genius* (New York, 2006). For Logan's account, see "Reminiscences of Deborah Norris Logan," transcript of original in the Historical Society of Pennsylvania in the archives of Independence National Historical Park; Edgar P. Richardson, Brooke Hindle, and Lillian B. Miller, eds., *Charles Willson Peale and His World*; Fanelli and Diethorn, *History of the Portrait Collection* (Upper Darby, PA, 2001); Wendy Bellion, *Citizen Spectator: Art, Illustration, and Visual Perception in Early National America* (Chapel Hill, 2011); and David R. Brigham, *Public Culture in the Early Republic: Peale's Museum and Its Audience* (Washington, D.C., 1995). On the buildings in this area, see Roger W. Moss, *Historic Landmarks of Philadelphia* (Philadelphia, 2008); Charles Coleman Sellers, "Peale's Museum," in *Historic Philadelphia: From the*

Founding Until the Early Nineteenth Century and *Philadelphia: Three Centuries of American Art—Selections from the Bicentennial Exhibition Held at the Philadelphia Museum of Art* (Philadelphia, 1976). On Jackson and the Bank Wars, see Bray Hammond, *Banks and Politics in America from the Revolution to the Civil War* (Princeton, 1991), and Robert Wright, *The First Wall Street: Chestnut Street, Philadelphia, and the Birth of American Finance* (Chicago, 2005). Charles Dickens's account is found in *American Notes* (London, 1842).

CHAPTER 6: SOCIETY HILL

Tatum, *Philadelphia Georgian*; "Christ Church, St. Peters, and St. Paul's," *Historic Philadelphia*, 187–98; T. H. Breen, *Marketplace of Revolution* (New York, 2004); Gary B. Nash, "The Free Society of Traders and the Early Politics of Pennsylvania," *PMHB* 89, no. 2 (April 1965), 147–73; Samuel Powel Account Books, HSP; Zara Anishanslin, "Portrait of a Woman in a Silk Dress: The Hidden Histories of Aesthetic Commodities in the British Atlantic World, 1688–1790" (Ph.D. diss., University of Delaware, 2009); David W. Maxey, A Portrait of Elizabeth Willing Powel, 1743–1830, *Transactions of the American Philosophical Society* 96, no. 4 (Philadelphia, 2006); Roger W. Moss, *Historic Houses of Philadelphia* (Philadelphia, 1998); Howard C. Rice, Jr., ed., *Travels in North America in the Years 1780, 1781, and 1782 by the Marquis de Chastellux*, 2 vols. (Chapel Hill, 1963); Mary Beth Norton, *Liberty's Daughters* (Ithaca, NY, 1996); Rosemary Zagarri, *Revolutionary Backlash: Women and Politics in the Early American Republic* (Philadelphia, 2007); Martha Washington Letters; Deborah Gough, *Christ Church Philadelphia*; Kosciuszko House; Gary B. Nash and Graham Russell Hodges, *Friends of Liberty: A Tale of Three Patriots, Two Revolutions, and the Betrayal that Divided a Nation: Thomas Jefferson, Thaddeus Kosciuszko, and Agrippa Hull* (New York, 2008); "Tadeusz Kosciuszko" in *American National Biography*; David W. Maxey, "Madeira, Quakerism, and Rebellion: Reviving Henry Hill," *Quaker History* 93, no. 2 (October 2004), 47–75; David Hancock, *Oceans of Wine: Madeira and the Emergence of American Trade and Taste* (New Haven, 2009); Amy H. Henderson, "A Family Affair: The Design and Decoration of 321 South Fourth Street, Philadelphia," in John Styles and Amanda Vickery, eds., *Gender, Taste, and Material Culture in Britain and North America, 1700–1830* (New Haven, 2006); Roger W. Moss, *Historic Sacred Places of Philadelphia* (Philadelphia, 2005). For Governor Gordon's quotation on the Catholic chapel, see minutes of the Philadelphia City Council, July 25, 1734; Dennis C. Burjack, "St. Joseph's and St. Mary's Churches," in *Historic Philadelphia: From the Founding Until the Early Nineteenth Century.*

CHAPTER 7: CITY TAVERN BLOCK

Adams recorded his arrival in Butterfield, ed., *Diary and Autobiography of John Adams* (Boston, 1961). On taverns in early Pennsylvania, see Peter Thompson, *Rum Punch and Revolution* (Philadelphia, 1998); and Thompson, "A Social History of Philadelphia's Taverns, 1683–1800" (Ph.D. diss., University of

Pennsylvania, 1989); Robert Earle Graham, "The Taverns of Colonial Philadelphia," in *Historic Philadelphia: From the Founding Until the Early Nineteenth Century*. For a more recent interpretation of the tavern's role in revolutionary Philadelphia, see Benjamin Irwin, *Clothed in the Robes of Sovereignty: The Continental Congress and the People Out of Doors* (Oxford, 2011). On Daniel Smith, see his Loyalist claims (AO 12/102/82 and AO 13/132/221) in the Public Record Office, London. My thanks to Kathy Ludwig of the David Library of the American Revolution for her assistance in locating copies of these records. On visitors to the tavern, see James Bear and Lucia Stanton, eds., *Jefferson's Memorandum Books* (Princeton, 1997), and Butterfield, ed., *Diary and Autobiography of John Adams*; Samuel Shoemaker records in the archives of INHP. On the Merchants' Exchange, see Roger W. Moss, *Historic Landmarks of Philadelphia; Philadelphia: Three Centuries of American Art* (Philadelphia, 1976); and Greif, *Independence*.

CHAPTER 8: CARPENTERS' HALL BLOCK

On the nature of early American neighborhoods, see Sam Bass Warner, *Streetcar Suburbs* (Boston, 1978); and Billy G. Smith, *"The Lower Sort": Philadelphia's Laboring People, 1750–1800* (Ithaca, NY, 1990). On the Carpenters and their building, see Charles E. Peterson, "Carpenters' Hall," in *Historic Philadelphia: From the Founding Until the Early Nineteenth Century*; Roger W. Moss, Jr., "The Origins of the Carpenter's Company of Philadelphia," in Peterson, ed., *Building Early American: Contributions Toward the History of a Great Industry* (Mendham, NJ, 1976); and Peterson, *Robert Smith*. On Benezet, see Maurice Jackson, *Let This Voice Be Heard: Anthony Benezet, Father of Atlantic Abolitionism* (Philadelphia, 2009), and George S. Brookes, *Friend Anthony Benezet* (Philadelphia, 1937). On the First Bank of the United States, see Stanley Elkins and Eric McKitrick, *The Age of Federalism: The Early American Republic, 1788–1800* (New York, 1993); Roger W. Moss, *Historic Landmarks of Philadelphia*; Gordon S. Wood, *Empire of Liberty: A History of the Early Republic, 1789–1815* (New York, 2009).On Dolley Todd Madison, see Catherine Allgor, *A Perfect Union: Dolley Madison and the Creation of the American Nation* (New York, 2006); John and Dolley Todd's lives as members of the Society of Friends are to be found in the records of various Friends' meetings, housed in the Quaker Archives at Swarthmore College. On the Todd and White houses, see the furnishings plans created by NPS staff, in the INHP archives. On the neighborhood, and Dock Creek's effect on it, see Charles Olton, "Philadelphia's First Environmental Crisis," *PMHB* 98, no. 1 (January 1974); and A. Michal McMahon, "'Small Matters': Benjamin Franklin, Philadelphia, and the 'Progress of Cities,'" *PMHB* 141, no. 2 (April 1992). On American Anglicanism, see Patricia U. Bonomi, *Under the Cope of Heaven: Religion, Society, and Politics in Colonial Society* (Oxford, 1986).

CHAPTER 9: THE DECLARATION HOUSE

All of the Jefferson quotations are found in Julian P. Boyd et al., eds., *The Papers of Thomas Jefferson* (Princeton, 1950–). My thanks to Elizabeth Chew, curator of

Monticello, for her help in identifying Jefferson's actions and possessions con-
nected to Philadelphia. On Virginia and the coming of the revolution, see Rhys
Isaac, *The Transformation of Virginia* (Chapel Hill, 1982); and Woody Holton,
*Forced Founders: Indians, Debtors, Slaves, and the Making of the American
Revolution in Virginia* (Chapel Hill, 1999). On Jefferson's life in Philadelphia, see
the Jefferson chronology in the Thomas Jefferson Library, International Center
for Jefferson Studies, Charlottesville; Bear and Stanton, eds., *Jefferson's
Memorandum Books*; and Dumas Malone, *Jefferson the Virginian* and *Jefferson and
the Rights of Man* (Boston, 1948, 1951). On Robert Hemings, see Annette
Gordon-Reed, *The Hemingses of Monticello: An American Family* (New York,
2008), and Robert Bear, *The Hemings Family of Monticello* (Ivy, VA, 1980); on the
Declaration House, see Doris D. Fanelli, *Furnishings Plan for Graff House,
Philadelphia, PA* (Philadelphia, 1988), and Penelope Hartshorne Batcheler's
Preliminary Development Plan of the proposed reconstructed building in the
archives of Independence National Historical Park. On the writing of the
Declaration, see Pauline Maier, *American Scripture: Making the Declaration of
Independence* (New York, 1997), and Whitfield J. Bell, Jr., *The Declaration of
Independence: Four 1776 Versions* (Philadelphia, 1986).

CHAPTER 10: INDEPENDENCE SQUARE

During the creation of Independence National Historical Park, NPS historians,
architects, and curators amassed a large collection of original accounts of the
appearance of the hall and square, now housed in the card file, INHP Archives.
Other firsthand accounts may be found in *Documents from the Continental
Congress and the Constitutional Convention, 1774–1789*, located online at
http://memory.loc.gov/ammem/collections/continental/; *Journals of the Continental Congress, 1774–1789*, ed. Worthington C. Ford et al. (Washington, D.C.,
1904–37); Paul H. Smith et al., eds., *Letters of Delegates to Congress, 1774–1789*,
25 vols. (Washington, D.C., 1976–2000); Penelope Hartshorne Batcheler,
"Independence Hall: Its Appearance Restored," in Charles Peterson, ed., *Building
Early American: Contributions Toward the History of a Great Industry*; Anna Coxe
Toogood et al., *Cultural Landscape Report: Independence Square* (Denver, 1994);
Edward M. Riley, "The Independence Hall Group," in *Historic Philadelphia:
From the Founding Until the Early Nineteenth Century*; Silvio A. Bendini, "'That
Awful Stage': The Search for the State House Yard Observatory," in Randolph S.
Klein, ed., *Science and Society in Early America: Essays in Honor of Whitfield J. Bell,
Jr.* (Philadelphia, 1986). On the coming of independence, see Kevin Kenney,
*Peaceable Kingdom Lost: The Paxton Boys and the Destruction of William Penn's Holy
Experiment* (Oxford, 2009); Richard Alan Ryerson, *The Revolution Is Now Begun:
The Radical Committees of Philadelphia, 1765–1776* (Philadelphia, 1978); Eric
Foner, *Tom Paine and Revolutionary America* (New York, 1976); Robert Gross,
The Minutemen and Their World (New York, 2001); David Hackett Fischer, *Paul
Revere's Ride* (Oxford, 1995); Benjamin L. Carp, *Rebels Rising: Cities and the
American Revolution* (New York, 2007); Andrew Jackson O'Shaughnessy, *An*

Empire Divided: The American Revolution and the British Caribbean (Philadelphia, 2002); Pauline Maier, *American Scripture: Making the Declaration of Independence* (New York, 1997). The Frazer quotation is drawn from the historic source card file, INHP Archives.

Chapter 11: Washington Square

On Adams, see L. H. Butterfield, Friedlaender, and Kline, eds., *The Book of Abigail and John: Selected Letters of the Adams Family, 1762–1784* (Lebanon, NH, 2002); Butterfield, ed., *Diary and Autobiography of John Adams*. Franklin's recollection of the founding of the hospital is found in his *Autobiography*; on the hospital, see Moss, *Historic Landmarks of Philadelphia*. For a biography of the hospital's founder, see Whitfield J. Bell, Jr., "Thomas Bond," in *Patriot Improvers: Biographical Sketches of Members of the American Philosophical Society, Vol. I* (Philadelphia, 1997). On revolutionary era soldiers, see Philip Katcher, *Rebels and Loyalists: The Revolutionary Soldier in Philadelphia* (Philadelphia, 1976), and *Sally Wister's Journal: A True Narrative—Being a Quaker Maiden's Account of Her Experiences With Officers of the Continental Army, 1777–1778* (Carlisle, MA, 1995). The colonists' recollections of early African American customs are found in John F. Watson and Willis Hazard, *Annals of Philadelphia, and Pennsylvania, in the Olden Time*, 3 vols. (Philadelphia, 1891). On the African American community during this era, see Gary B. Nash, *Forging Freedom: The Formation of Philadelphia's Black Community, 1720–1840* (Cambridge, MA, 1988); Julie Winch, *A Gentleman of Color: The Life of James Forten* (Oxford, 2002); see also the Cadwalader and Chew papers, HSP. On the square, see "Washington Square" research report, INHP archives; Dennis Rabzak, "Washington Square: A Site Plan Chronology, 1683–1984" (NPS, 1984), and Rebecca Yamin, *Digging in the City of Brotherly Love: Stories from Philadelphia Archaeology* (New Haven, 2008).

Chapter 12: Old City

For a firsthand account of Old City and the Revolution, see Elaine F. Crane, ed., *The Diary of Elizabeth Drinker*, 3 vols. (Boston, 1991); Edward H. Tatum Jr., ed., *The American Journal of Ambrose Serle, Secretary to Lord Howe, 1776–78* (San Marino, CA, 1940), and Jane Bonsall Clark manuscript diary, Friends Historical Library, Swarthmore College. The Franklin quotation is from his pamphlet *Plain Truth* (Philadelphia, 1747). On the British occupation, see John W. Jackson, *With the British Army in Philadelphia, 1777–1778* (San Rafael, CA, 1979); Judith Van Buskirk, "They Didn't Join the Band: Disaffected Women in Revolutionary Philadelphia," *Pennsylvania History* 63, no. 2 (Summer 1995); and Thomas J. McGuire, *The Philadelphia Campaign*, 2 vols. (Mechanicsburg, PA, 2007). On Old City's residents, see Marla R. Miller, *Betsy Ross and the Making of America* (New York, 2010); William Pencak, *Jews and Gentiles in Early America, 1654–1800* (Ann Arbor, 2005); on residences, see Bernard L. Herman, *Town House: Architecture and Material Life in the Early American City, 1780–1830* (Chapel Hill, 2005); Herman and Peter Guillery, "Negotiating Classicism in

Eighteenth-Century Deptford and Philadelphia," in Barbara Arciszewska and Elizabeth McKellar, *Articulating British Classicism: New Approaches to Eighteenth-Century British Architecture* (Aldershot, UK, 2004); Peter Guillery, *The Small House in Eighteenth-Century London* (New Haven, 2004); and Roger Moss, *Historic Houses of Philadelphia.* On the two surviving Friends meetinghouses, see Charles E. Peterson, "Notes on the Free Quaker Meeting House, Fifth and Arch Streets, Philadelphia, Built 1783–84" (Philadelphia, 1966); Lee Nelson and Penelope Hartshorne Batcheler, "An Architectural Study of Arch Street Meeting House" (1968); Susan Garfinkel, "Genres of Worldliness: Meanings of the Meeting House for Philadelphia Friends, 1755–1830" (Ph.D. diss., University of Pennsylvania, 1997); Roger Moss, *Historic Sacred Places of Philadelphia*; and Emma Jones Lapsansky and Anne A. Verplanck, eds., *Quaker Aesthetics: Reflections on a Quaker Ethic in American Design and Consumption* (Philadelphia, 2003).

CHAPTER 13: THE NATIONAL CONSTITUTION CENTER

George Mason's accounts are found in Rowland, *Life of George Mason,* 2 vols. (New York, 1892), 100–102. On establishing the NCC, see Michael Les Benedict, *The National Constitution Center* (Philadelphia, 2007). The critical source for any telling of the Philadelphia Convention is Max Farrand, ed., *The Records of the Federal Convention of 1787,* 3 vols. (New Haven, 1911); on the convention, see Richard B. Morris, *The Framing of the Federal Constitution* (Washington, D.C., 1986); Richard Beeman, *Plain, Honest Men: The Making of the American Constitution* (New York, 2009); David Waldstreicher, *Slavery's Constitution: From Revolution to Ratification* (New York, 2009); William G. Carr, *The Oldest Delegate: Franklin in the Constitutional Convention* (Newark, Del., 1990). On Philadelphia during the summer of 1787, see Edmund S. Morgan, "The Witch and We, The People," *American Heritage* 34, no. 5 (July–August 1983); on Madison, see Lance Banning, "James Madison," *American National Biography.* On James Oronoko Dexter, see Anna Coxe Toogood, "James Dexter, a Biographical Sketch," Independence Historic Research Study, Appendix F, www.cr.nps.gov/history; my thanks to Toogood, and to Dan Rolph of the Historical Society of Pennsylvania, for sharing their research.

CHAPTER 14: THE PRESIDENT'S HOUSE

On the presidency's decade in Philadelphia, see George Washington's *Papers* (available online through Washington's Mount Vernon) as well as Joseph E. Fields, *"Worthy Partner": The Papers of Martha Washington* (Westport, CT, 1994), Clarence L. Ver Steeg, "Robert Morris," in American National Biography online. On 190 High Street, see Edward Lawler, "The President's House in Philadelphia: The Rediscovery of a Lost Landmark," *PMHB* 126, no. 1 (2002), 5–95; and Lawler, "The President's House Revisted," *PMHB,* 129, no. 4 (October 2005), 371–410; Harold Donaldson Eberlein, "190, High Street (Market Street Below Sixth)—The Home of Washington and Adams 1790–1800," in *Historic Philadelphia: From the Founding Until the Early Nineteenth Century*; David John

Jeremy, ed., *Henry Wansey and His American Journal* (Philadelphia, 1970); Anne Hollingsworth Wharton, *Salons Colonial and Republican* (Philadelphia, 1900); and Catherine Allgor, *Parlor Politics: In Which the Ladies of Washington Help Build a City and a Government* (Charlottesville, 2000). My thanks to INHP historian Anna Coxe Toogood for sharing her extensive research on the Washingtons and their enslaved servants. On the Washingtons and slavery, see Henry Weincek, *An Imperfect God: George Washington, His Slaves, and the Creation of America* (New York, 2003); James Oliver Horton and Lois E. Horton, *Slavery and Public History: The Tough Stuff of American Memory* (New York, 2006).

CHAPTER 15: THE GERMANTOWN WHITE HOUSE AND ITS NEIGHBORS

On the yellow fever epidemic, see Worth Estes and Billy G. Smith, *A Melancholy Scene of Devastation: The Public Response to the 1793 Philadelphia Yellow Fever Epidemic* (Philadelphia, 1997); Kenneth Foster, Mary F. Jenkins, and Anna Coxe Toogood, "The Philadelphia Yellow Fever Epidemic of 1793," *Scientific American* 279, no. 2 (August 1998); J. H. Powell, *Bring Out Your Dead* (Philadelphia, 1993). On Germantown, see Stephanie Grauman Wolf, *Urban Village: Population, Community, and Family Structure in Germantown, Pennsylvania, 1683–1800* (Princeton, 1976); Charles Francis Jenkins, *Washington in Germantown* (Philadelphia, 1905); and Adolph B. Benson, ed., *Peter Kalm's Travels in North America: The English Version of 1770*, 2 vols. (New York, 1937). On these houses, see Roger W. Moss, *The American Country House* (New York, 1990); Roger W. Moss, *Historic Houses of Philadelphia* (Philadelphia, 1998); and Mark Reinberger and Elizabeth McLean, "Isaac Norris's Fairhill: Architecture, Landscape, and Quaker Ideals in a Philadelphia Colonial Country Seat," *Winterthur Portfolio* 32, no. 4 (Winter 1997).

CHAPTER 16: PHILADELPHIA AS THE NATION'S CAPITAL

William Maclay's reminiscences are found in Kenneth R. Bowling and Helen R. Veit, eds., *The Diary of William Maclay and Other Notes on Senate Debates, March 4, 1789–March 3, 1791* (Baltimore, 1988). On the legislative and judicial branches of the government, see Kenneth R. Bowling and Donald R. Kennon, eds., *The House and Senate in the 1790s: Petitioning, Lobbying, and Institutional Development* (Athens, OH, 2003); and Bowling and Kennon, eds., *Neither Separate Nor Equal: Congress in the 1790s* (Athens, OH, 2000); Elder Witt, "The First Century," in *Congressional Quarterly Guide to the U.S. Supreme Court* (Washington, D.C., 1990); David Waldstreicher, *Slavery's Constitution*; Stanley Elkins and Eric McKitrick, *The Age of Federalism* (New York, 1993); Joseph J. Ellis, *Founding Brothers: The Revolutionary Generation* (New York, 2001), and Gordon S. Wood, *Empire of Liberty* (New York, 2009). On Congress Hall, see Karie Diethorn, *Furnishing Plan for the First Floor of Congress Hall* (Philadelphia, 1992), and for all of the buildings on the square, see Roger Moss, *Historic Landmarks of Philadelphia*, and Toogood et al., *Cultural Landscape Report:*

Independence Square. On Congress' departure from Philadelphia, see Minute Book of the Philadelphia City and County Commissioners, May 17, 1800.

CHAPTER 17: THE LIBERTY BELL

For accounts of the bell in the eighteenth century, see Labaree, ed., *Papers of Benjamin Franklin*; Butterfield, *Book of Abigail and John: Selected Letters of the Adams Family 1762–1784; Pennsylvania Archives.* On the bell in history, see John C. Page, *The Liberty Bell: A Special History Study* (Denver, n.d.); David Kimball, *The Story of the Liberty Bell* (Fort Washington, PA, 1989); Gary B. Nash, *The Liberty Bell.* On nineteenth-century abolition, racism, and conflict, see Leonard L. Richards, *"Gentlemen of Property and Standing": Anti-Abolition Mobs in Jacksonian America* (Oxford, 1970); Ronald G. Walters, *The Antislavery Appeal: American Abolitionism After 1830* (New York, 1984); and Richard S. Newman, *The Transformation of American Abolitionism: Fighting Slavery in the Early Republic* (Chapel Hill, 2001).

Illustration Credits

ii–iii: New York Public Library. viii–ix: Library of Congress. xi: Library of Congress. xii: Philadelphia Free Library. xiv: Powel House. xviii–xix: Library of Congress. xx: Frank Margeson. 3: Historical Society of Pennsylvania. 4: Trustees of the British Museum. 5: American Philosophical Society. 7: Library Company of Philadelphia. 11: Top, Author's collection. Bottom, Dr. Bernard Herman, University of North Carolina at Chapel Hill. 12: Library of Congress. 13: Historical Society of Pennsylvania. 15: Top, Metropolitan Museum of Art. Bottom, Trustees of the British Museum. 16: Library of Congress. 18: American Philosophical Society. 20: American Philosophical Society. 23: Library of Congress. 24: Author's photograph. 26: Independence National Historical Park. 27: University of Pennsylvania Archives. 29: Library of Congress. 30: Library Company of Philadelphia. 35: Independence National Historical Park. 37: Library of Congress. 39: Library of Congress. 40: Frank Margeson. 43: Library Company of Philadelphia. 45: Frank Margeson. 46: University of Pennsylvania Archives. 49: Library Company of Philadelphia. 50: Author's collection. 51: Frank Margeson. 53: Independence National Historical Park. 55: American Philosophical Society. 58: American Philosophical Society. 59: Library Company of Philadelphia. 60: American Philosophical Society. 64: American Philosophical Society. 66: Private Collection. 68: American Philosophical Society. 69: Metropolitan Museum of Art. 70. Frank Margeson. 71. Rare Book Room, Van Pelt Library, University of Pennsylvania. 72: Independence National Historical Park. 73: Independence National Historical Park. 75: Independence National Historical Park. 76: Independence National Historical Park. 78: Frank Margeson. 81: American Philosophical Society. 82: American Philosophical Society. 83: American Philosophical Society. 84: Frank Margeson. 86: Stenton and The National Society of the Colonial Dames of America. 87: Top, American Philosophical Society. Bottom, Independence National Historical Park. 88: The Pennsylvania Academy of the Fine Arts. 89: Library of Congress. 90: Independence National Historical Park. 92: Library of Congress. 93: Library of Congress. 94: Library of Congress. 95: Library of Congress. 98: Frank Margeson. 100: Rare Book Room, Van Pelt Library, University of Pennsylvania. 102: Lisa Nagy. 103: Philadelphia Society for the Preservation of Landmarks. 104: Frank Margeson. 105: Philadelphia Society for the Preservation of Landmarks. 106: Independence National Historical Park. 107: Top, American Philosophical Society. Bottom, Lisa Nagy. 109: Library of Congress. 111: Library Company of Philadelphia. 113: Independence National Historical Park. 114: National Park Service. 116: Frank Margeson. 117: Library of Congress. 118: Library of Congress. 119: Thomas Jefferson Foundation, Monticello. 123: Frank Margeson. 124: Lisa Nagy. 129: American Philosophical Society. 131: Frank Margeson. 133: Library Company of Philadelphia. 135: Rare Book Room, Van Pelt Library, University of Pennsylvania. 136: Independence Seaport Museum. 137: Library of

Congress. 138: Rare Book Room, Van Pelt Library, University of Pennsylvania. 139: Top and bottom, Independence National Historical Park. 140: Independence National Historical Park. 142: Independence National Historical Park. 144: Library of Congress. 147: Library of Congress. 149: The Philadelphia Print Shop. 151: Author's Collection. 152: Independence National Historical Park. 153: Independence National Historical Park. 154: Independence National Historical Park. 157: Independence National Historical Park. 159: Independence National Historical Park. 160: Library of Congress. 162: Independence National Historical Park. 164: Independence National Historical Park. 165: Independence National Historical Park. 168: American Philosophical Society. 170: Frank Margeson. 172: Library of Congress. 173: Independence National Historical Park. 174: Library Company of Philadelphia. 175: Charles E. Peterson, collections of Independence National Historical Park. 177: Frank Margeson. 178: Thomas Jefferson Foundation, Monticello. 179: Library of Congress. 181: Frank Margeson. 183: American Philosophical Society. 186: Independence National Historical Park. 188: Independence National Historical Park. 189: Independence National Historical Park. 191: Historical Society of Pennsylvania. 192: Independence National Historical Park. 193: Library of Congress. 194: Independence National Historical Park. 195: Library of Congress. 196: Library of Congress. 197: Independence National Historical Park. 198: Independence National Historical Park. 199: American Philosophical Society. 201: Independence National Historical Park. 203: Independence National Historical Park. 206: Ken Thomas. 208: Library Company of Philadelphia. 209: University of Pennsylvania Archives. 211: Frank Margeson. 215: Friends Historical Library, Swarthmore College. 217: Library Company of Philadelphia. 220: Library of Congress. 224: John Milner Associates. 225: Library Company of Philadelphia. 227: American Philosophical Society. 228: Library of Congress. 230: Library of Congress. 231: Historical Society of Pennsylvania. 232–233: Library of Congress. 235: Library of Congress. 236: Library of Congress. 239: Frank Margeson. 243: Library of Congress. 245: National Portrait Gallery. 250: Library of Congress. 253: Left, Library of Congress. Right, Frank Margeson. 254: Frank Margeson. 257: Library of Congress. 258: Frank Margeson. 260: American Philosophical Society. 261: Independence National Historical Park. 262: Winterthur Museum and Garden. 263: American Philosophical Society. 265: Smithsonian Institution. 266: Library of Congress. 267: Library of Congress. 271: Independence National Historical Park. 272: Rare Book Room, Van Pelt Library, University of Pennsylvania. 274: Metropolitan Museum of Art. 276: Independence National Historical Park. 278: Independence National Historical Park. 279. National Archives. 280: Independence National Historical Park. 283: Independence National Historical Park. 285: Library of Congress. 286: Anna Coxe Toogood. 287: Library of Congress. 288: Independence National Historical Park. 291: Independence National Historical Park. 297: New York Public Library. 299: Rare Book Room, Van Pelt Library, University of Pennsylvania. 302: Independence National Historical Park. 303: American Philosophical Society. 306: National

Park Service. 309: Independence National Historical Park. 311: Library Company of Philadelphia. 312: Library of Congress. 313: Library Company of Philadelphia. 315: Library of Congress. 316: Library Company of Philadelphia. 318: Library of Congress. 319: Independence National Historical Park. 320: Library of Congress. 322: Library of Congress. 323: Downs Collections, Winterthur Museum and Library. 324: American Philosophical Society. 327: Independence National Historical Park. 329: Frank Margeson. 330: Library of Congress. 332: Frank Margeson. 333: Independence National Historical Park. 335: Library of Congress. 336: Library of Congress. 337: American Philosophical Society. 339. Independence National Historical Park. 341: Library of Congress. 343: Independence National Historical Park. 344: Library of Congress. 348: Independence National Historical Park. 349: Winterthur Museum and Library. 353: National Science Foundation. 357: Library of Congress. 359: Carl A. Kroch Library, Cornell University. 360: Independence National Historical Park. 361: Library of Congress. 362: Library of Congress. 363: Temple University Urban Archives. 364: National Park Service.

Index

Acknowledgments

This book would not have been possible without the help and support of the staff of Independence National Historical Park. Superintendents Mary Bomar, Dennis Reidenbach, and Cynthia MacLeod, as well as Joseph Becton, Doris Fanelli, Robert Giannini, Mary Jenkins, Jed Levin, Charles Tonetti, and Anna Coxe Toogood were integral to my research and writing this book. Penny Batcheler and Charles Peterson, both retired when I moved to Philadelphia and now deceased, provided invaluable information about the park's early days and the decisions made to preserve, restore, and interpret its sites. The staff of the library and archives at Independence National Historical Park provided invaluable help in finding materials and locating images; they preserve an amazing, often underutilized national resource. My eternal thanks to Andrea Ashby, Karen Stephens, and recently Christian Higgins for all they have done. Frances Kolb Delmar was there at the beginning and the end of this project. Chief Curator Karie Diethorn has been an inspiring researcher and dedicated sounding board during every stage of this book's progress.

Many other scholars have shared their research with me during the time I wrote this book. From the beginning, John Murrin, Bill Pencak, and Stevie Wolf offered wise counsel; Bill read the entire manuscript. Thanks also to Roger Abrahams, Matt Allison, Zara Anishanslin, Bob Bernstein, Libby Browne, Benjamin Carp, Elizabeth Chew, Elaine Crane, David Dashiell, Richard Dunn and Mary Maples Dunn, Linda Eaton, Sally Hadden, Stephen Hague, David Hancock, Amy Hudson Henderson, Bernie Herman, Laura Johnson, Cory Kegerise, Laura Keim, Susan Klepp, Edward Lawler, Margaretta Lovell, Edward Mauger, David Maxey, John McCurdy, Debbie Miller, Marla Miller, Charlene Mires, Gary Nash, Andrew Jackson O'Shaughnessy, Leslie Patrick, Dennis Pickeral, Justin Sarafin, Phil Seitz, David Silverman, Billy Smith, Patricia Stallone, Susan Stein, Carrie Taylor, Anne Verplanck, and Michael Zuckerman. At Penn State Harrisburg, my student Lindsay Volker offered outstanding assistance on the final manuscript revisions; my colleagues Kathryn Robinson, Margaret Rose Jaster, Patricia Johnson, Robin Veder, Julie Kearney, and William Mahar were of great help; my sincere regret is that my friend and colleague Louise Hoffman did not live to see this book published. Research and illustration funds provided by Dean Marian Walters aided this project greatly. Additional funding from the David Library of the American Revolution, Winterthur Museum and Library, and International Center for Jefferson Studies allowed time to research and write. At Westholme Publishing, Lucinda Bartley provided outstanding editorial comments and tough questions. My thanks to her, and to publisher Bruce H. Franklin and Noreen O'Connor-Abel for their splendid work on this book.

Many friends—some historians, some kind souls who were willing to listen to endless anecdotes about historic Philadelphia—offered sage advice and a kind ear. Very special thanks to Allis Eaton Bennett, whose friendship included a long-standing tutorial in art history and the material world of early America; Stephen Harp and Lisa Bansen Harp for now-too infrequent walks but regular Sunday talks that keep me thinking and writing; Judith Van Buskirk, who turned a hike along the Wissahickon Creek in 1994 into decades of good counsel; Dee and Bob Keller, my onetime profs at Manchester College who provided both encouragement over the years and an amazing porch in Maine where I made the final revisions to the manuscript, with the much-appreciated distractions of Dan and Celia Cook-Huffman and their kids, Jesse and Grace. My partners in the teachingfranklin team, Carol Baldridge and Ina Morrow, shared their love and knowledge of Philadelphia's history and joined me in trying out some of the ideas in this book with our Summer Scholars from around the world during our Benjamin Franklin teachers' workshops. Last, but not least, my friends John Makem, Stephen Paesani, Paul Artrip, Joanna Reiner, and Patrick Cargan pushed me to finish this book (many years before I actually did so).

Numerous archivists and librarians assisted in tracking down obscure materials and illustrative objects for this project, including Nicole Joniec, John Van Horne, and Jim Green of the Library Company of Philadelphia; Kathy Ludwig of the David Library of the American Revolution; John Pollack of the Rare Book Room at the University of Pennsylvania's Van Pelt Library; Roy Goodman, Charles Greifenstein, and Michael Miller of the American Philosophical Society Library; Sarah Haim and Lee Arnold of the Historical Society of Pennsylvania; Linda Stanley, now of the Union League but whose unmatched grasp of the HSP's collections proved to be a last-minute godsend; Susan Newton and Jeanne Solensky of Winterthur; Carrie Hogan of the American Swedish Historical Museum; Brandi Levine and Del Connor of the Philadelphia Society for the Preservation of Landmarks; and Alison Wright and the staff of the British Museum's Drawings and Prints Department. The Philadelphia Print Shop generously allowed me to use the Breton print of the Fourth Street Meeting House and School. Finally, Frank Margeson's and Lisa Nagy's original photographs provide excellent contemporary views of Philadelphia.

Finally, I thank my family. My sisters Mary, Vivian, Yvonne, Joanna, and Janice listened attentively (or pretended to) as a child historian rambled about American presidents and delayed family vacations while he examined old buildings. Paul Alles may not have bargained for the Continental Congress, the extended Franklin family, and a score of dead Quakers moving in with him, but he accepted it with good humor. He didn't get the dedication page of this book, but that will be one more IOU I have given him. Finally, the four people who are recognized on that page will, I hope, accept it as a small token of esteem too long overdue. My parents, Beverly and Lee Boudreau (who drove east from Indiana in 1976 so their kids could see the Liberty Bell and Independence Hall during the Bicentennial year), allowed me to pick my own paths and dream my own dreams, one of which was to be a historian. The mentor who guided me on that path, Professor David Waas of Manchester College, showed far more faith in me than I deserved at the time, and in the years that followed, he and his wife Rebecca Brightbill Waas served as guides, instructors, and most important, friends. Both taught me the importance of history, but a history that included diverse people, and a past that included great moments and terrible ones. I hope this story lives up to the faith they put into me as I wrote it.